How It Works®

Science and Technology

Third Edition

Marshall Cavendish
99 White Plains Road
Tarrytown, NY 10591

Website: www.marshallcavendish.com

Third edition updated by Brown Reference Group plc.

Library of Congress Cataloging-in-Publication Data
How it works: science and technology.—3rd ed.
p. cm.
Includes index.
ISBN 0-7614-7314-9 (set)   ISBN 0-7614-7331-9 (Vol. 17)
1. Technology—Encyclopedias. 2. Science—Encyclopedias.
[1. Technology—Encyclopedias. 2. Science—Encyclopedias.]
T9 .H738 2003
603—dc21   2001028771

Consultant: Donald R. Franceschetti, Ph.D., University of Memphis

Brown Reference Group
Editor: Wendy Horobin
Associate Editors: Paul Thompson, Martin Clowes, Lis Stedman, Dawn Titmus
Managing Editor: Tim Cooke
Design: Alison Gardner
Picture Research: Becky Cox
Illustrations: Mark Walker, Darren Awuah

Marshall Cavendish
Project Editor: Peter Mavrikis
Production Manager: Alan Tsai
Editorial Director: Paul Bernabeo

Printed in Malaysia
Bound in the United States of America
08 07 06 05 04   6 5 4 3 2

Title picture: The Cygnus Loop supernova remnant, see *Supernova*

How It Works®

Science and Technology

Volume 17

Superconductivity

Tin

Marshall Cavendish

New York • London • Toronto • Sydney

Contents

Volume 17

Superconductivity

Superconductivity is an absence of measurable electrical resistance exhibited by some materials at extremely low temperatures. At room temperature, the same materials have normal ohmic resistance behavior—their resistance falls gradually as temperature decreases. This behavior ceases at a transition temperature, called the critical temperature (T_c). At that temperature, resistivity suddenly falls to zero, and the material passes into its superconducting state.

The value of T_c varies from material to material and can vary over a range of a few degrees for different samples of nominally identical material. This variation is due to small differences in impurity levels and the presence of varying densities of structural defects in the crystalline lattices that materials that can superconduct assume.

In the superconducting state, electrical currents can flow without generating the heat that would arise in a normal conductor as a consequence of its resistance. Since the heat generated in normal conductors represents a loss of electrical energy and, in extreme cases, could cause the conductor to melt, superconductors are prized for their ability to avoid heat generation.

The potential advantages of superconductors are offset by the need to cool them to extremely low temperatures for their superconducting property to come into effect. The earliest superconductors to be discovered had T_c values only a few degrees above absolute zero, which is $-459.67°F$ ($-273.15°C$). For this reason, scientists in the field of superconductivity tend to use the Kelvin scale, in which absolute zero is 0 K and each degree interval is equivalent to $1°C$ ($1.8°F$).

Such low temperatures are achieved using liquid helium, which boils at 4.2 K ($-452.1°F$, $-268.9°C$). Great amounts of energy are required to obtain liquid helium by liquefaction and subsequent distillation of air, and thorough insulation is necessary to prevent ambient heat from boiling the helium at an unacceptable rate. These factors added expense, ensuring that early superconductors found few uses outside research laboratories.

Discovery

The basic phenomenon of superconductivity was discovered in 1911 by the Dutch physicist Heike Kamerlingh Onnes. Using liquid helium, he cooled mercury to within a few degrees of absolute zero and discovered the sudden onset of zero resistivity that is typical of superconductors. To dispel the doubts of sceptics, he set a current flowing in a ring of superconducting mercury and

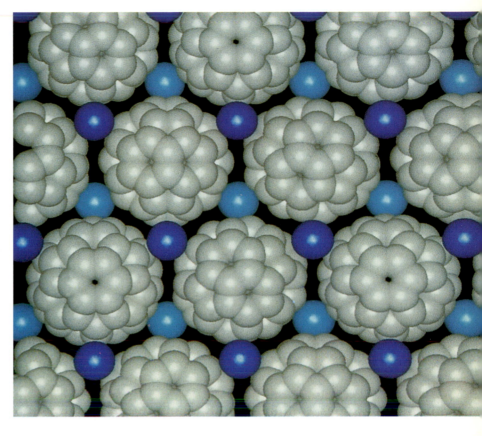

then measured the current again after a year. The current had not diminished in the slightest, indicating that the resistance of mercury had truly fallen to zero.

At this point, it is convenient to explain how a current is set flowing in a ring and subsequently measured. Since a ring has no start or finish to which terminals can be attached, it is impossible to use the two outputs of a battery to kick start the current—current from the battery would simply short out through the superconductor.

Instead, a changing magnetic field is used to produce a current by induction. For example, a permanent magnet can be placed within the ring above T_c and then removed when the material has been taken into its superconducting state. When the permanent magnet is removed, the lines of magnetic flux that cut through the superconducting ring induce a current in it, rather as a changing magnetic field induces current in the windings of a generator. Once the current is established, it creates a magnetic field that passes through the center of the ring at right angles to the plane of the ring. The strength of this field can then be used to quantify the current flowing in the ring. Modern experiments using this technique have confirmed that superconductors have no resistivity above the lower limit of measurement, which is currently around 10^{-25} Ωm.

▲ This image portrays the structure of potassium fulleride (K_3C_{60}), a compound shown in 1991 by researchers at AT&T Bell Laboratories to exhibit superconductivity at 18 K. The compound forms when potassium atoms diffuse into a sample of fullerene (C_{60}). Each of the large clusters represents a ball of sixty carbon atoms, while the smaller balls are potassium ions that occupy gaps in the fullerene lattice.

MAGLEV TRANSIT SYSTEMS

For years, scientists and engineers have been exploring the potential of magnetic levitation (maglev) to eliminate the friction between wheels and track that wastes much of the tractive power of conventional trains. The combination of maglev with linear-motor propulsion and braking also eliminates the susceptibility to poor adhesion that limits the performance of conventional trains.

Maglev vehicles stay aloft because powerful electromagnets in their undersides temporarily induce magnetic fields in conducting loops in the track beneath them, and the opposition between the original and induced magnetic fields produces a mutual repulsion between vehicle and track. The strength of the repulsion increases as the gap between the track and vehicle becomes narrower, with the result that the vehicle floats at a height where the repulsive force matches its weight.

The role of superconductors in maglev vehicles is in the coils in their electromagnets. If normal conductors were to be used, their coils would be around twice the size of superconducting magnets and they would waste much more energy.

The only maglev vehicle to enter regular public service to date was a low-speed internal shuttle that operated at Birmingham International Airport, England, between 1986 and 1997. Nevertheless, speeds as high as 343 mph (552 km/h) have been attained in 1997 on the Yamanashi Maglev Test Line, Japan.

▼ This diagram illustrates a maglev vehicle that uses strong superconducting magnets to stay aloft. Magnetic shielding is necessary to prevent interference with heart pacemakers and other magnetizable items in the train.

Passenger compartment

Liquid helium

Magnetic shielding

Aluminum thrust rail

Linear motor for propulsion

Concrete base

Aluminum guide rail

Superconducting electromagnet

Apart from discovering the existence of superconductivity and the critical temperature associated with its onset, Kamerlingh Onnes found that superconductivity depends on external magnetic fields. At any given temperature below T_c, there is a critical magnetic field strength, H_c, above which the material ceases to behave as a superconductor and normal conductive properties return. The value of H_c depends on how far the material is below its T_c—the colder the sample, the stronger the field needed to disrupt superconductivity.

Meissner effect

In 1933, the German physicist Walther Meissner discovered that a material in a superconducting state excludes magnetic flux, provided the external magnetic field is not stronger than a value H_c. He made this finding while studying magnetic fields within crystals of tin at 3.72 K (–452.97°F, –269.4°C).

This effect, since called the Meissner effect, has a consequence for superconductors that leads to one of the most spectacular aspects of their behavior—magnetic levitation. When a permanent magnet is

▼ The fine cable (right), when superconducting, can carry as much current as the copper block (left). This finding indicates the saving in space that can be made by use of superconductors.

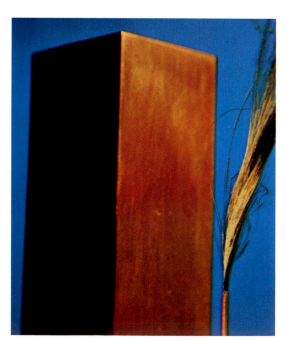

released above a superconductor, it will hover in place, because the superconductor generates an external magnetic field that opposes the field projected by the magnet; thus, the two fields cancel to zero within the superconductor.

The repulsive force that arises from the opposition of the two magnetic fields is what prevents the permanent magnet from falling, and the ability of superconductors to project equal and opposite magnetic fields in response to external fields has led to their being described as perfect diamagnets, since diamagnetism is the property of producing a magnetic field in opposition to an external field.

Flux pinning

The fact that a permanent magnet floats quite steadily over a superconductor—even if it is set spinning by a current of air—shows that some other factor is in operation. If the interaction between the magnet and the superconductor were purely repulsive, the magnet would tend to slip over the edge and fall to Earth.

The mystery factor is called flux pinning, and it is caused by imperfections in the crystal structure of all real

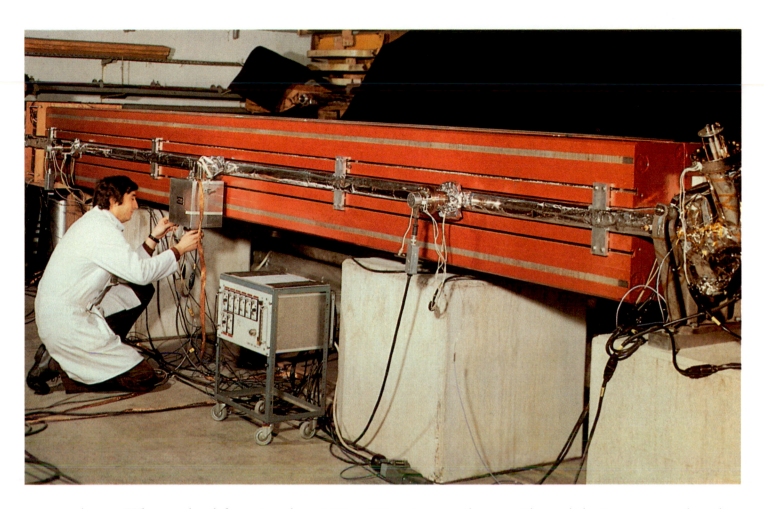

superconductors. Where such a defect exists, the perfect diamagnetism of the superconductor breaks down, and some magnetic flux from the magnet penetrates the superconductor. While this passage of flux causes sufficient attraction to hold the magnet in place over the superconductor, diamagnetism prevents it from getting too close, and thus, the magnet is held in suspension.

Type I and II superconductors

As Kamerlingh Onnes discovered, the superconducting properties (and also the diamagnetic properties) of materials below their T_c values can be extinguished by the application of a sufficiently strong magnetic field. With the early superconductors, the critical magnetic field strength for this phenomenon to occur was found to be quite weak, putting a rather tight limit on the density of current, measured in amperes per unit cross-sectional area, that such superconductors could carry. Because the current creates a magnetic field, too strong a current can quench the superconductivity. Materials that behave in this way are classified as type I superconductors.

Some of the more recently formulated superconductors have not one but two H_c values. When the field strength rises above the first critical value, H_{c1}, the resistance rises from zero but continues to be much less than it would be if

the material were behaving as a normal conductor. As the field strength increases through a second critical value, H_{c2}, all traces of superconductivity are lost.

BCS theory

Following the discovery of superconductivity, many attempts were made to provide a theoretical model to explain its existence and that of related phenomena, such as the Meissner effect. The first theory to gain general acceptance in this role was published in 1951. It is called BCS theory, a name derived from the surname initials of its inventors—the U.S. scientists Bardeen, Cooper, and Schrieffer. The trio shared the 1972 Nobel Prize for physics in recognition of their theory.

The BCS theory concentrates on interactions between moving electrons and phonons—packets of vibrational energy that permeate crystal lattices. When electrons move singly, as they do in normal conductors, their interactions with phonons impede their motion to some extent, resulting in the resistance observed for common conductors. The mechanism of this interaction is the electrostatic attraction between the negative charges of electrons and the centers of positive charge in the lattice, and it results in electrons losing momentum and kinetic energy to the lattice, which becomes hot in the process.

At extremely low temperatures, however, the electrons of superconductors unite in pairs, called Cooper pairs. The quantum states of these pairs are tied together by the coupling so that a property such as momentum cannot change for one electron of the pair in isolation. Therefore, as it is impossible for one member of the pair to lose momentum through its attraction to positive centers in the lattice, the pairs sail through the lattice of a superconductor without impediment.

Increasing temperature tends to split the electron pairs, resulting in the existence of T_c values—the loss of entropy sustained by forming an electron pair can only be sustained at low temperature. The influence of magnetic fields stems from the fact that each electron carries a magnetic dipole, and the dipoles in a pair must be opposed to allow their coexistence in a pair. The imposition of an external magnetic field causes one electron to line up with the field, giving it lower energy than its partner, whose dipole aligns against the field. Above H_c, this split in energy is sufficient to disrupt the pairing.

Superconducting materials

Some 27 elements in the periodic table are now known to exhibit superconductivity, but their T_c values are close to 0 K, and they also have low H_c values. The combination of these factors makes them useless in practical applications.

Many thousands of alloys have been prepared that have been shown to be superconductors. In 1961, for example, scientists at the Bell Laboratories in the United States discovered a group of alloys that exhibit type-II superconducting behavior. These materials were found to be capable of carrying high current densities in strong magnetic fields. Their critical field depends on the composition of the alloy, but the critical current can be increased enormously by suitable fabrication and heat treatment processes, because the introduction of structural defects into the material inhibits the growth of magnetic fields.

The most important alloys in this class of materials are based on niobium, which has the highest transition temperature and critical field of all the elements. (T_c = 9.2 K, and H_c = 0.2 tesla or 2,000 gauss.) The first such materials, alloys of niobium and zirconium, were superseded by various niobium–titanium alloys, which proved to be more ductile and easier to fabricate. These alloys were fabricated in the form of fine twisted-wire filaments embedded in a copper matrix.

Some of the best superconducting materials of this class, such as niobium–tin (T_c = 18 K, –427°F, –255°C), were found to be brittle and therefore difficult to fabricate, as well as being sensitive to

slight changes in composition. The optimization of these alloys required many years of intensive collaboration between physicists, materials scientists, and engineers. The same process was repeated for niobium–aluminum–germanium alloys, which were found to exhibit yet higher T_c values—up to 23 K (–418°F, –250°C).

High-temperature superconductors

The greatest breakthrough to date occurred by accident in 1986. Scientists at IBM Zürich, Switzerland, had been heating a sample of a potential new superconductor alloy in an oven. When they removed the sample, they noted a green coloration, which indicated that the sample had been oxidized in the oven. Since mixed metal oxides fall into the class of ceramics—materials noted for their high electrical resistance and often used as insulators—the initial prospects of the "spoiled" sample performing as a superconductor would have appeared slim. Nevertheless, when they tested the sample, it proved to have the highest T_c then known—30 K (–406°F, –243°C).

Following on from the Zürich team's discovery, several groups of researchers set about testing other types of ceramics to see if they had higher T_c values. The target at that time was a superconductor whose T_c would be above the boiling point of liquid nitrogen—77.4 K (–320.4°F, –195.8°C).

▲ This is an early example of a processor chip that uses Josephson junctions instead of semiconducting transistors to perform processor operations faster and with less energy loss. The chip operates when cooled to the temperature of boiling liquid nitrogen.

The significance of liquid nitrogen is that it costs around one-tenth the unit price of liquid helium and absorbs 20 times more heat than helium as it boils, making it a much more economical cooling agent. Furthermore, the higher boiling temperature makes it much safer to handle and easier to insulate effectively against ambient heat.

One of the first groups of superconductors to pass the liquid nitrogen limit were mixed oxides of yttrium, barium, and copper, following the approximate formula $YBa_2Cu_3O_7$. They have T_c values around 90 K ($-298°F$, $-183°C$), so they are well below their critical temperatures when cooled by liquid nitrogen. Even higher T_c values—around 110 K ($-262°F$, $-163°C$)—are obtained with ceramics that share the approximate formula $Bi_2Sr_2CaCu_2O_9$ and are called BSCCO superconductors. In both classes of ceramics, the copper ions form sheets, which are supposed to be the channels through which superconduction occurs. In addition, the superconductivity of such materials depends strongly on their orientation.

The greater the difference between T_c and the boiling point of nitrogen, the greater is the value of H_c, so higher-T_c superconductors can carry greater current densities without losing their superconductivity. For this reason, vigorous research continues into ever higher T_c values.

The task of developing new superconductors is complicated by the fact that there are so many variables in formulas of five or more elements. One approach that has been adopted to screen the largest number of formulations as rapidly as possible employs combinatorial chemistry. In this technique, a robotic device effects the synthesis of many hundreds of tiny samples in pits in a plate of an inert material, such as silicon. This procedure generates hundreds of samples in the time a human technician would use to prepare a single sample. The testing of the samples and result reporting is also automated. The vast numbers of samples that can be prepared in this way allow researchers to examine trends that indicate where they have to guide the research.

A future goal for superconductor research, one that remains distant at the present time, is a superconductor whose T_c is higher than 194.7 K ($-109.3°F$, $-78.5°C$). This is the temperature at which dry ice (solid carbon dioxide) sublimes, and its attainment would further simplify and reduce the cost of keeping superconductors below T_c.

Practical applications

Until the advent of high-temperature superconductors (HTSs), the use of superconductors was confined to laboratory environments and other situations where the benefits of superconductors justified the expense and effort required to keep them at extremely low temperatures. Such was the case with magnetic-resonance-imaging (MRI) scanners, which rely on the strong magnetic fields produced by superconducting electromagnets to form images used in medical diagnosis. Another example is the bubble chamber, where the paths of subatomic particles are deflected by the magnetic field from the superconducting coil. The direction of deflection indicates the sign of the charge, and the radius of curvature indicates the ratio of charge to mass. Particles that have no charge are not deflected, since their motion does not constitute an electrical current, and hence they produce no magnetic field.

The coils for such devices would be wound from superconducting tape or wire and immersed in baths that could be filled with liquid helium during the operation of the electromagnet. Magnetic flux densities up to around 14 tesla (140,000 gauss) could be attained from small coils, but much bigger magnets operating at lower fields were more typical.

Since the development of high-temperature superconductors, engineers and inventors are now applying superconductor technology in areas

JOSEPHSON JUNCTION

A Josephson junction is a superconducting version of a semiconducting transistor. In its simplest form, it consists of two overlapping strips of superconductor separated by a third layer of superconductor. When the device is in the "on" condition, current flows through with no resistance.

Current is prevented from flowing between the supply terminals by a control current that flows through a normal conductor atop the sandwich of superconductors. The materials are chosen such that the magnetic field from the control current is sufficient to disrupt the superconductivity of the middle layer, which then becomes an insulator. The advantages of this device over a conventional transistor are that less energy is wasted and current flows more rapidly, making for faster processing rates.

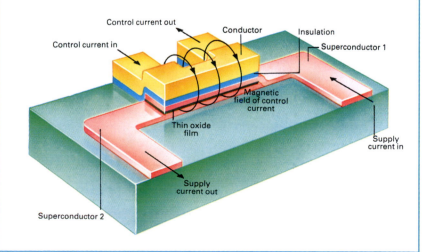

where it has long been known that its benefits could be reaped but where the cost of helium cooling was prohibitive. Furthermore, the much greater critical field strength of modern HTSs operating at the temperature of liquid nitrogen has increased the current density they can carry compared with earlier superconductors. This has had a marked effect in reducing the sizes of semiconductor coils, cables, and other devices.

Transportation. One of the most publicly visible applications of HTSs is in various experimental forms of transportation. High-speed maglev trains that rest on a cushion of magnetism produced by superconducting electromagnets are well into development and plans are underway to provide commercial services in Germany, Japan, China, and the United States by 2030.

Superconducting electromagnets have also found applications in marine propulsion. In the case of the Japanese experimental vessel *Yamato I*, launched in 1992, the coils produce a magnetic field that passes vertically through a water-filled duct that runs the length of the vessel below its waterline. When a current passes through the water between electrode on either side of the duct, water is propelled through the duct under the magnetohydrodynamic effect. In a more mundane system, the U.S. Navy demonstrated in 1998 a 104 horsepower (78 kW) electric motor

using HTS windings (coils). The advantage in this case is an increase in efficiency.

Power generation. Just as superconducting windings can make an otherwise standard electric motor run more efficiently, so they can increase the efficiency of an electrical generator to more than 99 percent. Since the heat generated—and energy lost—in conventional generator sets is a major limiting factor on their power output, the potential market for such devices is huge, and a 100 MW generator of this type is being tested by General Electric.

Power storage. HTSs can also help in the storage of power. An induced current can be set up in a superconducting storage ring when excess power is available and released whenever there is a failure or shortfall in power supply. Alliant Energy is currently installing a system of such devices, each of which will be able to deliver up to 3 MW of power at times of need.

Power distribution. The potential savings achievable by replacing conventional high-tension power lines with superconducting cables is enormous. Various power companies in the United States and Japan have small stretches of nitrogen-cooled BSCCO cables under test.

Electronics. Josephson junctions—devices in which current flows through superconductors but can be switched on or off like transistors—offer a potential route to a new generation of ultrafast processors. They switch between states faster and waste less energy than do transistors.

▲ A prototype marine-propulsion unit under test. The system comprises a superconducting generator (1), which could be driven by a diesel engine; a superconducting motor (2); and a cryogenic unit (3), which keeps the superconducting parts below their T_c.

FACT FILE

- *Resistivity in a mercury ring below the superconductivity transition temperature of about 4.25 K is so low that no one knows how long a current introduced into the ring would last.*

- *A large industrial scrap-metal electromagnet typically produces a magnetic field of less than 0.3 tesla. Niobium–titanium magnets, however, which operate at a temperature of 4.2 K and are therefore superconductive, create fields of 8 tesla, and niobium–tin produces fields of 16 tesla.*

- *Flux pinning can be used to create magnetic bearings, in which magnetic disks can rotate free of friction above a superconductor. The addition of traces of silver oxide (AgO) to a BSCCO high-temperature superconductor increases flux pinning to such an extent that a magnetic disk can even be suspended below a superconductor doped in this way.*

SEE ALSO: Alloy • Ceramics • Conduction, electrical • Electricity • Electromagnetism • Linear motor • Resistance

Supernova

A nova marks the violent explosive death of a star. In the case of a supernova, the explosion is much more violent and causes the star to rip itself apart, blowing its outer layers into space at many thousands of miles per second. A supernova may, for a brief period, outshine a whole galaxy. To get an idea of such an event, consider that Earth's galaxy, the Milky Way, contains a hundred billion ordinary stars like the Sun. Often, prior to the explosion, it is not easy to see these stars from Earth, and their sudden increase in brightness led observers to believe that they were new stars, hence the term *nova*, which is Latin for "new."

In the past, astronomers classified supernovas into two types. These two types were distinguished on the basis of their different light curves—the way in which they first brighten and then fade; their spectra—the way in which their light output varies with wavelength; and the peak brightness they attain. The current system of classification produces largely the same divisions but for different reasons; it separates supernovas into two basic types according to their physical characteristics rather than their light curves.

Type Ia supernovas occur in both spiral galaxies, like Earth's, and elliptical galaxies. These supernovas arise in some binary star systems—pairs of stars orbiting each other under the influence of their mutual gravity. The pairs of stars in binary systems that cause supernovas are white dwarfs and red giants.

A white dwarf is the remains of a star that is in the final phase of its life, having used up all of its fuel and contracted to a size approximately 0.01 times that of the Sun. A red giant is the phase in a star's life prior to becoming a white dwarf, in which the star, having used up much of its hydrogen, collapses into itself, causing the star to heat up once more and burn its remaining hydrogen. The burning of this hydrogen causes the star to expand once more but this time to an enormous size. If a white dwarf in such a binary system is inundated by material drawn from the much larger red giant, a nuclear explosion can be triggered. This explosion blows the star apart. The amount of material these supernovas eject into space when they explode is roughly equal to the mass of the Sun. The material is ejected at the enormous speed of about 6,900 miles (11,000 km) per second.

Unlike Type Ia, Type II supernovas are seen only in the arms of spiral galaxies. Because these explosions occur in spiral arms, where stars are currently being born, the stars must also be young. To be young and yet near the end of their life cycles, these stars must be massive, because massive stars undergo accelerated aging, burning up their nuclear fuel rapidly. In a Type II explosion, several solar masses are ejected into space at about 3,100 miles (5,000 km) per second.

The presupernova star in this case is a supergiant star of five or more solar masses. The supergiant is highly evolved, that is, nuclear reactions have converted much of its initial hydrogen into heavier elements. When the core of the star is mostly iron, no more energy can be extracted by nuclear reactions. The core cannot support the overlying layers of the star, so it contracts catastrophically in less than a second to form a core with a temperature of more than 100 billion degrees. This implosion creates an outward shock wave that blows away the outer layers of the star. The remaining matter in the core is so dense that it is made only of neutrons, the electrons and protons having also combined to form neutrons—hence, these stars are called neutron stars. If the original star is extremely massive—around 15 or more solar masses—it may instead collapse into a black hole.

▲ The Cygnus Loop supernova blast wave is the remnant of a supernova that occurred around 15,000 years ago.

THE FORMATION OF AN X-RAY PULSAR

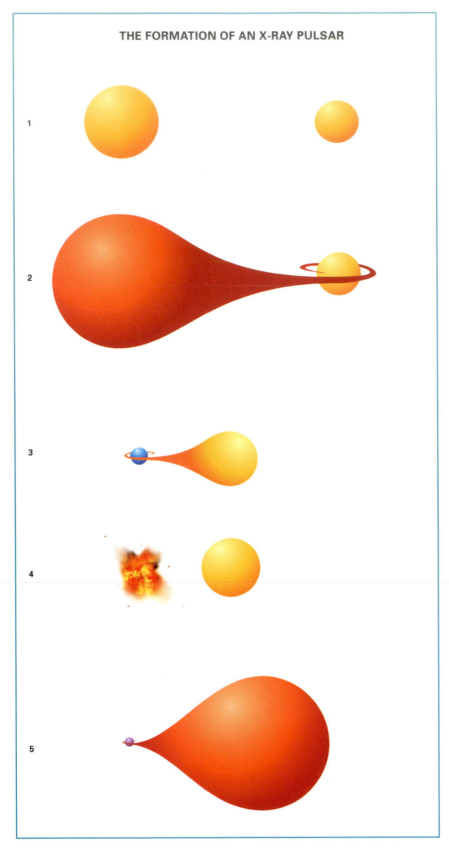

1

2

3

4

5

A further type of supernova, Type Ib, occurs in young stars that are so massive that their stellar wind causes them to lose their hydrogen atmosphere. This loss produces spectra that, like those produced by Type Ia supernovas, lacks hydrogen spectral lines, making them appear similar to Type Ia supernovas when in fact they are really Type II.

Supernova remnants

After a star blows itself to pieces, a collapsed star may be left, together with a supernova remnant. The supernova remnant is an expanding shell of gas. The shell contains gas ejected by the star and interstellar gas that has been swept up. The most famous remnant is the Crab nebula, a shell of gas so large that light, traveling at 186,000 miles (300,000,000 m) per second, takes ten years to cross it. Supernova remnants are generally faint when observed in visible light, but they emit intense radio waves and X rays. The radio emission, known as synchrotron radiation, is produced by high-energy electrons moving in a magnetic field.

Pulsars

In time a supernova remnant should fade into invisibility, but this process can be slowed if the collapsed star formed at the center of the explosion is a pulsar, or pulsating neutron star. Such an ultracompact star, only a few miles across, will be spinning very rapidly, perhaps as fast as 1,000 revolutions per second. The reason for this speed is not difficult to see—a contracting star rotates faster and faster for the same reason that ice skaters spin more rapidly when they pull in their arms.

▼ A before and after picture of a supernova that appeared in 1987 in the Large Magellanic Cloud. This was the first supernova in 400 years to be clearly visible to the unaided eye.

▲ In a binary system (1), which consists of a pair of stars, an X-ray pulsar forms when the heavier of the pair expands, becoming a red giant (2), and then starts to lose most of its mass to the other star, finally becoming a white dwarf (3). The other star then begins to lose some of its mass to the white dwarf, causing it to go supernova (4). The core of the supernova is a neutron star. Six million years later, the second star also begins to expand, becoming a red giant, and its gases overflow onto the neutron star (5). Heated by the fall, the gases emit X rays, which are directed into pulses by the spinning star's magnetic field: it is an X-ray pulsar.

Pulsars emit radio energy along a beam that sweeps past an observer with each revolution of the star, like the beam of a lighthouse. It is this energy that powers the supernova remnant. The rapidly spinning pulsar acts like a giant flywheel, gradually bleeding out the energy stored in its rotation during the first moments of the supernova explosion. All pulsars are therefore slowing down. The pulsar at the heart of the Crab nebula, for instance, is slowing at the rate of one part in a million per day.

Every element heavier than iron was created in the high temperature and pressure of supernova explosions. For example, our Sun, Earth, and even our own bodies contain supernova material. We are supernova remnants.

Every time a supernova occurs, space is seeded with heavy elements. So each successive generation of stars, formed from interstellar gas, is richer in heavy elements. Our own Sun is a second or third generation star—its composition is very different from the first generation of stars that formed when the Milky Way was young.

It may be that our Sun would not have formed at all if it were not for a supernova explosion. Compression of gas by an expanding supernova remnant—which can trigger the birth of stars in interstellar gas clouds—may have initiated the formation of our Solar System four and a half billion years ago.

Observations of supernovas

A number of supernovas have occurred in our galaxy, the Milky Way, in historical times. They have been noted chiefly by the Chinese, who watched the skies closely and called them guest stars. Europeans were less observant and seemed only to have noticed the supernovas visible in 1572 and in 1604. The supernova of 1572 is known as Tycho's star, for the Danish astronomer Tycho Brahe, and the one in 1604 Kepler's star, for the German astronomer Johannes Kepler.

Tycho's star was a Type I supernova which appeared in the constellation of Cassiopeia. At its peak, Tycho's star was as bright as the planet Venus. It remained visible to the naked eye for a total of 18 months. Kepler's star was also a Type I supernova. It appeared in the constellation of Ophiuchus and remained visible to the naked eye for over a year.

Additional supernovas were recorded by Chinese and Korean astronomers in C.E. 185, 393, 1006, 1054, and 1181. The supernova that appeared in Taurus in 1054 left the dramatic remnant we now know as the Crab nebula.

From observations of galaxies similar to our own, astronomers have determined that a star

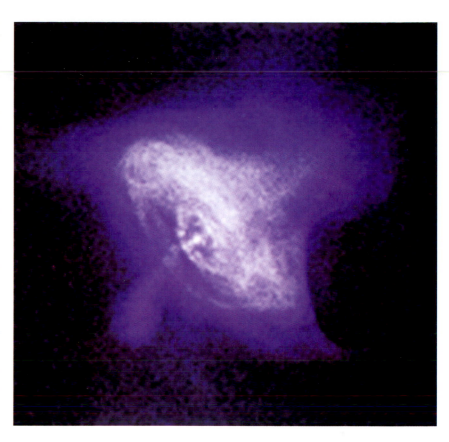

▲ An image of the Crab nebula pulsar taken by the Chandra X-ray observatory. The supernova explosion that formed the Crab nebula was seen from Earth in 1054 C.E.

should go supernova about once every 30 years in the Milky Way. Despite this expectation, however, only one—Supernova 1987A—has been spotted since the 17th century. One suggestion for the apparent paucity of supernovas in our galaxy is that they are obscured by dust. Huge lanes of dust cover large tracts of our galaxy, making it very difficult to see deep into the Milky Way.

Hypernovas

In 1998, the Polish astrophysicist Bohdan Paczynski working at Princeton University proposed the possible existence of hypernovas, which produce more than 100 times as much energy as supernovas. This theory was developed as a means of explaining the phenomenon of gamma-ray bursts (GRBs). Discovered in the 1960s, GRBs occur randomly in the sky, and once their burst fades, there are no more bursts from this location. In 1999, astronomers discovered what they believe may be the remnants of two hypernovas—MF83 and NGC5471B. Several possible explanations for hypernovas have been suggested. One is that a collision occurs between two stars in a binary system, causing the stars to merge; another proposes that hypernovas are produced by massive rapidly spinning stars with strong magnetic fields.

SEE ALSO: ASTRONOMY • ASTROPHYSICS • BLACK HOLE • FUSION • GRAVITY • OBSERVATORY • RADIO ASTRONOMY • SOLAR SYSTEM • TELESCOPE, OPTICAL • TELESCOPE, SPACE

Supersonic Flight

◀ An F-15B flying over the Mojave Desert. This supersonic aircraft is a two-seat version of the F-15 and is used for a variety of flight experiments.

Since the birth of powered aviation in 1903, flight speeds have increased from 40 mph (64 km/h) to well over 4,500 mph (7,242 km/h). Costs rise steeply with increases in speed, however, and there are also design problems associated with the velocity of sound waves in air.

Sound is a wave disturbance in the atmosphere, rather like the ripples that spread out when a stone is dropped into still water. The velocity of sound waves in air is proportional to the square root of the absolute temperature. At sea level, in temperate zones, where the average temperature is about 59°F (15°C), sound waves travel at 761 mph (1,225 km/h). The velocity falls with increasing height (because the temperature is dropping) until at just over 36,000 ft. (10.97 km) it is only 691.3 mph (1,112.5 km/h). Further increases in altitude, at least up to about 60,000 ft. (18.29 km), have no effect because the temperature of the atmosphere remains constant.

During the 19th century, an Austrian scientist, Professor Ernst Mach, studied the propagation of sound waves, and in recognition of his work, the speeds of aircraft flying close to the velocity of sound are described by their Mach numbers. At sea level, an aircraft traveling at 761.5 mph (1,225.5 km/h) is said to have a speed of Mach 1, and if it is traveling at 1,320 mph (2,124 km/h) at 40,000 ft. (12.2 km), its speed is Mach 2. Flight up to Mach 1 is described as subsonic, that above Mach 1 is supersonic.

During World War II, when piston-engined fighters were sometimes flown at speeds much higher than normal during test or in combat, their pilots would report severe buffeting or even loss of control. The greater performance of the early jet fighters brought with it increasing experience of these compressibility effects, as they were called, though their maximum speed still fell short of Mach 1.

Sonic boom

When an aircraft flies at a comparatively low speed, the air is able to move out of the way in a smooth manner, creating a region near the aircraft where the air pressure is slightly higher than normal, called a low-intensity pressure field. As the aircraft's speed increases, the pressure field increases in intensity, and regions of sudden pressure rise develop. When its speed approaches the speed of sound (Mach 1), these regions of sudden pressure rise become shock waves, which are, in effect, surfaces along which the air suffers an abrupt change in velocity and increase in pressure in its efforts to move out of the way of the aircraft. Shock waves, like other waves, are able to radiate away from their region of origin to a large distance from the aircraft.

At speeds near Mach 1, these shock waves radiate mainly in a forward direction, but as the speed of the aircraft increases above that of sound, the shock waves radiate outward at an increasing angle to the direction of flight. Their paths of movement are called rays. These rays are refracted, or bent, as they travel in the same way that light rays are bent as they pass through glass or water. Owing to the way temperature varies through the atmosphere, the rays are refracted upward so that, up to a Mach number of about 1.15—that is, 1.15 times the speed of sound, called the cut-off Mach number—they do not reach the ground for an aircraft in horizontal flight at high altitudes. Above this Mach number, however, the rays do reach the ground, and it is the arrival at the ground of the shock waves and their associated pressure field that create the sound called a sonic boom. At these speeds, the resistance of the air to the motion of the aircraft increases rapidly. If the aircraft is to travel even faster, more power has to be applied to overcome this drag, or resistance to motion. Associated with the formation of shock waves is a breakdown in the airflow behind them, which may destroy the effectiveness of the aircraft's controls.

An aircraft radiates shock waves all the time it flies at supersonic speeds. For a specific supersonic flight, the area on the ground over which sonic booms are heard is called the carpet; it extends from the region where the aircraft accelerates to supersonic speeds to the region where it decelerates back to subsonic speeds. Everyone within this carpet will hear a sonic boom just after the aircraft has passed overhead, although people at the beginning of the carpet may hear two booms or possibly a somewhat louder bang because of a tendency for the boom rays to converge when the aircraft is accelerating—called focusing.

Supersonic aircraft

The first aircraft to fly faster than sound was the U.S. rocket-powered Bell X-1, which—carried by a converted B-29 Superfortress bomber into the stratosphere in order to conserve fuel—attained Mach 1.06 on October 14, 1947. A few years later, employing the German idea of wing sweepback to reduce drag, jet fighters were able to exceed Mach 1 in a dive, though their engines were still insufficiently powerful to take them to the speed of sound in level flight. The F-86 Sabre in the United States and the Hunter in Britain were examples of these so-called transonic aircraft.

The first truly supersonic aircraft was the F-100 Super Sabre of 1953, which could reach Mach 1.25 in level flight. With its extremely thin wing, it had an even more streamlined shape than its predecessors. Such was the pace of development that only five years later the Lockheed F-104 Starfighter showed sustained speeds of Mach 2 to be not only technically possible but also militarily

realistic. It had a small wing, only a few inches thick, and edges so sharp that they had to be covered with felt when the aircraft was on the ground to prevent people from injuring themselves.

Today there is no particular difficulty in designing a fighter to fly up to Mach 2.5, though speeds above this call for the use of special metals to resist the high temperatures caused by the friction of air molecules passing over the structure. During the early 1980s, the fastest aircraft in the world were the Lockheed SR-71 reconnaissance vehicles and the Soviet MiG-25 interceptor, code named Foxbat in the West. Both cruise at heights of over 80,000 ft. (24.28 km) at Mach 3, about 2,000 mph (3,218 km/h) at that altitude. Fastest of all, however, was the rocket-powered X-15 U.S. research aircraft, which on October 3, 1967, flew at 4,534 mph (7,297 km/h), equivalent to Mach 6.72. The friction heating was so severe that parts of the airframe became red hot, and tough, very expensive Inconel (nickel-based) alloys were necessary to withstand the heat loads. Speeds above Mach 5 are described as hypersonic, to indicate that the nature of the airflow over the plane has changed again.

Wings designed to fly efficiently at supersonic speeds are invariably inefficient at low speeds; they generate high drag and low lift. Landing speeds are much higher than for subsonic layouts, calling for longer runways. In an effort to couple low drag at high speed with high lift at low speed, a number of combat aircraft have variable-geometry wings, the sweepback of which can be varied continuously to provide the best efficiency at any particular speed.

Supersonic transportation

Although it is relatively common for military aircraft to fly at supersonic speeds, the majority of passenger and transportation aircraft are restricted to operating at just below the speed of sound. Only the Anglo-French Concorde offers scheduled supersonic performance. This 128-seat airliner has a cruising speed of Mach 2.05 (around 1,400 mph, or 2,240 km/h) and a range of over

▼ The Lockheed SR-71 Blackbird reconnaissance aircraft is capable of flying at Mach 3. To slow its motion when landing, a drag chute is deployed.

◄ An artist's impression of NASA's experimental hypersonic aircraft—the X-43. This prototype may one day lead to the development of cheaper methods for launching satellites as well as much faster civilian air travel.

4,000 miles and is used mainly on intercontinental routes. The aircraft has a long (202 ft., or 61.66 m), narrow (9 ft. 6 in., or 2.63 m) fuselage with a slender, swept-back delta wing shape. This wing profile is a compromise that gives acceptable supersonic cruising drag—plus adequate lift for takeoff and at subsonic speeds. The lift characteristics vary with speed. Aircraft trim is maintained by pumping fuel between fore and aft trim tanks to adjust the center of gravity to match the lift and maintain good handling without the drag penalty resulting from large flap movements.

Adoption of a cruising speed just over Mach 2 means that the heating effects are kept to a sufficiently low level to allow the use of substantially conventional materials and construction. Higher speeds would have involved the use of a material such as titanium for the skin, whereas the Concorde uses aluminum alloys. The highest temperatures are encountered at cruising speeds and altitudes, with the nose reaching around 266°F (130°C) and the leading edges of the wings more than 212°F (100°C).

There is a sustained environmental opposition to the effects of sonic boom, however, and supersonic aircraft may well have to be restricted to routes that do not involve overflying densely inhabited regions. In addition, Concorde has been very expensive to operate, limiting its use to the luxury market. The increase in fuel costs since the 1970s have made this form of transportation economically impractical for general use. NASA, however, has a plan to build a supersonic passenger jet called the High Speed Civil Transport (HSCT). If built, this aircraft will fly as fast as Concorde but will be bigger and cheaper to operate.

Hypersonic flight

Increasing interest is now being shown in the possibility of developing aircraft that can travel at hypersonic speeds. NASA is currently working on a prototype vehicle, called the X-43, that will fly at speeds up to Mach 10. To achieve these speeds, the X-43 uses a scramjet rather than a conventional rocket or jet engine. Scientists at the University of Queensland's center for hypersonics in Australia are also working on developing scramjet technology in their HyShot project.

A scramjet has no moving parts and, unlike a rocket engine, does not carry a supply of oxygen but takes oxygen from the atmosphere to burn the hydrogen fuel. Scramjets use the sonic shock waves caused by the supersonic airflow to force air into the combustion chamber of the engine. The rapid airflow through the engine makes efficient combustion difficult to achieve, especially with liquid hydrocarbon fuels, and thus, hydrogen is used. Advanced materials will be needed to withstand the conditions in the engine and also for the airframe, which will have to withstand a greater heating effect.

One problem with these engines is that they must already be travelling at speeds greater than Mach 5 before they begin to work. Current testing involves accelerating the prototypes by attaching them to rockets. Scientists expect that scramjets will initially find use as cheaper methods for sending satellites into space.

SEE ALSO: Aerodynamics • Aerospace industry • Air • Aircraft-control engineering • Aircraft design • Aircraft engine • Airliner • Sound • V/stol aircraft

Surface Tension

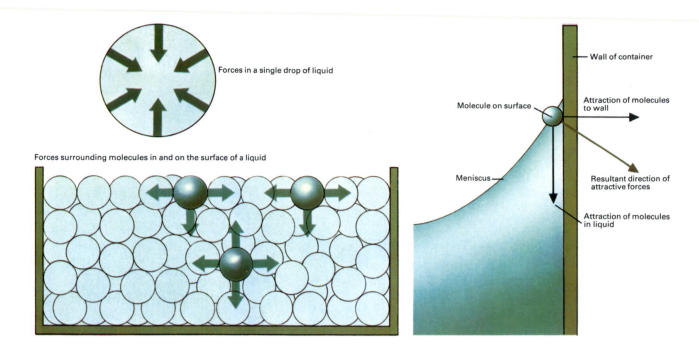

Forces in a single drop of liquid

Forces surrounding molecules in and on the surface of a liquid

Wall of container

Molecule on surface

Attraction of molecules to wall

Meniscus

Resultant direction of attractive forces

Attraction of molecules in liquid

The surface of any liquid behaves like an elastic sheet, pulling a drop of the liquid into the shape with the smallest possible surface area. In weightless conditions it forms a sphere, but on Earth the shape is modified by the surroundings, and even a falling raindrop is slightly flattened by air resistance. The explanation of this surface tension effect lies in the fact that, whereas the molecules of liquid within the drop are attracted equally in all directions by the other molecules, a molecule at the surface experiences only an inward force from the other water molecules. These intermolecular forces are electromagnetic. The outward attractive forces from the molecules of air or vapor outside the drop are much less strong, so the layer of molecules composing the surface behaves like an elastic skin.

Surface tension acts in such a way as to contract the surface area of a liquid, and it can be measured as the force acting at right angles to a line of unit length in the surface. For water the force is about 0.07 N/m—that is 0.0007 newtons for a line of one centimeter length. Although this seems a very small force, it is sufficient to float a steel needle placed carefully on water and also to support small insects, such as water striders, which live on the surface of ponds. The surface tension of pure alcohol is as low as 0.02 N/m, while mercury has a much higher value of 0.47 N/m. For all liquids, the surface tension decreases with temperature, mainly owing to the increase in density of the vapor above the surface—the increased attraction of the vapor molecules on the surface molecules of the liquid lowers the surface

tension, until at the critical point it becomes zero. In addition, an increase in temperature weakens the bonds between the molecules in the liquid and therefore decreases the surface tension.

The surface tension of liquids is also decreased by impurities, especially by detergents, which congregate at the surface of the liquid. A small amount of detergent added to water will reduce the surface tension so much that it will support neither a floating needle nor a water strider. The lower surface tension, however, does mean that a thin film of liquid is much less liable to disruption by the surface forces and that water containing detergent can form large, stable bubbles.

When a liquid is in contact with a solid, the attractive force between the molecules of the solid and those of the liquid may be stronger than that between the liquid molecules. It is this force, adhesion tension, that causes the surface of water to be pulled up where it is in contact with a glass surface to form a meniscus (curved surface). In a very narrow (or capillary) tube, the curvature means that there is a difference in pressure across the surface of the water.

To equalize the pressures inside and outside the capillary at the level of the outside water surface, water is pushed up the tube. The surface tension and the tube diameter affect the final height reached by the liquid—mercury is pushed downward, but water could rise to 33 ft. (10 m).

▲ All molecules attract other molecules, so a drop of liquid contracts as if it had a skin. If the molecules of a liquid are more strongly attracted to the molecules of which the wall is made than to each other, the increased molecular attraction at the edges causes an upward meniscus.

SEE ALSO: ATOMIC STRUCTURE • DENSITY • ELECTROMAGNETISM • MATTER, PROPERTIES OF • MERCURY • PRESSURE • WATER

Surface Treatments

◀ Continuous electrogalvanizing of sheet steel conserves more zinc than other methods. The sheet is fed into the galvanizing bath through a snout, which dips below the surface of the molten zinc and protects the surface of the steel against reoxidation, thus eliminating the need for fluxing.

In the production of manufactured goods made of metal, surface-finishing operations may be necessary at various stages. Original surfaces may need to be prepared for further processing—an example would be the descaling of a forging before it is machined. An intermediate surface may need to be cleaned or polished before final treatment, and a final surface often must be protected from corrosion—perhaps by painting or electroplating, which also serve as decorative effects. Surface finishing may be divided into preparatory treatments, which are mostly metal-cleaning operations, and final treatments, which offer protection, decoration, or an extremely hard or smooth surface to prevent failure in service—for example, the heat treatment and grinding to precise size of bearing surfaces on machine parts.

Fettling and descaling

After forging or casting, metal objects must often be treated to remove casting sand, metal scale, and rough edges before they can be cold worked by machine tools, otherwise dimensional accuracy may be difficult to achieve.

Grinding and wire brushing are undertaken with hand-held tools that are driven pneumatically or electrically. In barrel tumbling, the articles are tumbled with small, star-shaped pieces of cast iron in a barrel rotating at about 10 or 15 rpm, creating a burnished surface.

Various forms of blasting techniques have been developed to clean and smooth components at some stage during manufacture. The different techniques used are commonly referred to as

sandblasting and shot blasting, although sand is no longer used as an abrasive—silica sand, while inexpensive, generates toxic dust that gives rise to a risk of the lung disease silicosis. Generally, a stream of abrasive particles is directed over and against the part at high speed so that the abrasive impact cleans the surface thoroughly.

A wide range of abrasive media is available to suit different cleaning and finishing applications. Iron and steel grit are used for rust and scale removal and for deburring, while alumina abrasives offer fast cutting for surface cleaning. Steel shot gives a fine surface finish and is used for surface peening; glass beads have a similar but more gentle action. Plastic parts are deflashed with soft blast abrasives such as nylon and crushed fruit stones, which are also used for fine cleaning and paint removal.

Typical applications include the removal of sand cores and scale from castings before machining, surface preparation for painting, cleaning of used components for servicing or refurbishing, and the deflashing of plastics moldings.

Shot blasting consists of directing a steady high-velocity stream of shot (round or angular pieces of chilled cast iron) at the article to be cleaned. The stream is directed at the object through a flexible tube. Small objects are placed in a chamber that may have a window through which the operator can monitor the cleaning on a one-time-only basis, or the process may be automated with fixed nozzles in mass production.

The wet process of cleaning castings uses water jets at a pressure of 80 times the atmospheric pressure and a velocity of 186 mph (300 km/h).

▶ Plastic coatings on steel are available in many colors for making furniture, paneling, and other products where basic strength as well as a soft, durable surface is required.

The electrochemical method of cleaning employs an alkali liquor in an electrolytic tank.

Descaling is also accomplished by pickling, which consists of immersion of the metal stock in a solution of 5 to 10 percent sulfuric acid at 140 to 176°F (60–80°C). Because of its relative slowness, pickling has declined in favor of shot blasting for cleaning forgings. Pickling is also used, however, to clean hot-rolled stock in the steel mill. Whenever tight dimensional tolerance and smooth surface finish are required from metal stock, cold rolling is necessary, because it gives a smooth, dense surface. Pickled hot-rolled stock is often finished to size by cold rolling. To prepare hot-rolled product for cold rolling, to remove an oxide layer after hardening, or to roughen the surface of strip metal for special applications, a reel-to-reel strip grinder is sometimes used.

Coatings

Various coatings for decoration, corrosion resistance, or other purposes are applied to metal. Paints, lacquers, varnishes, and enamels are applied mechanically after degreasing with chemicals. Color or protection can also be applied by chemical and electric means. An oxide range of colors from pale gold to steel gray can be deposited on copper and brass articles by applying solutions of the appropriate soluble sulfides. Anodizing is the deposition of a thin film of synthetic oxide on a light metal, such as aluminum, to prevent the further access of air to the surface, preserving the luster and preventing corrosion. The article is made the anode in a 3 percent solution of chromic acid at about 104°F (40°C). Sulfuric and oxalic acid processes are also used, and the anodic film may be dyed various colors. Zinc is applied by electrolysis to steel for corrosion prevention in one of the processes for galvanizing and sherardizing. Paint is also used to prevent corrosion—for example, a stainless steel pigment has been claimed to reduce necessary repainting by 30 percent.

Metal surfaces are coated with metal to provide a more wear-resistant surface or to build up a worn surface so that it can be machined to size again. Machine parts that would be expensive to replace can often be repaired this way. Electroplating is one method; others are metal spraying and electric arc spraying. In metal spraying, the compounded metal particles, heated in the oxyacetylene flame, undergo an exothermic (involving evolution of heat) reaction that causes a fusion bond to the substrate. In electric arc spraying, the deposit metal is melted by the electric arc, and a compressed air blast atomizes it for projection on to the workpiece.

▶ Copper plating in a cyanide bath containing cuprous cyanide, sodium cyanide and carbonate, and sodium thiosulfate as a brightener.

Principles of electroplating

In electroplating, a metal coating is deposited onto a conducting surface by making the surface metal the cathode in an electrolytic cell, with a suitable electrolyte containing heavy metal ions—the plating metal. A low-voltage direct current reduces metal ions at the cathode to metal atoms, which adhere to the object being coated, known as the basis metal. The quantity of current is proportional to the weight of metal deposited, according to Faraday's law.

Simultaneously, metal will go into solution at the anode (a sheet or bar of the plating metal) if the anode is soluble. In some instances, however, an insoluble anode is used for practical reasons: lead anodes are used in chromium plating solutions and conduct electric current but remain virtually unaltered—the chromium is removed from the solution and replaced by adding more chromic acid. If the anode is soluble, the weight of metal dissolved from it is proportional to the quantity of current passed.

Throwing power

One of the most important properties of an electroplating solution is its throwing power, which is its ability to deposit a metal coating of uniform thickness on a cathode surface, not all areas of which are equidistant from the anode. Good throwing power enables recessed portions of an article of complicated shape (to which less current penetrates) to be covered with a coating of adequate

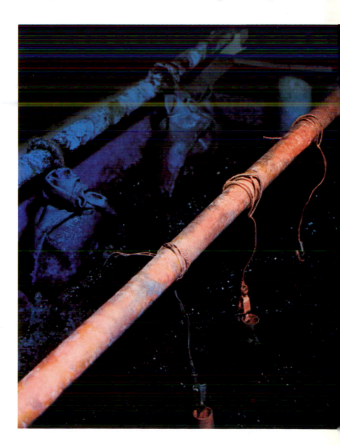

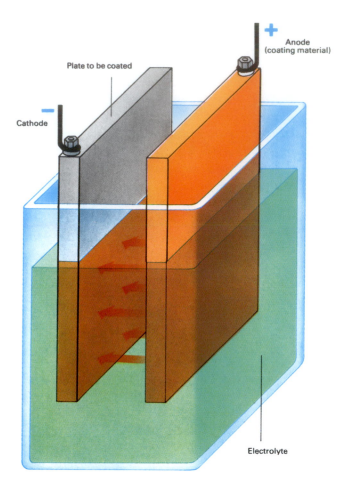

Plate to be coated

Cathode −

Anode + (coating material)

Electrolyte

▲ In electroplating, an electric current is passed between the two plates, and metal from the anode passes into solution in the electrolyte to be deposited on the surface of the cathode.

thickness. This property is of particular importance if the basis metal needs to be protected against corrosion. Solutions of ions formed by the combination of a simple metal ion with a neutral molecule normally possess a better throwing power than solutions of simple metal salts.

Commercial electroplating solutions

Commercial electroplating solutions consist of aqueous solutions of heavy metal and other salts to which various specific substances (normally organic compounds) have been added to obtain coatings of the desired properties (for instance, brightness, hardness, ductility, smoothness, and adequate thickness in recess).

Although nonferrous metals and alloys are often electroplated with coatings of various metals, the material most widely used as the basis metal for electroplating is steel. Most metals below aluminum in the electrochemical series can be deposited from aqueous plating solutions. The electrochemical, or electromotive, series is a list of metals in which a metal higher in the series will replace one lower down from a solution of its salts. In order of this series, the main metals are sodium, magnesium, aluminum, manganese, zinc, chromium, iron, cobalt, nickel, tin, lead, (hydrogen), copper, mercury, silver, platinum, and gold.

Nonaqueous plating solutions, using solvents or molten salts for the electrolyte, can be used in specialized applications—for example, plating with the more reactive metals such as aluminum and magnesium or applying coatings to metals, such as uranium.

In electroless plating, the solution decomposes on the surface to be plated (sometimes with the aid of a catalyst) to leave a metal deposit. Although sometimes used to plate metals, this process is especially important in the plating of plastics. A popular plastic for coating is polystyrene, which is frequently used for the production of small components, such as automobile door handles and trim. Examples of metals that are used for electroplating are mainly chromium and nickel but also include cadmium, cobalt, copper, gold, iridium, iron, lead, palladium, platinum, rhodium, silver, tin, and zinc.

Decorative and protective coatings

Decorative and protective coatings are usually bright, such as bright nickel–chromium finishes on automobile bumpers, hubcaps, and door handles and on various domestic fittings. In the past, bright finishes could be obtained only by mechanical polishing at various stages of the plating operation, a time-consuming and costly process that necessitated degreasing and cleaning after each stage. For this reason, bright plating solutions were developed, which contain organic additives to help the plated surface develop a mirror finish.

Plant for electroplating

Electroplating machinery can be automatic, semiautomatic, manual, or barrel treated. In the first three categories, the work is treated individually or at least is individually suspended on jigs. In the barrel process, bulk quantities of small items are plated in a rotating barrel, which is perforated to allow the electrolyte through and which provides the cathode connection.

Automatic plants process articles through the various pretreatment, plating, and posttreatment stages. Such plants are used for large-volume production. In semiautomatic baths, the work is transferred manually from bath to bath.

The size of plating vats can range from a few gallons for the electrodeposition of such costly metals as gold, rhodium, and platinum to several thousand gallons for the deposition of nickel and chromium in large automatic plants. The current used depends on the total surface area of the work being processed, so an important factor is the current density—current in amps (A) per unit area. Current density can vary from about 0.013 A per sq. in. (0.002 A/cm²) for some noble metals to 3 or more A per sq. in. for certain nickel solutions and chromium baths.

Polishing

A very good surface finish can be produced by electropolishing. This method is the opposite of electroplating—the workpiece is made the anode rather than the cathode, and the high points on its finish are removed. A wide variety of solutions is used—for example, phosphoric acid and butyl alcohol for stainless steel. The resulting finish can be comparable or even superior to mechanical buffing and can be used for parts having irregular surfaces that would be difficult to polish any other way, such as jewelry and automobile trim pieces.

Galvanizing

Galvanizing is the general name given to processes that apply a thin surface coating of zinc to iron and steel articles. With the exception of paint, it is the most widely used protective coating for ferrous (iron-containing) metal, its applications including structural steelwork for building, sheet metal, bolts, nuts, and wire.

The zinc coating affords the ferrous metal protection from the corrosive effects of atmospheric oxygen and water vapor in two ways. Firstly, it physically shields the iron in the galvanized article from contact with the surrounding air. In addition, if the zinc coating is broken to expose the iron base metal, the zinc surround-

◀ A castored blasting gun used to clean a large, welded steel box. Dust and debris are carried by a vacuum recovery tube to a reclaimer section. Here an adjustable air-wash and sieving system are used to cleanse the recycled blasting medium to ensure its quality is maintained.

ing the break provides a type of cathodic protection for the iron.

Chemically, rust corrosion is the formation of complex iron oxides at the surface of the metal. These iron oxides are essentially ionic compounds,

◀ A worker in protective clothing sandblasts an aircraft component to get the surface clean. Sandblasting consists of directing a steady high-velocity stream of abrasive at the article; because of the fluid nature of the stream, complicated shapes and internal cavities can be cleaned as easily as flat surfaces. The stream of abrasive particles is usually produced by feeding abrasive into compressed air, which carries them down a hose to the workpiece.

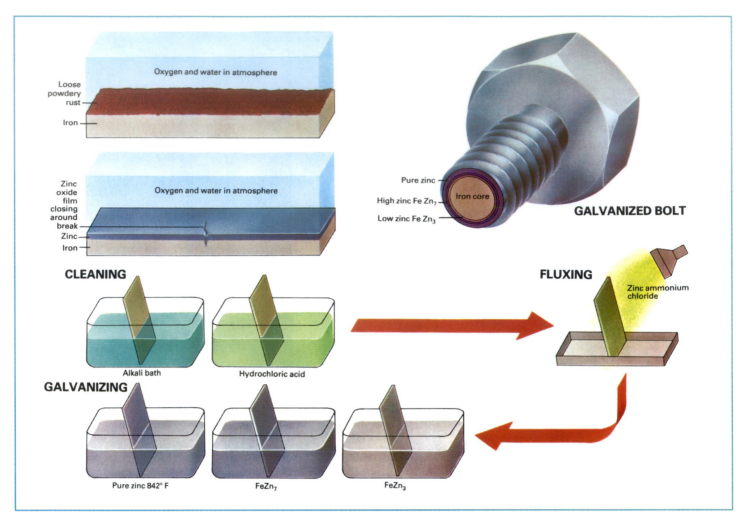

CLEANING

Alkali bath   Hydrochloric acid

GALVANIZING

Pure zinc 842° F   FeZn₇   FeZn₃

FLUXING

Zinc ammonium chloride

Pure zinc
High zinc Fe Zn₇
Low zinc Fe Zn₃
Iron core
GALVANIZED BOLT

Loose powdery rust
Iron
Oxygen and water in atmosphere

Zinc oxide film closing around break
Zinc
Iron
Oxygen and water in atmosphere

involving a transfer of outer-shell, or valence, electrons from the iron atoms to the oxygen molecules. Zinc, however, is more electropositive, that is, it is more prone to lose its valence electrons by reacting with another element to form a compound. The zinc coating will thus be preferentially attacked by the atmospheric water and oxygen, if it is in electric contact with the iron base metal.

In common with many pure metals, zinc is oxidized in air. The zinc oxide formed at the interface of the metal and the air is not, however, in the loose powdery form of iron rust. Rather, this oxide continues to adhere strongly to the metal surface in what is termed an oxide film. This oxide serves to seal off the rest of the metal, and therefore the underlying iron, from further attack. Iron rust, on the other hand, because of its powdery form, exposes even more of the raw metal to the corrosive effects of the air.

Most bulk commercial galvanizing is done by the hot-dip process, in which the iron or steel article is simply immersed in a bath of molten zinc at around 842°F (450°C). There are three distinct processes: galvanizing of fabricated or semifabricated articles, continuous galvanizing of steel sheet and steel wire, and automatic galvanizing of steel tubes.

Galvanizing fabricated articles

Because the surface of the article must be very clean, oil and grease residues are cleaned off in a preliminary alkali bath. The article is next descaled—that is, has any surface oxides and carbonates removed in another bath of hydrochloric or sulfuric acid. A fluxing solution of zinc ammonium chloride is applied before the article is dipped. The zinc coating that adheres to the article after it has been dipped is in fact a series of three layers. Beneath the outer covering of pure zinc there are two layers of iron–zinc alloys: a very thin low-zinc ($FeZn_3$) layer next to the iron, with a high-zinc ($FeZn_7$) layer above it. Although zinc itself is a ductile metal, the alloy layers are brittle and must be kept as thin as possible to prevent flaking. After immersion, the article is removed quickly, drained, and cooled in air or in water.

Other methods of applying zinc coatings to iron or steel base include zinc plating (by electric or mechanical methods), sherardizing, spraying, and painting.

▲ The article to be galvanized is cleaned in alkali and hydrochloric acid, sprayed with a fluxing solution, and then submerged in tanks containing successively purer solutions of zinc. The top two boxes show how a zinc oxide film protects iron.

SEE ALSO: Abrasive • Chromium • Corrosion prevention • Electrolysis • Metal • Metalworking • Nickel • Zinc

Surgery

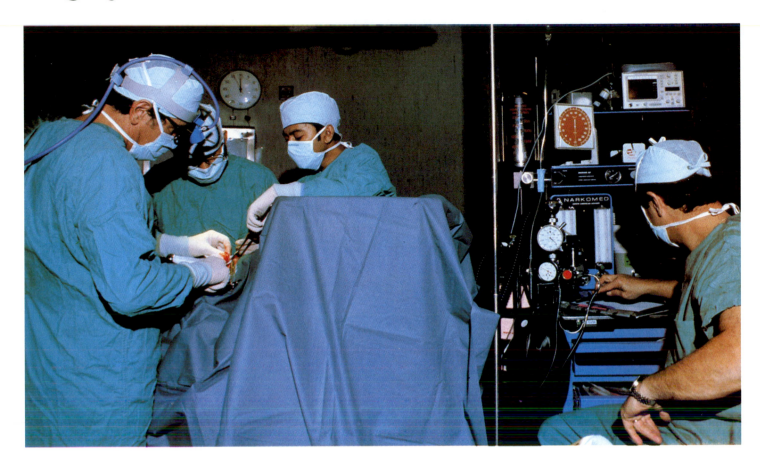

Surgery is the part of medicine that treats disease or injury by opening up the body. Diseased areas are cut out or repairs are made and the opening is closed up. Highly trained doctors called surgeons perform the operations, usually in a specially prepared room and using specially designed surgical instruments.

History

Surgery has been known since ancient times. The first records were found on ancient Egyptian papyrus scrolls, the Ebers Papyrus of about 1600 B.C.E. They describe the use of linen thread and animal sinews to suture battle wounds. Several operations were detailed, including trepanning—the boring of holes into the skull to relieve pressure on the brain. The Stone Age people trepanned the skull with flint implements, and the new bone on the skulls of some skeletons shows that many of the patients survived. Some operations were known to ancient Babylonians, Greeks, and Romans. The best early surgeons were the Hindus, who used at least 120 different surgical instruments. They also developed plastic surgery to replace cut-off noses and ears.

Among the many famous surgeons of the past was the Frenchman Ambroise Paré, who came to Paris as a barber's assistant and became the father

of military medicine. He reintroduced the use of ligatures and stopped the practice of controlling bleeding with boiling oil and cauterization, methods that were prevalent in the Middle Ages.

It was not until the middle of the 19th century, however, that surgery became more humane, and it was the discovery of anesthetics and antiseptics that brought about the changes. Before the discovery of ether and chloroform, operations were carried out without any anesthetic. The unfortunate victim was tied down, and any relief from pain came from the use of alcohol or opiates.

The first successful public demonstration of ether anesthesia was given in 1846 at the Massachusetts General Hospital in Boston and

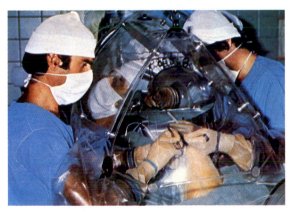

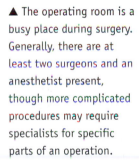

▲ The operating room is a busy place during surgery. Generally, there are at least two surgeons and an anesthetist present, though more complicated procedures may require specialists for specific parts of an operation.

◄ These surgeons are operating through a sterile bubble to prevent any bacteria from contaminating the wound. Aseptic conditions are important if the patient has a poor immune system or if the patient has a highly infective disease that could be passed on to the operating staff.

later the same year in Europe. Although operations could now be performed more safely and painlessly, many patients died from infection. Wounds did not heal, and patients often died from blood poisoning.

The 19th-century French chemist Louis Pasteur discovered that bacteria could transmit disease. Working on these ideas, the British surgeon Sir Joseph Lister investigated the cause of hospital gangrene and introduced the carbolic spray for use during operations. He also developed the principle of antisepsis: by sterilizing instruments before an operation, by the surgeon soaking his hands in a solution of carbolic acid, and by soaking dressings in carbolic acid, infection was reduced by one-third.

As surgery continued to progress, new techniques were mastered and new materials developed and refined. A significant advance was made when blood transfusions became safe. Karl Landsteiner, an Austrian pathologist, discovered blood groups in 1900, and this knowledge allowed blood to be matched between donor and patient. Despite antisepsis, many patients still did not recover from surgery because of infection. This position was changed only by the discovery of the sulfonamides and then of penicillin, the first of many antibiotics that are now used to control infection.

With safer conditions, the development of new materials, and improvements in postoperative care, great advances have been made in surgery. Today, surgeons can safely replace diseased

▲ Helium–neon laser beams bounced off tiny, throbbing blood vessels in the eye provide the best method of gauging blood flow, which is essential knowledge for the anesthetist.

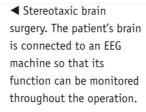

◀ Stereotaxic brain surgery. The patient's brain is connected to an EEG machine so that its function can be monitored throughout the operation.

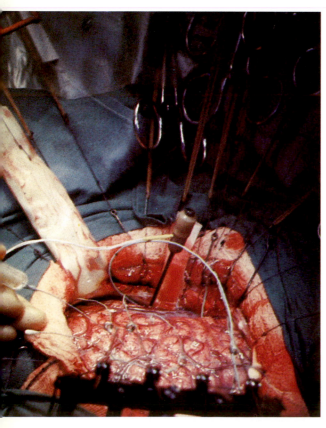

or worn-out parts of the body. Using operating microscopes, they can sew together tiny nerves and blood vessels. The trend is increasingly toward minimally invasive techniques that cause less trauma to the patient and reduce scarring. A great variety of operations can be performed.

Reasons for operating

Operations are performed to repair damage, remove growths, and correct abnormalities. After an accident, bones may be broken and organs and tissues damaged. Before corrective surgery is undertaken, the patient may need resuscitation, the wounds cleaned, and the damage assessed. It may not be possible for surgery to be performed until the swelling of the injured part has subsided and until any possible infection is under control. Wounds may be left open or sewn together until it is possible to perform the essential repairs. Metal screws, pins, and plates are used to repair badly fractured bones.

Abnormalities that are present at birth—such as club feet and heart defects—can now be corrected; these operations are often done within the first few months of life. Most operations are performed to support life, but many are done for cosmetic reasons. There have also been successful attempts to perform surgery on babies while still in the womb, though such procedures can increase the risk of miscarriage.

Growths and tumors can be either benign or malignant, and quite often they must be removed and examined under a microscope (biopsied) before the distinction can be made. Sometimes a growth can be removed simply, but in other cases, repairs to the organs where the growth originated need to be made. For example, if the tumor is in the bowel, the section containing the growth is removed, and the remaining ends of the bowel are sewn together. Sometimes reconstructive surgery is carried out at the same time, for example, if a woman has a breast removed.

How operations are performed

The patient who is undergoing surgery will always be given an anesthetic of some kind to remove pain. If a patient is given a general anesthetic, he or she will be asleep and will not be aware of what is happening. In the case of a local anesthetic, the area to be operated on is injected with a substance that blocks conduction in the sensory nerves from the operation site. Another method is to inject drugs into the spinal canal to produce loss of sensation below the level at which the injection is given but allowing the patient to remain conscious. Cesarean births and some types of brain surgery, where the surgeon needs to

▶ Many operations now make use of improved imaging systems to help surgeons locate the area on which they need to operate. This brain surgeon is using a viewing wand to beam images of small areas of the brain onto a television monitor.

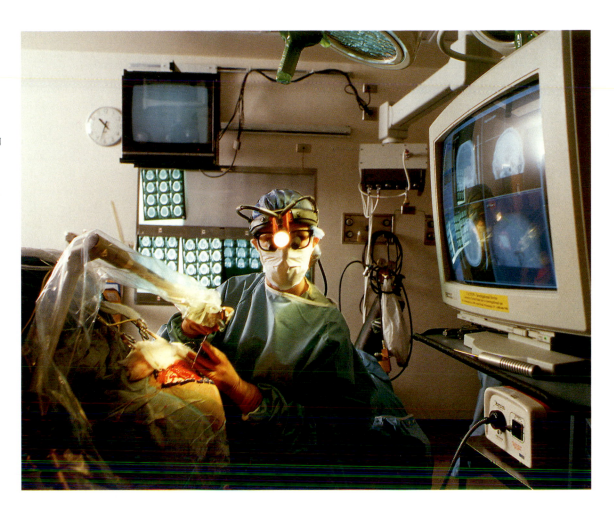

assess the patient's response to his actions, are commonly performed under local anesthesia.

All operations are performed under aseptic conditions, in which drapes and instruments must be sterile and the atmosphere clean. An incision is made in the skin to allow access to the part of the body that has to be operated upon. Fat below the skin is opened to reveal the muscle layer, which can either be cut through or dissected and separated. If the abdomen is being operated on, another layer, the peritoneum, a tough membrane, has to be opened to allow the surgeon access to the relevant organs. A stainless steel scalpel blade is used for most incisions, but work is proceeding with lasers for this purpose, and a diamond-edged knife is used for eye surgery.

As the tissues are cut, bleeding occurs, and it must be controlled. Bleeding from small blood vessels can be stopped by using a controlled source of heat, known as diathermy. Large blood vessels may be clamped with artery forceps, and a ligature can be tied around the bleeding vessels. Large blood vessels are identified before they are cut. They have two ligatures tied around them, and the cut is made between the ligatures. Nerves and tendons must also be identified and care taken not to injure them. Cotton packs moistened in warm saline are carefully placed over or around organs to keep them moist and prevent damage.

The surgeon uses many instruments, but a few basic ones are essential for any operation. The scalpel is a metal handle holding a stainless steel blade. The blades are of various shapes and sizes. Dissecting forceps help the surgeon to handle the tissues gently. Scissors are made of stainless steel and must be extremely sharp. Some are curved, others angled; some have sharp points, others round ends. When organs have to be kept out of the way to allow the surgeon clear access to the site of the operation, a retractor is used. Retractors come in a variety of shapes and sizes. Disposable equipment is also available for use on patients who are highly infectious.

Ligatures and sutures

During an operation, bleeding must be controlled and wounds repaired. Special materials have been produced for these purposes. Sutures can be made from natural materials or synthetic fibers. Some are dissolved by the body; others remain there permanently. The natural materials come from plant or animal sources. Catgut, for example, is a suture processed from the gut of sheep.

Synthetic sutures are made by processing a wide variety of polymers. They cause less reaction to the tissue than natural materials, and their performance in the body is more predictable. They are gradually replacing natural sutures.

Staples have also been developed for joining tissues together instead of sutures. They have evolved from a crude metal clip used to bring skin edges together and are now sophisticated devices assembled on an automatic loader.

The healing process

After surgery, cut or dissected tissues must be repaired. After an abdominal operation, for example, first the peritoneum is sewn together, then the muscle, then the fat layer, and finally the skin. If the chest has been opened by dividing the sternum (breastbone), it is repaired by using wire sutures. There is no muscle in this part of the body, so the subcutaneous layer is sewn together first, followed by the skin.

Once the tissues have been sewn together, the healing process starts, and the tissues begin to fuse together. Any excess of fluid will delay the healing process, and quite often, pieces of plastic tubing, varying in size according to the need, will be placed in the wound to allow fluid to drain away. As the amount of fluid decreases, the tube is gradually removed from the wound. Nutrition plays a great part in the healing process—if patients are too ill to eat normally, they are nourished by infusing special fluids into their veins.

The control of pain assists in the healing process, and physiotherapy and early mobilization help to prevent postoperative complications, such as chest infections and blood clots in veins. It also makes patients feel they are getting better. It has been demonstrated that by giving a patient adequate information before and after an operation, the healing process can be accelerated and the patient quickly discharged for home recovery.

◄ Vivid detail of a leaking blood vessel system in an eye is revealed by injecting a fluorescent dye into a vein in the arm and then filming it in the eye.

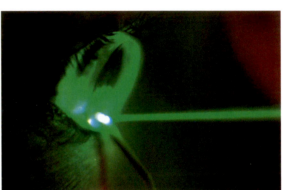

▲ An argon laser is fired in bursts of one-fifth of a second to cauterize leaking blood vessels that hamper vision without causing any pain in the process. The laser beam can travel straight through the lens to reach the back of the eye, reducing the risk of infection that cutting with a scalpel would entail.

Alternatives to surgery

Modern technology offers us faster and more accurate ways of diagnosing and treating diseases and, in some cases, eliminates the need for surgery. Flexible fiber-optic cables and microlenses can be inserted into various organs of the body without the need for a general anesthetic or an operation. These instruments (known as endoscopes) can be used to examine the trachea, bronchus, esophagus, stomach, colon, and bladder and to take small specimens of tissue for examination. Radiographic equipment such as image intensifiers, scanners, and ultrasound can eliminate the need for exploratory operations by assisting in the diagnosis of the disease. A fine tube with a tiny balloon attached to the end can, under X-ray control, be inserted into a blood vessel and passed into the coronary arteries. The balloon can be inflated, and as it passes along the arteries of the heart, it dilates them, so removing the need for surgery. Stones can be removed from the kidneys and gall bladder by a machine called a lithotripter, which uses sound waves to shatter them into tiny pieces that can be passed in the urine.

Drugs and radiotherapy, either singly or combined, are used to treat and cure cancer, again reducing the need for surgery. By using computers, it is possible to monitor and work out the precise dosage of drugs and radiotherapy, so avoiding many side effects. Stereotaxic surgery uses a 3-D system to fix the coordinates of tumors deep in the brain so that bursts of radiation, heat, cold, or chemicals can be directed at them without cutting the surrounding tissue. Lasers are also being used, particularly in the treatment of diseases of the eye and the cervix. Freezing of tumors by cryosurgery, particularly in the nose, pharynx, and larynx, is now replacing some operative procedures.

Minimally invasive surgery

Endoscopy is a generic name for various similar forms of viewing inside the body. A typical endoscope consists of a tube 10 mm in diameter containing a light, with optical fibers attached to a video camera and a pipe that blows carbon dioxide to separate the organs and allow a better view. Other optional facilities include tiny metal jaws to grasp hold of a piece of tissue and a laser beam that can accurately destroy the most minute piece of diseased tissue while leaving the surrounding healthy tissue intact. Specialized forms of endoscope include the gastroscope, for viewing the gullet, stomach, and duodenum; the bronchoscope, for viewing the lungs; the proctoscope, for viewing the rectum and colon; and the laparoscope, for viewing inside the abdomen. Laparoscopes used on babies and children are less than ¼ in. (5 mm) in diameter.

In a typical laparoscopic operation, such as gall bladder removal, the surgeon first makes four tiny punctures in the abdomen. An illuminated laparoscope is inserted through one hole, the instruments through another. The gall bladder is clamped off at both ends with clips inserted down a tubular instrument, a cautery is used to seal off any bleeding, and the gall bladder with its stone is removed though the largest hole, the one through which the laparoscope went. Before this innovation was introduced in 1987, surgeons needed to make a long incision, and the patient had to stay in the hospital 9 to 10 days, instead of 1 to 2 days, for the wound to heal.

Robot control

During laparoscopy, it is the task of an assisting doctor to point the laparoscope itself while the surgeon carries out the operation. A new development, however, involves a robotized pointing system. Tiny sensors on a headband pick up any movements of the surgeon's head.

Instead of instructing the assisting doctor how to move the camera, the surgeon simply makes natural movements of the head while watching a TV screen. The laparoscope moves accordingly, as if it were the surgeon's eyes.

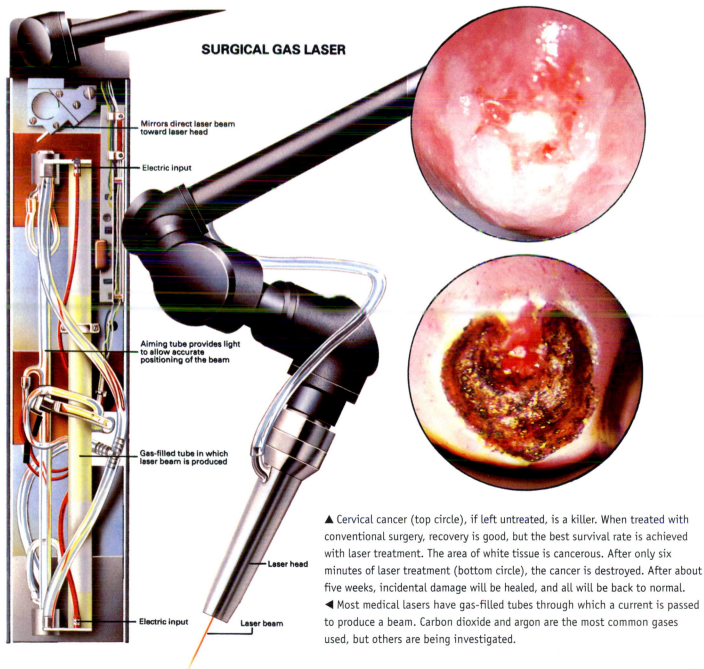

SURGICAL GAS LASER

Mirrors direct laser beam toward laser head

Electric input

Aiming tube provides light to allow accurate positioning of the beam

Gas-filled tube in which laser beam is produced

Laser head

Electric input Laser beam

▲ Cervical cancer (top circle), if left untreated, is a killer. When treated with conventional surgery, recovery is good, but the best survival rate is achieved with laser treatment. The area of white tissue is cancerous. After only six minutes of laser treatment (bottom circle), the cancer is destroyed. After about five weeks, incidental damage will be healed, and all will be back to normal.
◄ Most medical lasers have gas-filled tubes through which a current is passed to produce a beam. Carbon dioxide and argon are the most common gases used, but others are being investigated.

Eventually, robots may actually wield the surgical instruments themselves, either under the control of the surgeon while watching an endoscope or scan image or automatically on a chosen route into the patient. The first use of such a system, using a device called Robodoc, took place in 1992. Since then, the concept of telesurgery, using a combination of computers, videoconferencing, telecommunications, and surgical robots, has been advanced to the point where, in 2001, the technique was used to perform a number of operations in which the surgeon and patient were on different continents.

Endoscopes are also used to operate inside joints and to repair hernias and remove kidneys and uteruses. Organs such as kidneys are encased in a strong plastic bag and macerated into small pieces so that they can be removed through the

▶ An operating room must be scrupulously clean—this one uses a filter to remove harmful particles from the air.

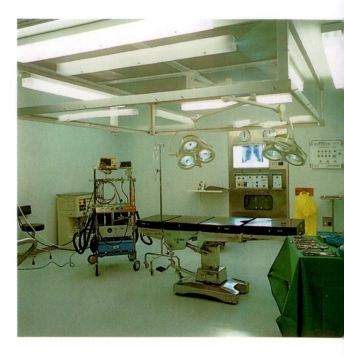

hole made for the endoscope. In theory, almost any operation except a transplant can be done endoscopically; it may even be possible to avoid heart bypass surgery by using an endoscope and a laser to drill tiny holes in the heart muscle so that it gets oxygen as it pumps blood.

The medical use of lasers has brought further advances in surgery. Lasers are used to drill tiny holes in the iris of the eye to relieve the pressure of glaucoma or to weld a detached retina to the back of the eye, to burn away precancerous cells of the cervix, to remove tattoos and birthmarks, and to alter the shape of the cornea to correct nearsightedness and astigmatism.

Virtual surgery

Surgeons are now benefitting from the huge advances that have been made in computing power and graphical interfaces, particularly virtual reality (VR) applications. VR packages are under development that will train experienced surgeons in new operating techniques and allow junior doctors to practice their skills before they are allowed to touch a real patient. One potential application, a virtual cadaver, would reduce some of the problems of obtaining and storing bodies. A virtual cadaver would have the added benefits of allowing repeated dissections and the study of specific pathologies, such as heart disease, on different ages and genders of patients. VR is also proving useful for improving hand–eye coordination in laparoscopy training.

FACT FILE

■ *Argon lasers are used to aid nerve repair by causing the patient's own blood to form a protective tube around the damaged area. The red blood absorbs nearly all the laser light wavelengths, making the blood coagulate and adhere. The white nerve tissue reflects the laser light and is completely unaffected.*

■ *Researchers at the University of Sheffield in the United Kingdom are developing an anatomically correct virtual hand that can move and flex like a real hand. The model will be used to assess how implanted rubber knuckle joints cope with the types of repeated movements that a hand undergoes while performing everyday tasks.*

■ *A quarter of a million U.S. citizens receive total joint replacements each year, usually for arthritic conditions. Current research is investigating 3-D computer graphics for possible use, together with radiography, in designing perfect replacements for each patient. It is envisaged that installation will eventually be carried out by "robot surgeons," with cutting machinery controlled by microcomputers.*

SEE ALSO: ANESTHETIC • BIOENGINEERING • BONES AND FRACTURE TREATMENT • CANCER TREATMENT • ELECTRONICS IN MEDICINE • ENDOSCOPE • HEART SURGERY • MEDICINE • MICROSURGERY • OBSTETRICS AND GYNECOLOGY • OPERATING ROOM • OPHTHALMOLOGY • OTOLARYNGOLOGY • PLASTIC SURGERY • TRANSPLANT • UROLOGY

Surveying

Land surveying is the three-dimensional measurement of natural and artificial features on Earth's surface for representation in maps and plans. The first people to develop surveying techniques were the ancient Egyptians—a tomb at Thebes shows two men apparently surveying a field. Also, the pyramids could not have been built without quite advanced surveying. The Romans used surveying extensively for fixing boundaries and marking out land for new cities, roads, and aqueducts.

There are two basic types of surveying: geodetic surveying, which takes into consideration Earth's curvature, and plane surveying, which assumes that the features to be surveyed lie on a horizontal plane. All large-scale surveys are geodetic, but for areas with perimeter dimensions of less than 10 miles (16 km), plane surveying is usually accurate enough.

Topographic surveying refers to the fieldwork required to collect data for the production of maps. Maps depict all the main features of the country and indicate changes in the topography by contours or color shading.

Cadastral surveys are usually carried out for legal purposes, normally related to the location of property boundaries. In many countries, there is a legal requirement for such property boundaries to be permanently marked.

Engineering surveys relate to the positioning of predesigned structures—roads, factories, bridges, tunnels, and dams—before construction.

Hydrographic surveying covers mapping of port and harbor areas and of inland and offshore waters. It includes sea-bottom mapping, oil-rig positioning, control of dredging operations, and the pursuit of marine resources.

Surveying methods

In its simplest form, surveying can be described as the science of determining position in three dimensions through the measurement of angles or distances, or both. The method of operation and equipment used vary with the task and the accuracy required in the results. Extremes can range from, on the one hand, distances less than 300 ft. (90 m) with accuracy of a few inches and angles to a few minutes of arc on a house plot to, on the other hand, lengths of 55 miles (90 km) with a few inches' accuracy and angles to seconds of arc as the basis of a national mapping network.

Much is based on the continual positioning of one point in relation to previously located points through the geometry of triangles and use of a

◀ The Wild Heerbrug D13S is an automatic machine capable of measuring slope and distance to 0.2 in. (5 mm) accuracy.

rectangular coordinate system. It may be either plane or spherical geometry, depending on whether or not the task requires allowance for the curvature of Earth rather than approximating a small area of it to a plane surface.

To locate a point C in relation to two already fixed points A and B, one can either measure distances AC and BC or distance AC and angle CAB or angles CAB and CBA. Once C has been located, similar techniques can be used to extend to D, and so on.

In measuring distances, the first consideration is which distance between the points is required. The natural one—indicated by stretching a tape measure between the points—is likely to be an inclined measure, but for producing a map or a plan, the equivalent horizontal distance is needed. There is a simple relation between the two—so long as it is possible to determine either the angle of slope or the difference of height between the two points.

Where distances are long—as, for example, between two towns—it is the straight-line distance that is required for mapping purposes. It is seldom possible to measure long distances all at once because of obstructions such as buildings, hills, trees, and the general topography. The geometry has to be extended—normally through linked triangles, quadrilaterals, or polygons. Where a large area is to be covered, a framework of interlinked triangles or quadrilaterals (triangulation or trilateration) will be set over the area, using high points such as church towers and hilltops to produce intervisibility. This framework then forms the skeleton to which the required detail will be related.

Alternatively, it might be necessary to map a highway through a forest. Here, linked triangles cannot be used, and the polygon approach, known as traversing, can be adopted. By measuring every side and angle within the polygon (and knowing the parameters of the starting point), the three-dimensional coordinates of all corners of the polygon can be determined, and a similar skeleton can be formed.

Detail

Once the skeleton has been formed, the items of detail—houses, roads, trees, fence lines, and any other relevant points—can be tied to it by various techniques. For small areas, it is simplest to locate, say, a tree in relation to the skeletal line AB—as being so far from A toward B and so much at right angles to AB. This position can then be plotted directly, or its coordinates can be computed for later automatic plotting.

Alternatively, a plane table or small board mounted on a tripod could be taken around the area and the detail recorded directly in the field. This technique was widely used in the past for making small-scale maps of much of Africa and Asia but has since been superseded by point radiation, where from selected positions of a theodolite

and electronic distance measurement (EDM) instrument, measurements of angle and distance are taken to each required point, and the information is automatically recorded into a data-recording unit for later processing.

Photographic techniques can also be used. In aerial photogrammetry, photographs are taken from an aircraft, and the prints are manipulated in a stereoscopic plotting machine to provide all the detail for the map. As with plane tabling, however, the detail is still tied to the basic framework of control points.

Aerial photographs are taken with the axis of the camera nearly vertical and so that each photograph overlaps the previous one along a strip by about 60 percent. If several strips are required to cover an area, each overlaps the neighboring one by about 25 percent. In this way, it is possible to form a three-dimensional image in the plotting machine, allowing contouring to be mapped as well as the positioning of detail.

Specialist applications abound for similar photography taken with cameras on tripods where the axis of the camera is more nearly horizontal than vertical. Obvious applications are in the recording of monuments and façades. Such photography can also be applied in areas of medicine, such as dentistry and general surgical research, that have a need for contouring parts of the body and in the automobile industry for the shape of a car body. In all cases, there is still the need for a framework

▼ Measuring height differences between two points (X and Y) by leveling. A telescope is horizontal at position 1. The operator looks back to staff A, reads off the height and repeats this step with staff B, C, and so on.

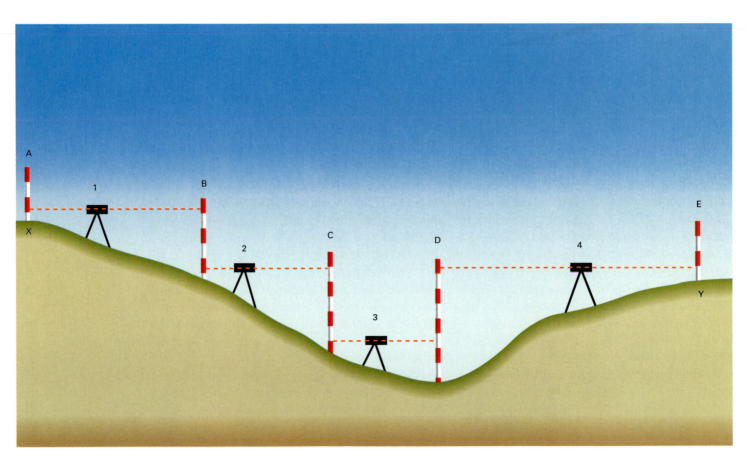

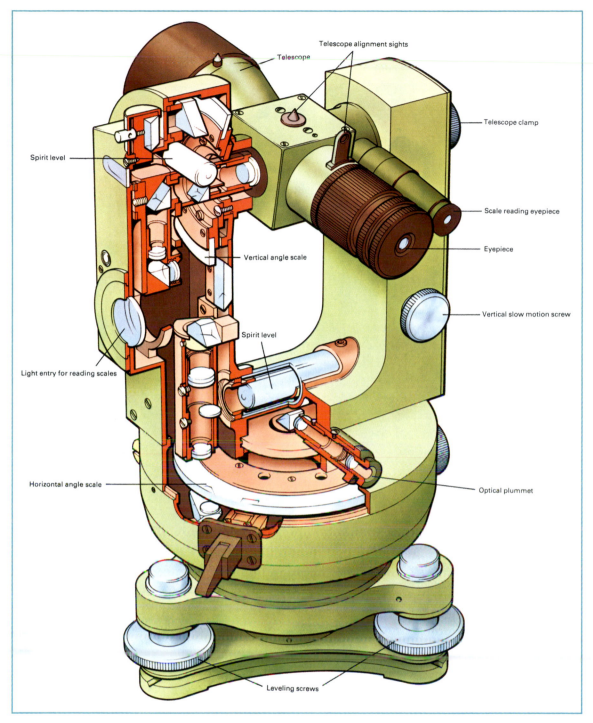

Telescope alignment sights

Telescope

Spirit level

Vertical angle scale

Spirit level

Light entry for reading scales

Horizontal angle scale

Telescope clamp

Scale reading eyepiece

Eyepiece

Vertical slow motion screw

Optical plummet

Leveling screws

◀ In a surveyor's theodolite, the scales are read through an eyepiece positioned next to the main telescope eyepiece. The vertical and horizontal angle scales are illuminated by daylight, which is directed through the window on the left by means of a mirror (not shown). The light is split into two beams, which are conducted to the scales and finally into the telescope head by reflection through a system of lenses and prisms.

of fixed positions to which all required information can be related. The use of infrared and false-color photography provides a wide range of remotely sensed information on topics ranging from diseased areas of woodland to mapping the outline of hot-water outflow from a power plant.

Leveling

The third dimension in mapping relates to height. It may be shown on maps as contours or as spot heights, but in either case, the technique of producing them is called leveling. From a datum such as mean sea level, a network of points of known elevation (benchmarks) are established across the country. For any area of interest, the surveyor seeks out the nearest benchmarks—usually every few hundred yards in urban areas—and by using a level and graduated staff, he or she can determine the height of any required points. Absolute heights across the country can be found in this way to within a few inches, and relative heights between neighboring points established to accuracies as small as $^4/_{10,000}$ in. (0.01 mm).

Other methods are available, such as the use of an aneroid barometer, which operates on changing air pressure with changing elevation, or the measurement of vertical angles between the points of interest—trigonometric leveling. These methods give lower accuracies than ordinary leveling, being more susceptible to vagaries of the atmosphere.

A level instrument consists of a telescope system mounted on a tripod so that it can rotate in a horizontal plane. The telescope contains a crosshair and focusing arrangement, and the whole can be set accurately horizontal. The staff is first set on a benchmark, or other known height point, and a reading is taken on it from the level, which determines the height of the telescope axis. If the staff is then placed on an unknown point and another reading taken, a simple calculation produces the height of the point. This process can be extended over any size of area, with periodic checks to other benchmarks.

Linear measurement

Linear measuring equipment comes in many forms. The simplest is a steel chain of 100 links, each 7.9 in. (20 cm) long. Improvements on this equipment are the linen, plastic, and reinforced tapes of 65 or 98 ft. (20 or 30 m) lengths. For accurate work of a general nature, a steel band 65, 98, 164, or 328 ft. (20, 30, 50, or 100 m) long can be used and corrections applied to its readings for the effect of changes such as temperature and sag. An even better material is invar—a nickel–steel alloy of very low coefficient of expansion.

Several forms of optical measurement based on the rangefinder principle have been developed, but they are now mostly superseded by electronic distance measurement (EDM), which was introduced in 1948. From the known velocity of a light or radio wave (v) and the recorded time (t) for a beam to travel from A to B and back, the distance (d) is given as $d = v \times t/2$, with various small correcting terms. Distances from a few yards to more than 100 miles (160 km) can be measured in minutes to great accuracies generally and even greater ones for specialist purposes. In principle, the EDM systems use either amplitude or frequency modulation techniques to compare the emitted and returned signals.

Angular measurements

The basic instrument for measuring angles is the theodolite. It is mounted on a tripod, can be accurately leveled, and is capable of rotation in the horizontal plane. The viewing telescope can also rotate in the vertical plane, thus allowing angles in both planes to be determined typically to a few seconds of arc or specially to 0.1 second.

Traditionally, the theodolite incorporated two highly accurate protractors set at right angles to one another for recording these angles. Electronic theodolites have optically sensed, coded circles capable of comparable accuracies. Some, known as total stations, now incorporate an EDM system with an automatic data-recording unit for direct transmission of the observed values to a computer processing unit and automatic plotter.

At a lower level are simple hand-held measuring devices such as the magnetic compass (which is of particular use on exploratory surveys) and the abney level, which is used for the measurement of slopes. For coastal hydrographic work, the sextant is still sometimes used but only rarely, because it is being overtaken by more accurate electronic devices.

Aerial surveying

Airplanes have long been used in aerial surveying but usually only to take photographs at a height of a few thousand feet above sea level. Since the late 1990s, the National Aeronautical and Space Administration (NASA) has used a modified U2 plane flying at about 12 miles (20 km) above sea level to provide data about the Earth's surface and atmosphere. The plane carries sensitive optical sensors—called airborne visible/infrared imaging spectrometer (AVIRIS)—that collect information about the visible light and infrared radiation emitted from Earth in swathes 7 miles (11 km) wide. Known as imaging spectroscopy, this information is used in a range of applications, such as mineral mapping and exploration and land-management studies.

Global positioning system

The age of the satellite brought a whole new dimension into surveying. The position of any point can be measured using the global positioning system (GPS)—a network of satellites that transmit exact details of their positions, enabling the location of a portable ground station to be found relative to the satellites. In 2001, there were 24 satellites orbiting 12,500 miles (20,000 km) above Earth in the GPS; the signals from four satellites are needed to plot the position of any particular point on Earth.

A line of sight along the ground is no longer necessary for precise position, and the accuracy of this system is measured to a few parts per million of the distances involved. So the

▼ A self-reducing telemeter used for measuring the horizontal distance between two points—vital when producing an accurate map or plan.

◀ A theodolite fitted with distomat equipment (orange). The theodolite measures vertical and horizontal angles, and the distomat uses an infrared beam to measure distances up to 1.2 miles (1.9 km).

relative positions of two points, say, a mile (1.6 km) apart can be found to within a few millionths of a mile—about 0.1 in. (2.5 mm).

The information a GPS receiver provides is the latitude, longitude, and altitude of its current position. Most receivers then combine this information with other data, such as maps stored in the receiver's memory.

Surveying by satellite

Satellite data provide invaluable information about the Earth and its atmosphere. Satellites observe the planet for changes in such things as temperature, forestation, ice-sheet coverage, and population density and produce remotely sensed images. The most famous are the Landsat series, first launched in 1972 and now in its seventh generation, *Landsat 7*, launched in 1999.

The Landsat satellites are in orbit about 438 miles (705 km) above Earth. They are equipped with an instrument package, called Enhanced Thematic Mapper Plus (ETM+), that acquires data in the visible, near infrared, middle infrared, and thermal bands. These data provide high-resolution images of Earth's surface that are each 115 miles (183 km) wide by 106 miles (170 km) long.

Surveying other planets

The principles of the science of geodesy—studying the shape and size of Earth and its gravitational field, its precise orbit, and the movement of the poles—are also used in the study of the surfaces of other planets.

The principal mission of the *Magellan* spacecraft, launched in 1989, was to map the surface of Venus with a synthetic aperture radar (SAR). Here, *aperture* refers to the length of the radar's antenna. The longer the antenna, the more information can be gained about an object and therefore the higher the resolution of the image obtained. It is too expensive to fit very large radar antennas in space, so scientists use the spacecraft's motion and advanced signal-processing techniques to simulate a larger antenna. A SAR antenna transmits several hundred radar pulses while its parent spacecraft passes over a particular object. The radar responses are manipulated to produce an image that looks as if the data were obtained from a large, stationary antenna. In this case, the synthetic aperture is the distance traveled by the spacecraft while the radar collected information about the object. Images of 98 percent of Venus's topographic relief were produced at resolutions better than 330 ft. (100 m).

The 2001 *Mars Odyssey* spacecraft carries equipment that will, among other things, map the mineralogy of Mars and which elements are found on the surface. A camera will take images of surface features and of the entire planet, enabling scientists to study changes in the Martian atmosphere and surface. A thermal emission spectrometer, which measures infrared energy, will study the composition of rock, soil, ice, atmospheric dust, and clouds. An orbital laser altimeter—which measures the time it takes for a laser beam to reach an object such as a cloud or the planet's surface, reflect, and return—will enable scientists to determine the height of the surface, resulting in a topographic map of Mars.

The laser altimeter can also be used to measure the height of water and clouds. Together with other data, the laser altimeter will enable scientists to study the surface processes of Mars, such as the formation of polar ice caps; provide information about the structure and evolution of the interior of Mars, such as the release of carbon dioxide to the surface; calculate the volume and changes in the polar ice; and measure the altitude and distribution of water and carbon dioxide clouds.

Other investigations by *Mars Odyssey* will include measurements of changes in the planet's orbit, which will allow a model of Mars's gravitational field to be made, and studies to determine the strength and orientation of a magnetic field on Mars, if indeed it has one.

SEE ALSO: AERIAL PHOTOGRAPHY • BUILDING TECHNIQUES • CIVIL ENGINEERING • GLOBAL POSITIONING SYSTEM • MAPMAKING TECHNIQUES • ROAD CONSTRUCTION • STEREOSCOPY

Suspension System

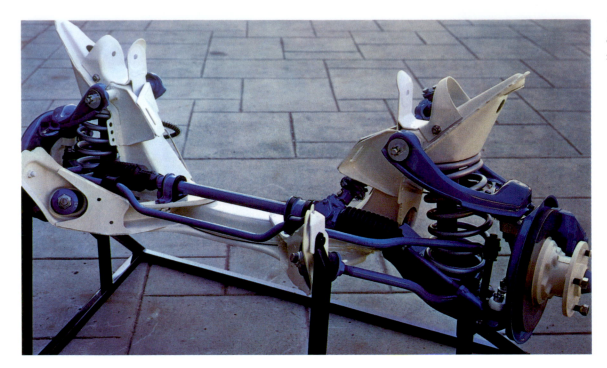

A road-vehicle suspension system performs the dual function of protecting the occupants and contents of a vehicle from rough rides while ensuring that the wheels stay in contact with the road to give adequate grip for accelerating, braking, and steering. Suspensionless vehicles, such as basic carts where solid-beam axles attach to a chassis through bearings, would not only be extremely uncomfortable but also unstable at anything more than a moderate walking pace. The term *suspension* derives from the fact that the bodies of early horse-drawn carriages hung by straps from the chassis extremities.

Pneumatic tires

A British engineer called Robert Thomson patented a type of pneumatic (air-filled) tire in 1845, but John Boyd Dunlop is generally given credit for its development. Dunlop was the first to realize that replacing a solid rubber tire with a pneumatic tire not only made a bicycle more comfortable but also reduced its rolling resistance, making the bicycle easier to propel. He developed his tire to absorb some of the road shocks on his son's tricycle, but it gradually became clear that tires have another important advantage over solid wheels: their ability to develop a substantial cornering force when turned from the direction of travel, enabling corners to be taken safely at much higher speeds.

Until the 1920s, pneumatic tires were of narrow cross section and ran at relatively high air pressures. As technology improved, tires were made wider and designed to operate with lower pressures. The wider tire made greater contact with the road surface at a more uniform pressure, so giving a better grip, and the lower pressure made a softer spring, giving more comfort.

Springs and dampers

Pneumatic tires alone would not provide much comfort; some form of sprung suspension is necessary between the wheels and the body. An early design was the leaf spring, first used on horse-drawn vehicles. The most basic form of leaf spring consists of two curved bars, called leaves, joined together at their two ends so that the leaves bow out from each other in the middle. The body rests on the upper leaf, while the lower leaf transfers the weight of the body to the axles.

A leaf spring deforms to absorb vertical relative motion between the body and axle, but a single leaf is prone to bounce the body up and down long after a bump is passed. Multileaf springs reduce bounce by virtue of the friction that occurs between leaves when the spring deforms. Leaf springs have the advantage that they hold the horizontal position of the axle fixed relative to the body, and they are still used for the rear-axle suspension of many automobiles.

The other most common type of spring is the coil spring, a helically wound rod of spring steel, which operates in torsion rather than bending. Closely allied to the coil spring is the torsion bar, which is a straight, metal bar of great elasticity. One end of a torsion bar is clamped in a crank that connects it to the axle; the other end of the bar connects to the chassis. As the axle rises relative to the chassis, it twists the torsion bar, which responds by producing a restoring force.

If an automobile had undamped springs, a single road shock would set it bouncing for a very long time. Bouncing would not only be disturbing to the occupants but would be unsafe, since it might result in the wheels leaving the road. Hence, an effective damping system is necessary. Early damping systems were of the friction type, consisting of a pivoted arm attached to the axle so that its movement turned one disk pressed tight against another. Friction between the two disks inhibited the bouncing motion.

Modern dampers, or shock absorbers, are usually hydraulic, consisting of a piston inside a sealed cylinder, one attached to the chassis and the other to the axle. Holes in the piston allow fluid (oil) in the cylinder to leak from one side of the piston to the other, effectively absorbing energy in the process. In some other designs, the shock absorber is combined with a spring to give a single unit that performs both functions.

Some types of springs take advantage of the elasticity of substances other than spring steel. Rubber and gases, such as air and nitrogen, have some advantages over spring steel. Rubber can be varied in shape and composition to allow it to work in shear as well as compression, for example (shear is a strain or stress in which parallel planes of a substance remain parallel but are allowed to move parallel to each other). Also, rubber can be formulated to make it less bouncy and therefore self damping. This type of rubber is called high-hysteresis rubber (hysteresis is the delay in the response of a material to a stimulus that affects it).

There are two basic types of air springs—high and low pressure. They are rounded like balloons, and thus, they can act only as springs and are unable to locate, or keep within a tolerable range of positions, any part of the suspension system. The stiffness of a pneumatic spring depends on three basic factors: internal pressure, volume, and load-carrying area. A low-pressure spring will typically operate around 70 psi (48 kPa); a high-pressure device might operate at ten times that pressure but be much more compact.

Pneumatic springs can be combined with hydraulic systems to give suspensions that can be readily adjusted to meet varying loads and road conditions. For example, in the hydropneumatic system used by the French manufacturer Citröen, the wheel is supported by a hydraulic piston coupled to an air spring. Pumping additional oil into the piston allows the ride height to be adjusted, both to increase overall ground clearance and to level the automobile when loaded. All four wheels' suspension units are coupled together to improve ride, especially on rough surfaces. Simpler hydropneumatic systems connect the front and rear suspension units to give good roll and pitch characteristics with a soft ride.

Active suspensions are essentially hydropneumatic systems in which a microprocessor continually monitors signals from accelerometers to assess suspension requirements. Individual wheel suspension units can then be made firmer or softer by pumping fluid to or from their cylinders. Active suspension makes for a better ride—particularly on tight curves—but is expensive and increases fuel consumption as a consequence of the energy requirement of the fluid pumps.

Axles

The tires, springs, and dampers provide the carrying and comfort function of the suspension system; the axles and other linkages, however, provide handling stability and roadholding—factors critical to safety. The axle elements control the movement of the body with respect to the wheels and the road (the suspension geometry). The overall characteristics of a suspension—comfort, capacity for loads, steering response, and so on—are the results of compromise, and the outcome depends largely on the choice of axle.

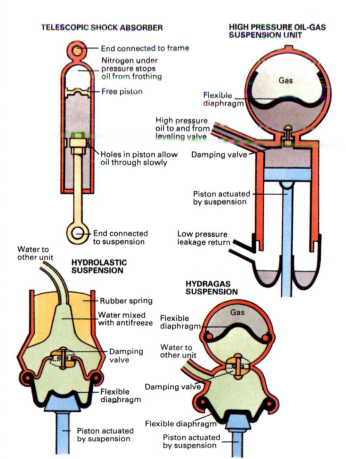

◀ A variety of suspension units that use gases and liquids.

TELESCOPIC SHOCK ABSORBER
- End connected to frame
- Nitrogen under pressure stops oil from frothing
- Free piston
- Holes in piston allow oil through slowly
- End connected to suspension

HIGH PRESSURE OIL-GAS SUSPENSION UNIT
- Gas
- Flexible diaphragm
- High pressure oil to and from leveling valve
- Damping valve
- Piston actuated by suspension
- Low pressure leakage return

HYDROLASTIC SUSPENSION
- Water to other unit
- Rubber spring
- Water mixed with antifreeze
- Damping valve
- Flexible diaphragm
- Piston actuated by suspension

HYDRAGAS SUSPENSION
- Gas
- Flexible diaphragm
- Water to other unit
- Damping valve
- Flexible diaphragm
- Piston actuated by suspension

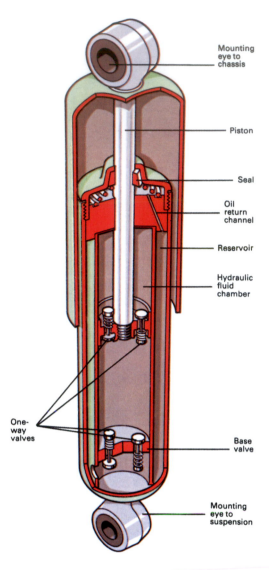

Mounting eye to chassis

Piston

Seal

Oil return channel

Reservoir

Hydraulic fluid chamber

One-way valves

Base valve

Mounting eye to suspension

◀ This hydraulic shock absorber works in tandem with a spring to reduce its bounce. Changes in the extension of the spring force fluid through the one-way valves that link the chambers of the shock absorber. This activity creates turbulence and then increases the random motion of the hydraulic fluid, which increases its temperature. Hence, the energy of the bounces dissipates as heat.

▶ The trailing arm is a form of independent rear-wheel suspension.

little used owing to its jacking-up effect—when cornering, the body rolls around the heavily laden outside wheel, which then adopts the wrong angle to the road, and cornering power is lost.

Most modern automobile designs feature independent suspension of the front wheels. One type of independent suspension is the twin wishbone layout. In this arrangement, two wishbone-shaped springs—one above the other—connect each wheel to the chassis at four movable joints that form an approximate rectangle. Double wishbones allow large vertical wheel movements while giving good cornering characteristics and a tight steering radius. Similar performance characteristics apply to the widely used MacPherson strut, which combines a lower wishbone with a damper-and-coil unit as a triangulating locating member in place of the upper wishbone of older twin wishbone arrangements.

Independent rear suspensions include the semitrailing arm type, which is geometrically a combination of swing axles and trailing arms. Such layouts, if well designed, give acceptable camber change and are compact and lighter than the more traditional beam axle.

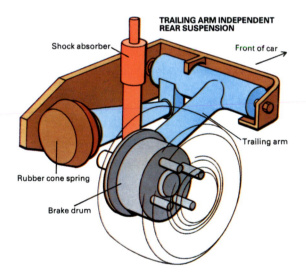

TRAILING ARM INDEPENDENT REAR SUSPENSION

Shock absorber

Front of car

Trailing arm

Rubber cone spring

Brake drum

The solid-beam axle is still in wide use, both in front (common on trucks) and in the rear. In the former case, stub axles swivel on kingpins to allow steering to take place. At the rear for a rear-wheel-drive vehicle, a live axle includes the final drive differential and may be carried on leaf springs, which provide both fore and aft and sideways location. Further location—essential if coil or pneumatic springs are used—can be provided by devices such as trailing arms. A trailing-arm system supports the rear wheels on levers that sweep back and down from a movable rod mounted in the chassis. A second lever attached to the same rod presses against a rubber spring that resists the upward motion of the rear wheel.

Disadvantages of beam axles are that a bump on one wheel tends to affect the opposite wheel on the same axle and that they tend to be heavy, thus increasing the ratio of sprung to unsprung weight and decreasing comfort. On the other hand, the beam axle keeps the wheels rigidly upright, providing better cornering. The swing axle is essentially a beam axle that has been divided in half and hinged at the center. It is now

▶ This type of suspension uses the friction between two concentric drums to damp the oscillations of a leaf spring. Other systems use friction between two adjacent disks.

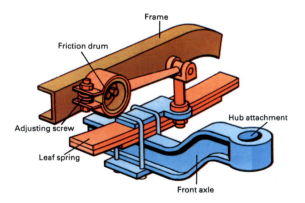

Frame

Friction drum

Hub attachment

Adjusting screw

Leaf spring

Front axle

SEE ALSO: Automobile • Braking system • Spring • Tire

Switch

A switch is a device used to close (make), open (break), or divert an electric circuit. Switches may be mechanical or electronic (such as transistors and valves). Switches are intended to operate under normal working conditions—as opposed to circuit breakers, which are designed to break a circuit when the current flow exceeds a preset limit. Indeed, a switch often has to be able to carry overload currents without failure.

Types

Switches are manufactured in many shapes and sizes. Essentially, however, they consist of two contacts that are connected together for the on state and disconnected for the off state. With power switches, the mechanism must be able to carry the rated power continuously without overheating and is often designed to take temporary overloads, such as the high starting current required by an electric motor. In addition, the switch has to provide good insulation when in the open position. Isolating switches are designed to be operated when there is no current flowing in the circuit. They are designed to isolate, or separate, sections of the circuit or to establish a circuit ready for use if required. Load switches are designed to operate while carrying current—with the make and break being made rapidly to minimize the effects of arcing across the contacts. Where high voltages are involved, special designs are used to break the arc as the switch is opened.

The three-way switches commonly used in the home are a development of the ordinary light switch. In this instance, two switches operate a single system so that if the light is off, either switch may be used to turn the light on, and vice versa. The switches used have three terminals rather than two.

Contacts

One of the most common designs is the knife switch, in which the moving contact is a blade moved between the jaws of a fixed contact. These jaws have a spring action to ensure that good contact is achieved and are normally arranged as a pair of springy fingers that grip on either side of the blade. The magnetic forces associated with the current flow through the contacts act to increase the contact pressure, so ensuring that the switch will stay closed under high currents (such as those that are due to a short circuit).

Butt contact switches can be used where the ratio of starting current to normal current is high. They have flat contact faces. A fast switching action is provided by an overcenter spring system that also provides a suitably high force between the closed contacts. Sliding contact switches are normally rotary in action—with sprung fingers making the connection to the contacts. In the mercury switch, the connection between a pair of contacts is made by a pool of liquid mercury.

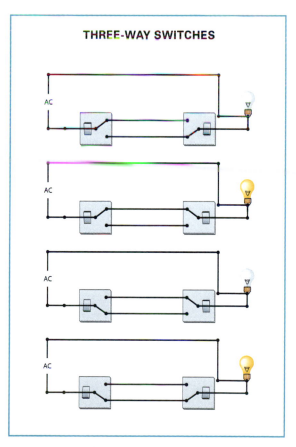

THREE-WAY SWITCHES

◀ In three-way switches, each switch has three terminals and either switch can be used to turn the light off or on.

SEE ALSO: ELECTRICITY • POWER SUPPLY • SOLENOID • THERMOSTAT • THYRISTOR

Synthesizer

A synthesizer is an electronic device designed to generate sound. Synthesizers come in many different types: conventional keyboard-based instruments, drum machines, drum synthesizers, guitar synthesizers, woodwind synthesizers, samplers, and so on. Older synthesizers use analog technology, but the latest generation uses digital technology.

Synthesized music has been around for more than 2,000 years, though these early instruments were mechanical rather than electrical. In the third century B.C.E., the Greek engineer Ctesibius built the hydraulos, a type of pipe organ in which pressurized air was sent to different pipes by mechanical levers. The electric harpsichord was invented in 1759 by a Frenchman, Jean-Baptiste de Laborde. It had a short keyboard and used static electricity to charge the clappers to strike bells. Shortly afterwards the panharmonicon, perhaps the earliest forerunner of a sampling machine, was built by Johann Maelzel, who persuaded Beethoven to write a piece of music for it. The panharmonicon was a keyboard instrument that automated the playing of various woodwind, brass, string, and percussion instruments.

Development continued in 1867 with the invention of the electromechanical piano, in which the keyboard was used to activate electromagnets that in turn activated dynamos to produce sounds. The Singing Arc, the first truly electronic instrument, was based on the carbon-arc lamp, a precursor to the lightbulb. The lamp was unpopular because of its tendency to emit noises varying from a low hum to a high-pitched whistle. An English physicist, William Duddell, discovered that the greater the amount of electricity supplied to the lamp, the higher the pitch of note it produced. Although his prototype instrument toured the country as a novelty, it was never developed further.

The first true synthesizer was built by RCA in 1954, but its commercial success (and therefore its widespread use) was held back until the development of cheap semiconductors. Semiconductors allowed a modular approach to electronic systems and voltage-control capabilities. Since 1954, the synthesizer has become progressively simpler to use, cheaper, and better sounding. It now looks like a musical instrument rather than a piece of electronic hardware.

During the 1950s and 1960s, synthesizers were huge, costly machines notorious for going out of tune and needing difficult setting-up procedures. This position changed in the late 1960s when Dr. Robert Moog, a U.S. physicist, introduced his Mini Moog, an instrument that can still be seen in use today. With the Mini Moog—a small and comparatively cheap portable instrument—the synthesizer had broken away from its role as a recording studio novelty.

Sound generation

Robert Moog amply described analog synthesizers when he said that a synthesizer needs to have a circuit to generate a vibration, a filter to shape the overtones, and an amplifier module to shape the overall loudness. Further control of the sound is accomplished by envelope generators, which add characteristics such as attack and delay.

In analog synthesizers, the sound is wholly synthetic—at best, it can be made to resemble real sounds closely. The reason for this limitation is that the starting point is a sine wave from the oscillator. Very few natural sounds are sine waves, so the shaping tools built into an analog synthesizer have to work very hard if real instruments are to be imitated convincingly. Square waves and sawtooth waves can also be generated to exploit their particular qualities—square waves consist only of the component tones of the natural harmonic series, whereas sawtooth waves comprise fundamental tones and all related overtones.

The other alternative is to use digital recording—which is used in recording studios and in the production of compact discs. Digital synthesizers use binary codes to represent the sounds of actual instruments or objects. Digital synthesizers sound more realistic than analog instruments because digital codes closely follow the exact waveforms produced by musical instruments. Sounds are encoded in the synthesizer's circuitry or are held in plug-in memory cartridges. The musician can either use these sounds as they are or modify them, but digital synthesizers are not really designed to allow the musician to change the supplied sounds—they are difficult to program.

Digital synthesizers can be divided into two categories—those that have sounds encoded by the manufacturer and those that allow musicians to sample any sound they wish. Sampling instruments have been used to create various effects,

► Electronic pianos are able to produce many sounds that an ordinary piano cannot. Many incorporate computer processors and high-quality sound cards that enable composers to store a piece of music in the instrument's memory, add other instruments and effects, and then play it back.

▼ Electronic dance music has triggered an interest in reviving original analog sounds. This digital synthesizer has a 16-note step sequencer that can reproduce the manual functions of pattern sequencers found in early analog synthesizers. The user can program up to 128 voices and add chorus, delay, flanger, and phaser effects to the track.

including a choir of musically meowing cats, and have had a profound effect on the sound of popular music since the 1980s.

An accurate sample can need a great deal of memory, so samples are generally short, lasting up to two seconds. Once stored in the machine, the binary code can be manipulated. In this way pitch can be altered and a tuned scale can be made from the most unlikely sounds—practically anything that the musician wishes to sample. The sound can be altered as much or as little as necessary. The possibilities are almost limitless. Samples can be stored in the way computer data are stored, on disks for later use or manipulation.

Until the mid-1970s all synthesizers were monophonic—they could play only one note at a time. This restriction severely limited their musical capabilities, because chords are commonplace in all kinds of music. Today almost all musicians use polyphonic synthesizers.

Tape synthesizers

Another type of analog synthesizer popular in the 1960s used magnetic tape that moved past a playback head whenever a note on the keyboard was depressed. The Mellotron and its American counterpart the Chamberlin employ a separate piece of three-track tape for each note. Each track has its own sound, for example, a flute, whose pitch corresponds to the note being played. When the key is depressed and released, the piece of tape is pulled back to its starting position by a spring, giving the sound attack and decay characteristics. Selecting a track on the front panel moves the playback heads across the tape. Blended effects are obtained by positioning the heads across two tracks. Such instruments are effectively samplers and were the precursors to the modern digital sampler.

Triggering

In theory, a synthesizer can be triggered by any kind of switch or signal—even by a series of simple light switches. In practice, the keyboard

remains the most popular way of playing a synthesizer instrument. A piano keyboard can be looked upon as a bank of 88 switches.

Guitar synthesizers are altogether more complicated, because an infinite number of notes can be played between the top and bottom of the instrument's range. At the front end of a guitar synthesizer, there is an analog-to-digital converter. Aside from this added complexity, synthesizer manufacturers have found it difficult to make their instruments respond quickly enough to the input from a guitar. Consequently, notes can be lost, and the instrument becomes less than satisfying to play.

Drum synthesizers are triggered when drum pads are hit with drumsticks or hands. Sometimes complete drum kits are replaced by electronic drums, but more often a number of electronic drums are used as an addition to a conventional acoustic drum kit. The sounds produced by drum synthesizers are generally percussive—different from the more familiar sounds produced by keyboard-based synthesizers.

Sequencers and drum machines

Sequencers are a means by which a sequence of notes may be played back. A real-time sequencer plays back exactly what a musician plays on an instrument. A step-time sequencer is sometimes seen as a composing aid and works by the musician playing a tune a note at a time—in steps. During playback, the tempo can be speeded up or slowed down, and the sound characteristics of the notes can be changed as required.

The earliest sequencers used punched paper tape. The tape was fed into a tape reader, and the dot patterns were converted into electric impulses. Other early experiments used a light beam to scan scores. The system could be used to convert patterns on paper into music but was too crude to stand the test of time. Today sequences are stored in exactly the same kind of memory chips found in computers.

Drum machines are a cross between a step-time sequencer and a synthesizer. Rhythm patterns are programmed into them and then played

▶ Modern synthesizers (top and below) are highly portable, polyphonic instruments that come with built-in rhythm patterns and modulators to alter sounds.

back at will. The number of patterns and the duration of the rhythm tracks that can be stored in drum machines are increasing as the cost of semiconductor memory falls. The sounds produced by drum machines may resemble those of snare drums, tom-toms, and bass drums, as well as cymbals, handclaps, and Latin percussion. The sounds of the best drum machines are almost indistinguishable from those produced by a human drummer—except when the machine is asked to do the physically impossible.

Computers and music

Perhaps the most serious developments in electronic music have come from the introduction of the digital computer. Synthesizers and computers now talk in the same language—binary 1s and 0s. MIDI—Musical Instrument Digital Interface—is a software protocol that links computers and synthesizers and provides a way of passing codes between different pieces of equipment. Musicians also use MIDI to trigger one instrument from another. For example, two synthesizers can be set to produce different sounds but can be played simultaneously from one keyboard. MIDI also allows a musician to connect a drum machine to a keyboard and synchronize a rhythm track with the melody.

MIDI uses a system of codes representing notes and ways of modifying notes. Using a standard interface for connecting all the different kinds of equipment, musical information can easily be passed from one instrument (or computer or other musical device) to another in a fraction of a second. MIDI files do not actually play recorded music but act as a set of instructions on how to play a sequence of notes, rather like the roll of paper in a player piano. For example, to

◀ This digital drum kit can produce 75 different sounds and 100 rhythms from its seven touch-responsive drum pads.

This inventor uses sensors on the bow and the body of a digital violin to input sounds to a computer. The computer then digitally enhances the data to make it sound as if the music is being played by an expert musician on a higher quality instrument.

reproduce the note G on a flute, the sequence would contain digital information to tell the synthesizer that a note has been selected, that the note is G, what octave it is, that it is a flute sound, whether it is loud or soft, and when the note stops. MIDI files can be played back only on a synthesizer, which is usually found on the sound card of a computer. The quality of the sound produced is heavily dependent on the playback device, and often what sounds good on one computer may sound tinny on another. The drawback with MIDI files is that they cannot synthesize vocal sounds.

Computer sound cards play MIDI files in two ways, according to type. Frequency modulation (FM) synthesis, found on older or cheaper sound cards, approximates the sound using a built-in synthesizer and produces an obvious synthetic sound. Wave-table cards, however, contain samples of real instruments, so a piano instruction will result in a real piano sound. Up to 128 instruments are sampled on these cards, but the time-consuming process of recording all these samples makes them much more expensive.

It is easy to use a computer as a sequencer, because it is an electronic memory device. Indeed, even the most inexpensive personal computer has advantages over a dedicated sequencer. The memory in a computer is cheaper than that in a sequencer owing to economies of scale in production, and the computer can be used for other things besides sequencing. It all depends on the design of the software that is running on the microcomputer. For example, patches—synthesizer settings for a variety of instruments—can be stored ready for use at any time. Using a sequencer is like using a word processor—the file can be edited, cut, copied, and pasted.

Some of the possibilities of MIDI include playing music in a new way. A computer-literate person who has had no musical training can now produce serious music on many different instruments. MIDI makes it possible to play music by composing on a computer monitor and sending the information to the musical instrument to be played. Similarly, sounds from digital instruments can be input directly to a computer where they can be changed to produce sounds not normally available when playing the instrument manually.

MIDI has also updated the old image of the one-man band. Solo musicians can now give performances with a full orchestral accompaniment provided by a single computer. Some electronic pianos have a built-in computer processor that allows the musician to record tunes that can then be edited and modified with different instrument sounds. The finished tune can then be copied onto a disk and played back on a computer.

SEE ALSO:	ANALOG AND DIGITAL SYSTEMS • MUSICAL SCALE • ORGAN, MUSICAL • OSCILLATOR • SEMICONDUCTOR • SINE WAVE

Synthetic Crystal

The term *synthetic crystal* refers to a manufactured solid whose crystalline properties make it valuable in industry or as a gemstone or both. It excludes a multitude of synthetic solids that happen to be crystalline but that have no added value for that property. Such is the case of manufactured common salt (NaCl).

A synthetic crystal often has the same chemical composition, internal crystal structure, and physical properties as its natural counterpart but may be more economical to manufacture than the natural crystal is to extract. In some cases, a synthetic crystal has no equivalent in nature or its natural equivalent might contain impurities that make it useless in its intended industrial application. An example is the element silicon, which in nature occurs in compounds, such as quartz and sand, but can be extracted from these substances and produced as entirely pure crystals for the manufacture of semiconductors.

Often, the valuable feature of a synthetic crystalline material is that it is produced as huge single crystals that have uniform physical and chemical properties throughout. Another important type of synthetic crystal is the whisker, a long crystal of very small diameter used to reinforce composite materials.

Synthetic gemstones

All the most important and valuable gemstones—diamond, ruby, sapphire, and emerald—have been synthesized, but their value as gems is only a fraction of that of the natural stones. All except emerald have important industrial uses. The masses of these stones are sometimes measured in carats (ct), and one carat is 0.007 oz. (200 mg).

Diamond. Diamond, an allotrope of carbon, is the hardest substance known—a property that makes it useful as an abrasive and in cutting tools. However, it is also exceedingly difficult to manufacture. Industrial diamonds were first manufactured in 1953 by the Swedish company ASEA. The process subjected graphite to pressures of

▲ This Czochralski unit is used to produce pure single crystals of gallium phosphide (GaP). A seed crystal rotates as it is slowly withdrawn from molten gallium phosphide, and a long single crystal forms below it.

around 97,000 atmospheres (1.4×10^6 psi, or 9,800 MPa) and temperatures of around 3600°F (2000°C). Industrial diamonds are now manufactured by subjecting solutions of graphite in iron to these conditions and subsequently dissolving the iron using acid. Such diamonds tend to be golden or smoky in color due to impurities, such as traces of iron.

Ruby and sapphire. Both ruby and sapphire are slightly impure forms of corundum (aluminum oxide, Al_2O_3). Rubies have dark red colors owing to traces of chromium oxide (Cr_2O_3); although the term *sapphire* is usually associated with blue forms of corundum, it is the name for any impurity-tinted form of corundum except ruby.

Ruby was first synthesized in 1904 by the French chemist Auguste Verneuil. In his process, Verneuil sifted a mixture of alumina (aluminium oxide) powder with traces of chromium oxide through an oxygen–hydrogen flame. The heat of the flame fused the powder to form droplets that accumulated as a pear-shaped boule (drop) on a pipe-clay stem below.

Verneuil's first boules of ruby weighed approximately 15 carats (0.11 oz., or 3 g) each. Nowadays, individual boules weighing several hundreds of carats are routinely made by the flame fusion process. Flame fusion of a mixture of alumina with traces of oxides of titanium and iron produces blue sapphire. The annual production of gemstones by this method runs to several millions of carats.

Emerald. Emerald is essentially a mixed oxide of beryllium, aluminum, and silicon (formula $Be_3Al_2Si_6O_{18}$). Its distinctive green color derives from the presence of around 2 percent by weight chromium or sometimes vanadium. Emerald is now generally synthesized by crystallizing hot aqueous (waterborne) gels of the appropriate mixture of oxides near the boiling point of water (212°F, 100°C). The resulting gems often have more consistent structures than natural emerald, and they are used in jewelry.

Czochralski method

The most widespread method of crystal synthesis is the most direct: it forms crystals from a liquid of the same composition and so is essentially a freezing process. A practical technique was developed in 1917 by the Polish chemist Jan Czochralski, who used it to make pure crystals of metals.

The Czochralski method starts with a tiny seed crystal of the target material and a crucible of molten liquid of the same composition. The crystal dips into the surface of the liquid, and matter starts to solidify on its surface. The structure of the seed crystal acts as a template, so the newly deposited material follows its structure. The seed crystal is then drawn slowly upward as more and more solid accumulates. One of the benefits of this technique is that any undesirable impurities remain in the molten liquid. The seed crystal usually rotates slowly during the drawing process, helping ensure the uniformity of properties of the resulting single crystal.

The advantages of a single crystal over a polycrystalline sample of the same material are numerous. Single crystals have a consistently repeated lattice structure throughout, so there are no boundaries between regions where the orientation of the lattice changes. This property is particularly important for crystals that will be used in optical devices. Furthermore, single crystals exclude impurities, making them useful for producing semiconductor substrates, which are extremely sensitive to impurity levels.

Important materials manufactured in large quantities as single crystals by the Czochralski method include silicon, germanium, and gallium arsenide for semiconductors; lithium fluoride for X-ray prisms; and synthetic ruby and yttrium–aluminum garnet for lasers. Single crystals of sapphire are grown by this process and subsequently sliced into wafers for use as substrates for gallium nitride (GaN) light-emitting diodes. Lithium niobate ($LiNiO_3$) and barium titanate ($BaTiO_3$) are grown for study and use of their optoelectronic properties, as are pure and doped mixed oxides of bismuth and silicon.

Zone refining

An alternative to the Czochralski method is called zone refining. It is particularly useful for removing impurities and for the formation of single crystals in small quantities. In this method, a sample of the impure target material is sealed in a heat-resistant ampoule. Heat is applied at one end of the ampoule, often by use of radio-frequency radiation. Once the end of the sample melts, the heating zone starts to move slowly along the ampoule. The part of the sample that melted first solidifies as a single crystal, and any impurities are carried along with the molten zone. At the end of the process, any impurities solidify in a narrow band at the end of the sample and can be sawn off to leave a pure single crystal.

Epitaxy

Epitaxy is an increasingly important procedure for depositing thin layers of single crystal onto substrates for the manufacture of semiconductor devices. Typical substrates include silicon, sapphire, and spinel ($MgAl_2O_4$); they must be etched and cleaned with solvents to provide suitable surfaces for deposition.

In one example of vapor-phase epitaxy, a silicon substrate is heated to around 930°F (500°C) by induction coils. A vapor-phase mixture of hydrogen, silicon tetrachloride, and the required dopant then streams over the substrate. Contact with the hot substrate then causes the following reaction, which releases nonvolatile silicon:

$$SiCl_4 + 2H_2 \rightarrow Si + 4HCl$$

The silicon so released crystallizes on the substrate, trapping the dopant with it. The advantage of this process over diffusion, whereby dopant penetrates the surface of silicon, is that the layer has a uniform concentration of dopant.

Abrasives

Two important abrasives are made by crystal synthesis. The first, Carborundum (silicon carbide, SiC), was first synthesized in 1891 by Edward Acheson, who designed a furnace in which silicon and carbon react together at 3632°F (2000°C). The second, cubic boron nitride (BN), is made by subjecting a graphitelike form of boron nitride to high temperatures and pressures. The resulting crystal has the same structure as that of diamond but is significantly less hard.

◀ Synthetic diamonds such as these have widespread use in cutting tools. Their coloration, caused by impurities, makes them worthless for jewelry.

SEE ALSO: ABRASIVE • CRYSTALS AND CRYSTALLOGRAPHY • DIAMOND

Talking Clock

Talking clocks are used in many countries to provide an accurate time check over the public telephone service. Typically, a caller to the service will hear an announcement of the form "at the third stroke, it will be ten forty-six and ten seconds," followed by a set of time pips, or tones. Announcements are usually made every 10 seconds, and the system may work on a 12- or 24-hour basis.

Recorded messages

In early designs, the messages were stored as optical recordings on rotating glass disks with a pendulum timing mechanism. To ensure accuracy, the time settings were checked against national standards every hour, giving a maximum error, over each hour, of 100 milliseconds (0.1 seconds). This design was superseded by one based on quartz crystal oscillators that offered an accuracy to within 10 milliseconds every hour.

The oscillator is temperature controlled to produce a very accurate 100 kHz sine wave that is divided to give a 50 Hz sine wave and used to drive a synchronous motor. This motor rotates a magnetic drum (which carries a series of recorded message phrases stating the time of day) at a rate of two seconds per revolution.

Since the time announcements are repetitive, only a limited number of phrases are needed to make up any messages. For a 12-hour clock system, these phrases are the initial "at the third stroke..."; 12 "-hour" phrases ("it will be..."); 60 "-minute" phrases ("o'clock" and 1 to 59); and 6 "second" messages. Each phrase is laid down as a separate track on the drum.

Reading heads are positioned along the length of the drum and stepped along it at regular time intervals to select the phrases corresponding to the time at any instant. To supply the time message, the heads are selected in sequence on the next full rotation of the drum with the concluding time signals being triggered by a photocell system linked to the drum. Typically, the signals consist of three 100-millisecond bursts of a 1 kHz tone at intervals of one second. Paired clocks are usually used to ensure reliability, with monitoring systems to check for errors and sound an alarm.

Solid-state units

In the more recent designs of talking clock, such as the Chronocal Speaking Clock developed by the British national telephone service, the electro-mechanical and magnetic recording systems have been replaced by solid-state electronics. The Chronocal clock is a compact self-contained unit that can be fitted into a standard 19 in. (48 cm) instrument rack in a telephone exchange and left to run unattended.

◀ Installing a microprocessor-controlled clock in a telephone exchange; the clock has its own high-accuracy, temperature-controlled crystal oscillator to ensure precise timekeeping.

In this unit, the time reference is still provided by a temperature-stabilized crystal oscillator, the system being controlled by a microprocessor. The message is built up from a series of speech segments encoded in pulse-code-modulated form and held digitally in read-only memory (ROM) chips ready for selection by the microprocessor. Since the telephone lines have a restricted available bandwidth, an upper frequency limit of only 4 kHz is adequate for the digitization process, thus reducing the storage requirements. The original source for the speech segments is a recording made by an announcer. This approach is adopted because it offers a better speech quality than a synthesized voice and can be used to make announcements in any language. The time signals are generated by stepping down the high-frequency signal of the clock oscillator.

A pair of clocks can be coupled together to give high reliability, with one clock being "live" while the second is on "standby." The outputs from the two clocks are constantly compared, and if there is a discrepancy, a decision system sounds the alarm, checks both clocks for possible errors, and selects the one more likely to be correct to continue the service. The digital design gives a very reliable system, though, with no routine maintenance being needed.

To maintain accuracy, the time setting can be automatically corrected to national standards on a daily basis. For example, the talking-clock service in Britain offers a highly accurate and convenient method of checking the time via a recorded message controlled by two pairs of clocks, situated in Liverpool and London. A one-second synchronizing pulse from an atomic clock is sent to the clocks by land lines and used to reset the talking clocks by stretching or shrinking one of the signals. The adjusting system allows for the time lag owing to transmission of the signal and allows the clocks to maintain an accuracy of 5 milliseconds.

The digital design also makes it easy to make alterations to allow for changes to and from daylight saving time, which can be programmed in up to a year in advance. Similarly, corrections can be made to allow for the "leap seconds" used to match absolute timekeepers, such as atomic clocks, to world time, called coordinated universal time (UTC), based on Earth's rotation. Indeed, the accuracy of today's talking-clock systems is such that the error owing to fluctuations in the rotation of Earth is greater than that of the clocks.

In the United States, this public service is cooperatively provided by the two time agencies: a Department of Commerce agency, the National Institute of Standards and Technology (NIST),

◀ Mechanical talking clocks (left and foreground) have now been replaced by far more compact microprocessor controlled clocks (right).

and its military counterpart, the U.S. Naval Observatory (USNO). Readings from the clocks of these agencies contribute to UTC. The Time and Frequency Division, part of NIST's Physics Laboratory, maintains the standard for frequency and time interval for the United States, provides official time to the United States, and carries out a broad program of research and service activities in time and frequency metrology. The division broadcasts standard time and frequency signals using radio, Internet, and telephone links.

◀ A printed circuit board from a talking clock. Microprocessors assemble the correct sequence of phrases from a series of segments held in read-only memory chips.

SEE ALSO: Clock • Oscillator • Sine wave • Telecommunications • Telephone system • Time

Tanker

Tankers are ships that are designed to carry bulk liquid cargoes such as crude oil or gasoline without the use of barrels or other small containers—instead, the liquid is piped into large cargo spaces. Other types of cargo include molasses, molten asphalt, wine, and LPG (liquefied petroleum gas).

Tankers vary in size from about 200 ft. (60 m), used in coastal waters, to ¼ mile- (0.4 km) long supertankers. The cost of transporting oil obviously decreases as the size of the tanker increases. However, the limiting factor is the capacity of shore facilities rather than the engineering capabilities of shipyards. In addition, huge supertankers have maneuverability problems and can present a hazard to other shipping.

The evolution of the tanker

The first bulk carrier was the brig *Elizabeth Watts*, which in 1861 took the first large consignment of oil, in large wooden barrels, from Pennsylvania to London, England. By 1864, over 7.5 million gallons (28 million l) of oil were being shipped over that same route. The wooden barrels, however, were not totally successful as a method of storage. Owing to the stresses and strains of the long sea voyage, many of them split and leaked oil into the timbers of the ship. By 1869, a new vessel, the

Charles, had been fitted with iron tanks, which were rectangular in section to fit the shape of the ship's hold. Each hold contained a number of containers, but in the following years, the containers grew to fill the entire hold.

The first custom-built oil ships were the *Atlantic* and the *Vaderland*. These ships were both iron hulled and built in Britain, on the Tyne River, in the early 1880s. The *Atlantic* was a sailing ship, but the *Vaderland* pointed to the future by adopting steam power. The most successful tank ship of the era was the *Glücklauf*, which could carry 3,500 tons (3,150 tonnes) of oil.

Experiences with the *Glücklauf* and similar vessels led to the development of the trunk deck steam tanker, which was the most important design in the early 20th century. The trunk deck solved the problem of the free surface effect, where movement of the ship caused waves to build up on the surface of the oil in the hold, making the ship unstable. The trunk was built over the main deck of the ship, and the hold filled until the oil entered the trunk. The effect of this design was to limit the oil's free surface area to less than half of that of the main

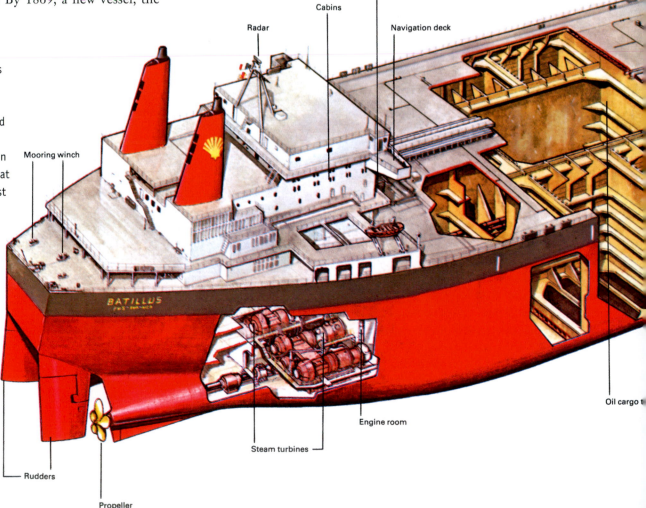

▶ Ultra Large Crude Carriers (ULCC) can be as large as 500,000 tons (450,000 tonnes); this ship's steam turbines and two five-blade, 52-ton (47-tonne) propellers can drive it through the sea at 15 knots; it takes at least three miles to stop.

Mooring winch

Radar

Cabins

Navigation deck

Cargo pump room

BATILLUS

Rudders

Propeller

Steam turbines

Engine room

Oil cargo t

tank. This design also allowed for the cargo to expand in warmer climates, so alleviating another problem. Then in the early years of the 20th century, tankers began to change from coal-fired to oil-fired boilers.

In the 1920s, the trunk deck vessels were superseded by summer tank designs, so-called because extra tanks that could be used in the Summer Load Lines zones—the waterline to which a ship may be loaded in warmer waters—were fitted alongside the trunk.

Modern tankers

The modern tanker was introduced in the 1930s. The essence of the design were the twin longitudinal bulkheads fitted in the tank space, which not only stopped cargo movement but also, when compared with the summer tank design, saved on materials. The main

cargo space in the bow. The remainder of the capacity is taken up by ballast tanks and fuel tanks. For safety reasons, the cargo holds are separated from the rest of the vessel by empty, watertight compartments called cofferdams. The main cargo compartment is subdivided into smaller compartments, approximately 40 ft. (12 m) in length; these compartments stop the cargo from moving around and help to stabilize the ship.

Pipelines and pumps

Pipelines and pumps are a very important part of the design of a tanker—they are used for loading and unloading the cargo quickly, safely, and efficiently. The pipeline layout on a modern tanker

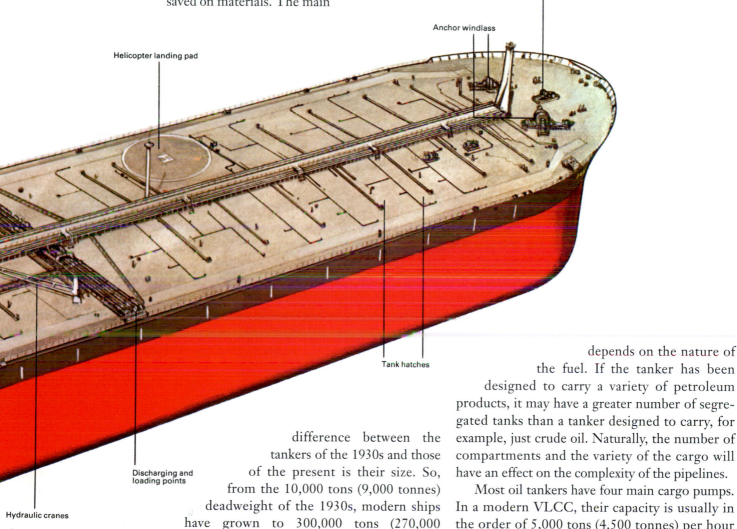

Mooring winches

Anchor windlass

Helicopter landing pad

Tank hatches

Discharging and loading points

Hydraulic cranes

difference between the tankers of the 1930s and those of the present is their size. So, from the 10,000 tons (9,000 tonnes) deadweight of the 1930s, modern ships have grown to 300,000 tons (270,000 tonnes)—called VLCCs (very large crude carriers)—and can be as large as 500,000 tons (450,000 tonnes)—ULCCs (ultra large crude carriers).

Below deck level in a modern tanker, the engine and steering gear are usually located at the stern. Some 60 percent of the tanker capacity is liquid cargo space and is located in the center of the craft. In addition, most tankers have a general

depends on the nature of the fuel. If the tanker has been designed to carry a variety of petroleum products, it may have a greater number of segregated tanks than a tanker designed to carry, for example, just crude oil. Naturally, the number of compartments and the variety of the cargo will have an effect on the complexity of the pipelines.

Most oil tankers have four main cargo pumps. In a modern VLCC, their capacity is usually in the order of 5,000 tons (4,500 tonnes) per hour per pump. The capacity of the pumps is dictated by the need to discharge the cargo as rapidly as possible. Most ship designers aim to use pumps that can empty or fill a ship in about 12 hours so that the total port turnaround time is less than 24 hours. The pumps, powered by steam turbines or electric motors, are usually two-stage centrifugal types, which are highly reliable.

A supertanker under construction in a Japanese shipyard; the dry dock in which the hull was built has now been flooded, ready for the ship to be launched.

In addition to a pumping system, a tanker has to have a ventilation system, because without it, particularly during filling and emptying, the tanks may distort. Venting systems fall into two categories—common-main and independent.

Common-main systems use gas lines leading from each tank into a main vent running along the length of the ship, whereas independent systems have a separate vent for each compartment. Both types need to stop the highly flammable gasoline vapor from escaping. The end of the vent may be fitted with a pressure vacuum (PV) valve.

Tanker safety

Regulations governing tankers are constantly evolving because of continuing pressure from environmental and safety groups and governments. An accident involving a tanker carrying oil products or liquefied petroleum gas (LPG) can be a major disaster, attracting much adverse press coverage and often polluting large areas of coastline, causing harm to wildlife, and making beaches unusable.

In 1948, the United Nations set up the Inter-Governmental Maritime Consultative Organization—IMCO. In 1978, the Maritime Pollution Protocol on Tanker Safety and Pollution Prevention—TSPP 1978—made six important recommendations on tanker design and modifications to existing tankers. New tankers were to have segregated ballast tanks to reduce pollution of the world's oceans. It was common practice to fill cargo tanks with seawater to act as ballast when a tanker was traveling empty; almost without exception, tankers are laden only in one direction of their journey, owing to the geographical distribution of the world's oil fields and the impossibility of carrying other kinds of cargo. Unfortunately, the use of seawater for ballast and

cleaning cargo compartments caused more pollution than the highly publicized tanker disasters.

To control pollution, regulations have been brought in to design separate ballast tanks so that seawater brought on board does not become polluted with oil products. These ballast tanks are placed along the sides and bottom of the ship to protect the cargo tanks from puncturing.

Existing tankers were also covered by the new regulations. New segregated ballast tanks were to be installed, or if this was not possible, some existing cargo tanks were to be given over to ballast only. Whichever course was chosen, the cargo capacity of the tanker was inevitably reduced.

Cleaning tanks of heavy oil residues is a continuing problem for tanker operators. In order to reduce pollution, operators spray the tanks with the oil cargo itself under high pressure so that the dislodged heavy sediments can be pumped out along with the oil. This kind of cleaning is only possible when the tanker is docked. During discharge, regulations demand a minimum of cross-connections in pumping systems that might cause the ballast tanks to become polluted.

Tankers above 100,000 tons (90,000 tonnes)—those with a capacity of 10 million sq. ft. (283,000 m³)—need to have two remote-steering control systems that can be operated separately from the navigating bridge. The main steering gear must also have at least two identical power units.

Under a program that began in 1993, all new tankers over a certain tonnage are also required to have double hulls to provide extra safety.

Liquefied gas vessels

Gas tankers are designed to carry LPG, propane, butane, anhydrous ammonia, and other liquefied gases in specially designed tanks, which may be rectangular or spherical. A typical gas tanker has a design similar to a bulk carrier, but it has gas tanks built into the hull that rest on chocks and are keyed to prevent movement when the vessel is rolling or pitching. The liquid gas temperature in the tanks may be well below zero; this condition will cause severe thermal stressing when the liquid moves, and therefore, the tanks will alter in shape owing to temperature changes. The tanks are made from a low-temperature carbon steel or aluminum alloy, which must withstand impact at low temperatures and thus not be susceptible to brittle fracture. In some vessels, the gas tanks are not refrigerated but are insulated with 4 in. (10 cm) of polyurethane foam.

 SEE ALSO: Freight handling • Marine propulsion • Oil exploration and production • Oil refining • Rudder • Ship

Taxidermy

The word *taxidermy* is derived from two Greek words—*taxis*, meaning "arrangement," and *derma*, meaning "skin." It is applied to any process by which animal bodies are preserved (other than in liquids) for display. The early development of taxidermy—the art of hanging a preserved skin on a false body to reproduce as closely as possible the look of the original specimen—is usually credited to the Dutch. A collection of tropical birds was put on display in Amsterdam in 1517. However, it was not until the middle of the 18th century—when public and private museums appeared and when unknown creatures were being brought back to European shores from distant lands—that taxidermy really became established.

Traditional techniques

Early techniques were very crude. Animals, whether mammals, birds, reptiles, amphibians, or fish, were simply skinned and stuffed, normally with tow or sawdust. Skins of mammals and birds were wired so that the head, tail, and limbs were supported, and the wires were bound together in the animal's body or pushed through a central cork. This method often resulted in grotesquely distorted representations of the living animals.

One taxidermist working during the latter part of the 19th century, Montague Browne of Leicester Museum in Britain, described a method for mounting a tiger. A plaster mold was made of the skinned body and cut into six sections. Layers of tissue and brown paper were glued onto the inside of each section and allowed to harden. The glued paper shapes were then removed from the molds and glued together to form an accurate model (called the manikin) over which to arrange the preserved skin. A U.S. taxidermist, Carl Akeley, later developed this technique, sculpting a model of the animal in clay, using measurements of the carcass as a reference. He then molded the model in sections and made a cast from the completed mold to produce an accurate model to receive the skin.

Methods and materials

The initial model is usually made in modeling clay, and glass fiber is normally used to make the mold. The number of sections needed depends on the complexity of the animal's position—with three being a bare minimum. For intricate models, undercutting is avoided by using a much larger number of sections. Glass fiber molds can be bolted securely together, and the manikin is cast in polyurethane foam, which is supplied as a two-part fluid. It is mixed rapidly and poured into the mold, where it quickly expands to fill the mold completely. When it sets, the mold is dismantled, flash lines are removed, and the manikin is ready to receive the skin. The advantages of this method are that an accurate model can be sculpted in clay or modeling clay and that the foam manikin is light and yet hard. The skin is tanned and, when arranged over the manikin, it follows its contours exactly. Anatomically accurate manikins

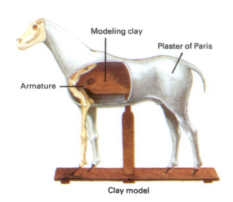

Modeling clay

Plaster of Paris

Armature

Clay model

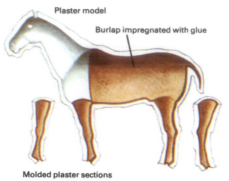

Plaster model

Burlap impregnated with glue

Molded plaster sections

Hollow burlap form

Tanned skin

The manikin

are now mass produced in a wide range of sizes and poses for different species, reducing the amount of time needed to mount the animal.

For the preparation of birds, the principle is the same—a rigid model is made over which to arrange the skin. This model ensures that the skin is given exactly the right shape and retains it indefinitely. Some limb bones are retained with the skin, and those of the wings lie on each side of the pointed back. The legs are attached at the sharp tail end of the body. Wires pass down the back of the legs and attach the bird to its base. Bare parts of birds such as beak, legs, and eyelids are painted because their colors change soon after death and continue to do so over a long period of time.

Many different methods of mounting have developed to complement the more usual techniques. Game heads, for example, are traditionally wall mounted, but today freestanding game heads are also common. Freestanding poses show the animal head mounted on a base and surrounded by an arrangement of materials, such as branches or moss, from the animal's natural habitat.

For scientific purposes, study, or cabinet, skins, are prepared. These skins are not intended to represent the living animal but are merely preserved and stored for research purposes. Small mammal skins are normally mounted on card, and bird skins are loosely and neatly filled and normally mounted on sticks to facilitate handling. All such skins are accompanied by their relevant data, including a series of measurements and details of when and where the animal was obtained.

Freeze-drying
In the 1960s, a technique for preserving specimens by drying was introduced. The specimen is set in a lifelike posture, frozen solid, and then transferred to a vacuum chamber at a temperature of about $-40°F$ ($-40°C$). Water is slowly removed from the animal by sublimation. Although complete animals or their parts can be prepared in this way, the results are rarely as convincing or as permanent as when conventional techniques are used by a com-

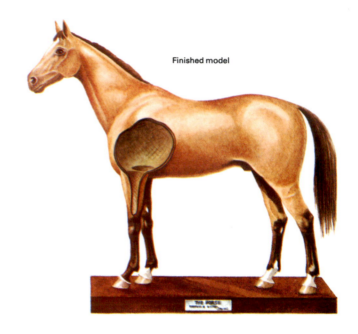

Finished model

petent taxidermist. Freeze-drying can be used to preserve bare fleshy parts, such as combs and wattles of game birds and poultry—but here, too, better results are achieved by molding the parts and casting them in polyester or epoxy resins.

Recent developments
In the field of fish taxidermy, it is increasingly common for taxidermists to make a copy of a fish from fiberglass or graphite, because anglers have become aware of the adverse effects on fish populations of taking large fish from the wild. Now it is possible to use photographs and measurements of the fish to produce a replica based on premade molds that match the dimensions of the specimen. Sometimes custom-made molds are made from the actual fish and then made into a highly accurate replica. The reason for using this technique is that fiberglass replicas are much more durable than animal skins, which decay, and fish scales, which eventually fall off a mounted specimen.

▲ Preserving a horse's body. The skull and leg bones are mounted on an armature. The structure is built up with wire mesh and clay and covered in plaster, which forms a mold for the final manikin.

SEE ALSO: CRYOGENICS • DISTILLATION AND SUBLIMATION • GLASS FIBER • LEATHER

Taximeter

A taximeter is a device to determine the correct fare to be charged for a taxicab journey. It was developed by the German inventor Wilhelm Bruhn in 1891. The word *taximeter* derives from the French word *taxe*, meaning price, and the Greek word *metron*, meaning measure, and has given rise to the modern word *taxi*, an alternative name for a cab.

The fare charged for a taxicab journey has to depend not only on the distance traveled but also on the time spent waiting for the passenger or in traffic. In addition, different tariff rates may apply on different occasions—for example, after a particular time at night or for certain journeys. The taximeter must therefore take all these factors into account. At the same time, it must be easy to operate but tamperproof.

In a typical taximeter, these requirements are met by combining the outputs from an internal clock and from a distance recorder that is linked to the cab's speedometer drive. In the case of mechanical units, an adaptor takes a drive from the speedometer cable to the taximeter input shaft, where it drives a set of adjustment gears chosen to match the speedometer cable ratio (rotations for a given distance traveled). The drive from the adjustment gears turns a shaft that carries a set of counters to give a permanent record

▲ Taximeters can be programmed for fares that vary with time of day, time taken in traffic, or distance traveled.

▶ A digital taximeter as found in modern cabs. These devices are able to print fare receipts and some can take payment by credit card.

of the total distance covered, the number of trips, and similar information.

A transmission system driven by this shaft allows different ratios to be manually set according to the tariff to be charged. The movement is transmitted to a cam unit through a freewheel mechanism. Drive from the internal clock is also transmitted to the cam through a freewheel system, and the final movement of the cam is determined by the faster of the two drives. An electromechanical system actuated by the cam then drives a ratchet system that operates the fare display.

Adjustment of the tariff rates is a complex operation that involves replacing the transmission box. Regular maintenance is needed (and often imposed by regulatory authorities) to ensure accuracy and reliability. The application of microprocessor systems has led to the introduction of electronic taximeters that are more reliable and more flexible. Tariff changes can be made by simply replacing a memory chip in the meter, and internal calibrations allow ready adjustment to suit the vehicle. Electronic transducers simplify connections to speedometer cables. However, the mechanical counter systems are generally retained to provide a record of essential information such as the total and paid distances and the fare units charged.

Modern taximeters can be programmed and configured to operate a printer for passenger fare receipts and credit-card transactions, and can also be fitted with a GPS (global positioning system).

SEE ALSO: CAM • DIGITAL DISPLAY • GEAR • SPEEDOMETER AND TACHOMETER • TRANSDUCER AND SENSOR

Telecommunications

Telecommunication is the act of exchanging information—sound, still or moving images, and computer data, for example—over long distances. It uses some of the most remarkable examples of modern technology, yet some form of telecommunication is used on a daily basis by practically every person in the developed world.

The media for carrying information in telecommunications networks are diverse, ranging from copper wires and more modern optical fibers to radio waves and microwaves. The latter travel through earthbound relay networks and between satellites and their associated ground stations and ground-based receiver sets. Information travels through these media in analog or digital form, and the format determines the nature of the equipment used to transmit, relay and receive it. The nature of the information—audio, video, or computer file—also has a bearing on the transmission and reception equipment, which must interconvert images, sounds, or files with signals of a suitable format for transmission.

Cable networks

Cable telephony is more than a century old, yet the volume of information transmitted through cable networks continues to grow at a fantastic pace. The types of information that pass through networks has also diversified.

In the first instance, cable networks were set up to carry analog sound signals between telephones. The caller would signal to an operator, who would attend the call and physically connect the caller's wire with that of the intended receiver by means of plugs and sockets on a switchboard. This process became automated, allowing callers to instruct the automatic exchange using a code of pulses generated by a rotary dial. This level of automation increased the speed and ease of connection but not in the capacity of the networks—each call still needed its own line.

This situation changed with digital multiplexing. In this system, the analog sound system from a telephone is digitized by sampling. This process measures the signal intensity many times per second and assigns the digital value closest to that measured for the signal. That value is then transmitted as a pulse. The fact that the pulse duration is much shorter than the interval between pulses makes possible a process called time-division multiplexing, whereby the pulse streams from several calls are interleaved and sent down a common wire. At the end of that wire, equipment separates the individual pulse streams and sends

them down separate wires to further switching offices or to equipment that reverts the signal to analog form for sending to a receiver. The process multiplies the capacity of wire networks without causing interference between calls. Digital signals have the additional advantage of being able to be amplified without distortion at booster stations on long-distance routes.

Cable networks started to be used to transmit television signals in the latter half of the 20th century. At first, these networks were rediffusion systems. That is, they collected signals from distant television antennas and boosted the signal strength for transmission through cable networks in communities where antenna reception was poor. Numerous signals would reach each subscribing household through separate wires, and a wall-mounted selector allowed the user to choose channels by connecting the appropriate wire.

In the late 20th century, cable television networks became digitized, allowing simultaneous transmission of tens of channels through a single coaxial cable. A decoder unit isolates the required channel and converts it into a suitable signal to drive a standard television receiver. The introduction of digital cable networks also paved the way for telephone signals to be multiplexed between television signals, providing competition for the conventional cable networks.

Fiber optics

The number of signals that can be multiplexed together through a single route depends on the frequency of the carrier signal, because the signal

▲ The *Mercury* is one of the world's most modern cable-laying vessels. Cable plays out continuously from the modified prow as the ship moves slowly across the surface. Booster stations can be fitted and tested on deck before going overboard.

pulses can be so much shorter when high-frequency carriers are employed. Higher capacity is the main reason why optical fibers are now being laid in place of copper wires: the laser-generated optical signals they convey can carry many thousands of times the traffic that can be transmitted by electrical impulses through copper.

The first transatlantic telephone cable to use optical fibers, TAT-8, has linked the United States with the British Isles and France since 1988. The cable is 4,114 miles (6,620 km) long and has 130 optoelectronic repeaters to boost the signal at intervals of about 30 miles (50 km) all along the cable. TAT-8 carries television, telephone, and computer data and is expected to have a lifetime of 25 years. It can handle up to 37,500 simultaneous telephone conversations.

Data transmission

The transmission of data through cable networks has a longer history than telephony—the Morse code and other telegraphic codes used pulsed signals to convey information, as did telex machines. However, modern data-intensive applications require much faster rates of transmission than were previously possible. For example, a 100-kilobyte image file would take almost 23 minutes to transmit at the 75 bps (bits per second) rate that was typically used for telex transmissions.

The first major improvement in transmission rates came with the introduction of facsimile (fax) machines. These machines scan printed pages line by line and produce modulated audio signals that can be transmitted through conventional telephone lines. At the remote end of the connection, a second fax machine interprets the audio signal and instructs a printer to reproduce the original page. The disadvantage of using analog transmission for this process is that noise on the line confuses the interpretation of the audio signal, leading to spots and lines on the reproduction.

Fax technology evolved into that of the computer modem (*mo*dulator-*dem*odulator), which converts digital data streams into audio signals for telephone transmission. The maximum rate of transmission for a conventional modem is around 56 kbps (kilobytes per second), so the 100-kilobyte image file cited in the earlier example could in theory pass through a standard modem-to-modem link in less than two seconds.

High-speed data transfer

Increasing sophistication in the multimedia files available on the Internet has created a demand for ever faster rates of data transmission. At first, the transfer of files was accelerated by the use of com-pression programs that strip out unnecessary information from signals. Despite this processing, it was still only possible to view movies in real time at extremely low resolution using a 56 kbps modem, and better resolution required lengthy file downloads prior to viewing.

One approach that seemed to offer improved data-transmission rates was ISDN (Integrated Services Digital Network). This system requires replacement of the local loop—the twin copper wires that link users with their local exchanges—with ISDN-compatible connections. By cutting out the digital-to-analog and analog-to-digital conversions used by conventional modems, a single ISDN connection can achieve 64 kbps, and a paired connection 128 kbps.

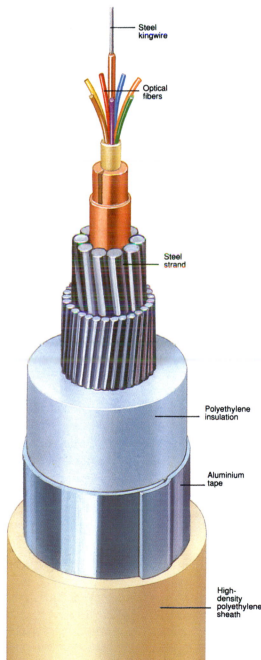

Steel kingwire

Optical fibers

Steel strand

Polyethylene insulation

Aluminium tape

High-density polyethylene sheath

◀ An optical fiber cable for undersea telephone links. The optical fibers, resin coated for protection and color coded for ease of identification, cluster around a central steel king wire. This assembly is surrounded by a double-layer copper tube and two layers of steel wires that reinforce the cable and carry the current for booster stations along the cable. A sandwich of polyethylene and aluminum sheet prevent electric fields from radiating out into the sea and attracting sharks, and an outer sheath of high-density polyethylene protects from shark bites and excludes moisture.

► Satellite receivers have brought television signals to remote locations, such as this one in the Amazon region of Brazil, for many years. Similar technology is now bringing access to mobile telephony and broadband Internet.

ISDN was conceived when conventional modems were much slower than they have since become, and a new type of connection has now been developed that seems likely to make ISDN redundant. That development is DSL—digital subscriber line. DSL systems differ from standard modems in that they use more of the space available on a conventional line, yet they do not always require a new connection.

For telephone calls, telephone cables use the frequency range from 400 Hz to 3.4 kHz; faxes and conventional modems use the same range. The standard telephone line can carry signal frequencies up to 1.5 MHz, however, and the various versions of DSL exploit the higher frequencies in order to cram more information down the wire.

One form of DSL uses a technology called DMT (*d*iscrete *m*ultitone), which divides the frequency spectrum of the line into 248 channels, each 4 kHz wide. Voice and fax signals are carried on the 0 to 4 kHz channel, and the associated equipment is protected from interference by low-pass filters that screen out any signal above 4 kHz. The remaining 247 channels are for data transmission, so the DSL system effectively works like 247 conventional modem connections. In ADSL (asymmetric DSL), the majority of channels are assigned to incoming data, since most users download much more information than they upload. Basic ADSL can provide download rates of 8 Mbps (megabytes per second) in this configuration, almost 150 times the rate of a conventional modem. Its disadvantage is that it only works where the local loop is less than 18,000 ft. (5,500 m) from the exchange, since longer loops include amplifiers that destroy the ADSL signal.

The alternative fast-download system for cable subscribers is a cable modem. Cable modems make use of the fact that the coaxial cables that take cable-television signals from the supplier to the home can carry frequencies up to hundreds of megahertz. Thus, they have hundreds of times more bandwidth than telephony cables. Each television channel occupies a band that is 6 MHz wide, and cable providers allocate further 6 MHz bands for modem connections, allowing around 35 Mbps of data transmission each. The disadvantage of a cable modem is that the information capacity of each channel is shared between all the users who connect to it, so the quality of connection is directly related to the number of users online per channel.

Earthbound radio systems

The major disadvantage of the cable-based networks so far described—their dependence on a physical connection between the user's equipment and the network—is overcome by the use of radio-frequency and microwave links.

Radio communication. Long-standing examples of radio links include ship-to-shore radio-telephone links and two-way radios for communicating in sparsely populated regions where there is no telephone network. Similar systems keep air-traffic controllers in touch with pilots, allow communication between ships, and form the basis of citizen-band (CB) radio.

Such devices operate within a range of frequencies permitted by national or international authorities. The parties in a communication share a frequency to the exclusion of other users and control the direction of signal flow by switching between receive and transmit modes according to agreed upon vocal instructions.

Cellular telephony. Cell phones are closely related to two-way radios, although their functioning is much more sophisticated; they are thus much easier to use. Rather than using radio frequencies, cellular telephone systems use low-power microwave transmissions to convey calls between handheld transceivers and omnidirectional microwave transceiver stations near the geographical centers of their cells.

The cells of a mobile telephone network form a honeycomb pattern. In urban areas, each cell has a radius of around 1.5 miles (2.5 km); this radius is somewhat greater in rural areas, where there is less interference and less telephone traffic. Each cell uses one-seventh of the total number of channels allocated to its operator, as do its six neighboring cells. The channels are organized so that there is no conflict of frequencies between adjacent cells. While it is on standby, a cell phone "listens" for signals from cell transmitters and registers the frequencies it can use to make a call. Each telephone also sends out signals to make the network aware of its location for receiving calls.

A call starts when the network receives an incoming call for one of its users or when a user sends a number to be dialed to its local cell. At this point, the local MTSO (mobile telephone switching office) allocates two frequencies for the use of that call. One frequency is reserved for transmissions from the user to the cell antenna, the other for transmissions in the reverse direction. If the user moves from one cell to another during a call, the responsible MTSOs coordinate the handover by allocating new frequencies in the cell that the user is entering. Once the new channels are ready, the handover is completed by a control signal that instructs the handset to switch frequencies to the new channels.

Cell phone transmissions occur in frequency bands around 800 MHz and 1,800 MHz (Europe and Asia) or 1,900 MHz (U.S.). Each of these bands is split into more than 800 channels, each of them 30 kHz wide and separated from its neighbors by 45 kHz. Early cell phone systems used analog transmission. More recent systems use digital transmission, partly for increased clarity and partly because digital signals allow each frequency to be used simultaneously by three callers using a multiplexing system called time-division multiple access (TDMA). The scope of cell phone technology has expanded from simple telephone calls and answering services to include small messaging services (SMSs) and wireless access protocol (WAP) Internet access.

Long-distance telephone routes. Another use of microwave transmissions is in providing wireless long-distance routes for telephone networks. They use highly directional microwave transmitters and receivers to convey huge numbers of calls. Such arrangements replace copper wire or optical fiber connections between regional exchanges, or they relieve some of their traffic. Their only restriction is the need for a clear line of sight between transmitting and receiving antennas.

Satellite links

Communications satellites are essentially microwave relay stations that occupy geostationary orbits high above Earth's equator. They have long been used for military communications, for retransmitting television signals beamed up to them from ground stations, and as relay stations for international telephone networking.

A typical satellite of this type might have 50 or so transponders receiving signals around 6 GHz and retransmitting them at 4 GHz to prevent interference between the inbound and outbound signals. Bandwidths of 500 MHz in each direction are sufficient to transmit one television channel or around 1,000 voice channels for telephony.

Recent advances in satellite technology include shifts to higher frequencies, such as the Ku band (14 GHz uplink, 11 GHz downlink) and spot broadcasting, whereby the downlink is focused on a small target area. It is now possible to make direct links through satellites using mobile telephones and even to achieve Internet connections at 500 kbps (download transfer rate) and 50 kbps (upload rate).

► The ability to upload news reports to satellites from remote and hostile locations has had a revolutionary impact on news broadcasting.

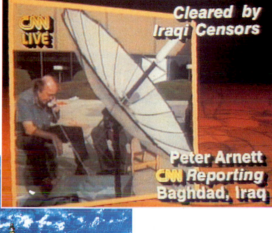

CNN LIVE

Cleared by Iraqi Censors

Peter Arnett
CNN Reporting
Baghdad, Iraq

◄ *Intelsat VI*—seen here in 1992 being captured by the crew of NASA's space shuttle *Endeavour* for the fitting of a new booster—is an example of the telecommunications satellites that relay back to Earth television signals, telephone calls, and even Internet data streams.

SEE ALSO:	CELLULAR TELEPHONE • COMPUTER NETWORK • FIBER OPTICS • MODEM AND ISDN • RADIO • TELEPHONE SYSTEM • TELEVISION RECEIVER

Telegraph

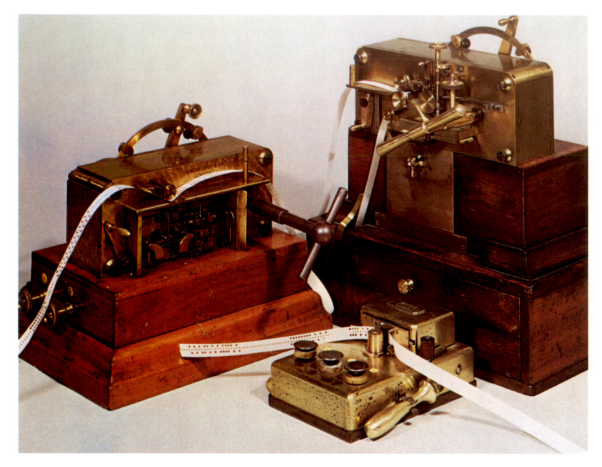

The word *telegraph* means literally "writing at a distance." Humans have practiced the art of passing messages without having to carry them by hand or word of mouth over many centuries. The methods they used include signal fires, tom-toms, heliographs, and church bells. They are primitive signaling methods limited in range and cannot carry complex messages. The development of industrialized societies demanded better communications, those able to pass messages quickly and accurately over great distances.

The first semaphore system was developed in 1794 in France by the brothers Ignace and Claude Chappe, and a British system was established by the Admiralty in 1795. A semaphore machine is a type of mechanical telegraph or signaling machine in which movable arms on a central post follow a table of signs to spell out a message. This message can be relayed over long distances in clear weather by a chain of stations on high points of land, each within sight of the next.

Electric telegraph

At the beginning of the 19th century, it seemed that the semaphore was the best system available. Even as the early semaphore systems were being planned and built, early experiments were showing that electricity could travel along a wire, apparently instantaneously. While the semaphore systems, mail coaches, and messengers on horseback continued to carry the growing volume of military and commercial messages, experiments continued in an effort to find a practical method of using electricity to carry information along a wire.

The need for a rapid communication system was emphasized by the development of railroads, where means were required to signal ahead of a train traveling at a (relatively) high speed. By around 1830, when the first public railroad was opened, the necessary technology had been developed, and shortly afterward, telegraph systems were introduced in England and the United States.

In England, William Cooke and Charles Wheatstone designed first a five-needle telegraph (1837) and then a two-needle telegraph (1839) for use on the railroads. With trained operators, the system could achieve a rate of up to 22 words per minute. By 1852, there were more than 4,000 miles (6,400 km) of telegraph lines in use throughout Britain.

It was soon appreciated that electric telegraphy could be usefully applied to other matters than simply railroads, and public telegram services and extensive press networks developed.

The Morse system

In the United States, one of the most famous names in telegraphy began work on the problems at about the same time as Cooke and Wheatstone. Samuel Finley Breese Morse, a painter, was intrigued by the challenge of using an electromagnet as the receiving element in a practical telegraph system. Morse had the original idea of using an electromagnet to deflect a pen so as to mark a strip of paper passing it. By 1835 he had constructed his first model, which used an electromagnet to deflect a pendulum carrying a pen. This design did not work well, but a later version—produced with the assistance of Alfred Vail—was able to receive signals at a distance of about 3 miles (5 km).

This version—and the following developments by Morse and Vail—moved the pen toward or away from the paper and (in place of Morse's original zigzag recording) drew patterns of dots and dashes on the paper tape.

An essential element in the use of such a system was the prearranged code by which the combinations of dots and dashes were assigned to letters and numerals. Vail—who had helped redesign the original Morse recorder—also improved the original Morse proposals for coding the messages. He noted the ratios of the numbers of different letters in use. He found 12,000 *E*s, 9,000 *T*s, 8,000 *A*s, and so on down to 200 *Z*s—the least frequently used letter in the English alphabet. The famous Morse code allocated the simplest patterns of dots and dashes to the most frequently used characters.

As in Europe, once the benefits of electric telegraphy were appreciated by the government, railroads, and newspapers, there was an explosive growth in its use. By 1866, the Western Union Telegraph Company had some 75,000 miles (120,000 km) of telegraph line in use, and the first transatlantic cable was laid in the 1850s.

In time, it became obvious that skilled operators could read Morse receptions by listening to the sound of the electromagnets without having to see the dots and dashes linked on paper tape. This idea led to the simplest of all electric telegraph systems, one that needed only a Morse key, battery, line, and sounder. The sounder is simply an electromagnet whose armature, when it is attracted to the electromagnet, hits a stop and thus makes a click. Speeds of about 20 words per minute were usually obtained with Morse equipment, and speeds of 30 to 35 words a minute could be achieved by experts. Because it used simple equipment and only one wire to carry the signal, the Morse system became the most widely used telegraph system in the world.

The paper-tape system

Wheatstone designed a system of automatic machines to increase the speed of Morse operation by introducing the idea of punched paper tape. This system provided a method by which a message could be stored and then transmitted by a high-speed transmitter that read the holes in the tape. The system designed by Wheatstone could transmit at speeds of up to 600 words per minute, though the transmission line usually limited operation to much lower speeds. The punched tape was originally produced on a small machine called a stick perforator, which formed the dots, dashes, and spaces when the operator struck one of three plungers with rubber-tipped mallets. The tape (or slip) was then transferred to a transmitter. Several operators were needed to keep one high-speed transmitter busy.

At the receiving end, the electromagnet moved an inked roller against the tape to produce the dots and dashes. Later, by about 1915, a further range of machines (designed by the Canadian-born Frederick Creed in Scotland and the Morkum–Kleinschmidt Company in the United

▼ Below left: Thirty-six codes were used for the semaphore machine developed by the Frenchmen Ignace and Claude Chappe. Messages were sent by a team of three. Each sign took about 20 seconds to send, so transmitting lengthy messages over a long distance—for example, via a series of towers between Paris and Lille—could be a time-consuming process. Below right: A section view of a mechanical telegraph tower. It was based on a beam 12 ft. (4 m) long with pivoted arms at both ends, which were operated by means of ropes, pulleys, and counterweights.

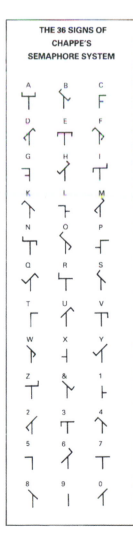

THE 36 SIGNS OF CHAPPE'S SEMAPHORE SYSTEM

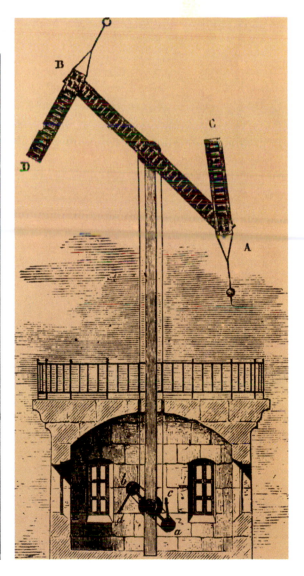

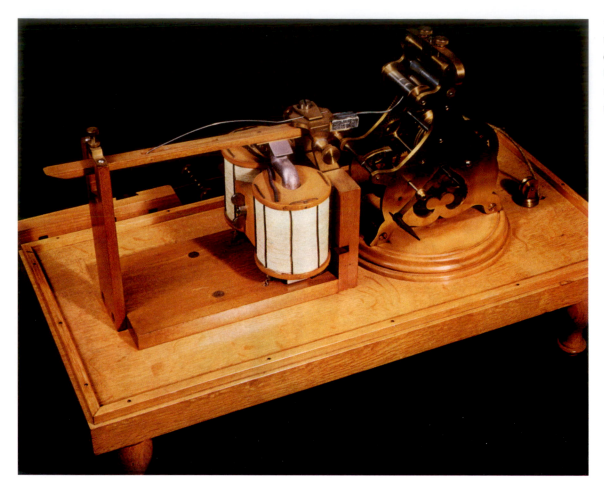

States) allowed typewriter-style keyboard operation for perforating the tape, and the reperforator machine punched the received tape instead of inking it. The latter development allowed the reperforated tape to be used to retransmit the message on another circuit.

The reperforated tape could also be used by a Morse printing machine that read the perforations and printed plain-language characters onto a gummed paper tape. The paper tape was then stuck down onto the message forms for final delivery, and the laborious manual transcription of telegrams was avoided.

This type of system—with a typewriter keyboard perforator, an automatic transmitter, and at the receiving end, a reperforator and a tape printer—represented the highest point of development of the Morse telegraph system for general message work.

Creed's system formed the embryo teletypewriter system of today, but the first teletypewriter, as we know it, came from the United States. The Morkrum Teletype machine operated on a five-unit start–stop signaling code and was a direct printer—it recorded messages directly from the incoming line signals, instead of from tape. The Morse code cycle length was variable, whereas the length of the five-unit code was fixed, making it much easier to handle on a machine.

Many teletypewriters are equipped with paper-tape punches and readers. When the tape is punched, the same five-unit code is used. A hole is punched for each mark element of a character, so a letter-shift (in which all the elements are marks) appears as a row of five holes across the tape with a sprocket hole between numbers two and three. The sprocket holes are used to feed the tape through the tape reader.

The operator can prepare punched messages, again from the keyboard, for transmission at high speed later. There are several advantages for the operator—the message can be prepared without transmitting anything on the exchange circuit (the machine is said to be operating in "local"), any mistakes that may have been introduced can be corrected, and the tape reader can be used to transmit the tape at the most opportune time. On the later generation of teletypewriters, a tape can be prepared while the machine is transmitting a message on line.

The telex network

Telex was introduced in Europe during the 1940s as a separate public exchange network to provide standard communications facilities on a circuit-switching basis. In the 1950s, the network spread to the United States and Canada. In the next 30 years, the network spread throughout the world, and in 1985, there were about 1.5 million subscribers worldwide. Satellite communications enabled telex terminals to be used on board ship as well as in businesses.

Telex operates in much the same way as the telephone network. Subscribers may rent or buy telex machines, and charges depend on the distance the message travels and on the number of characters sent—in effect, on the length of the call.

Telex messages are sent by dialing the receiving subscriber's number. There is no audible response from the switching equipment, so a call button illuminates, indicating when to dial. Because there is no need for anyone to be present at the receiving end, the exchange automatically generates a signal known as "Who are you?" in the calling machine. It results in a responding signal, the "answerback" of the called machine, which is printed on the calling telex machine, confirming the correct connection. The operator now transmits the message from the keyboard.

Telex coding

Pressing each key on the keyboard produces a series of five holes in the paper tape. A hole represents a binary one—no hole represents a zero. Each keyboard symbol is represented by a five-unit code of ones and zeros. As the punched tape is fed through the telex machine's tape reader, the reader registers the sequence of punched holes and produces a corresponding signal that can be sent down the phone lines. The opposite process is carried out at the other end to convert the transmitted signal into printed words. A major drawback of early telex systems was that the process was time-consuming, partly because transmission itself was slow, but mainly because of the need to wait until the receiving machine had finished printing out its message before another message could be sent. Later versions of telex machines have memories that can store incoming messages while another message is being printed out, avoiding connection delays.

Teletex and facsimile

By the mid-1980s, telex had a rival—teletex—a service that allows any electronic terminal with an appropriate interface to send or receive messages over telecommunications lines about 40 times faster than telex is capable of doing.

Facsimile transmission (commonly known as fax) is so called because it allows photocopylike facsimiles of paper sheets to be transmitted electronically. Facsimile machines have a reader that rapidly scans the sheet to be transmitted and converts the image it sees into a stream of binary information, which is based on the presence or absence of markings at a series of points on each scan across the page. The information is reconstituted at the other end.

Although facsimile has the advantage of allowing graphics to be transmitted, it may take several minutes to reproduce a page. Another problem is that equipment produced by different manufacturers is not always compatible, though standard protocols have largely alleviated this problem.

Electronic mail

What all electronic media have in common is the fact that they handle information in digital form, as a binary code. Binary-coded information can be transmitted quickly and reliably over long distances via telecommunication links. It can be stored in compact form in many different electronic memory devices. Most important of all, once information has been converted to binary form, it can be transmitted, received, and manipulated by a whole range of computer-based devices: word processors, microcomputers, specially designed terminals, and sophisticated electronic typewriters.

Electronic mail (e-mail) systems enable computer owners to use their machines as terminals. With this cheaper and more advanced alternative to telex, no specialized equipment is needed—anyone with a modem for connecting their computer to the telephone system and an Internet service provider (ISP) can subscribe to e-mail.

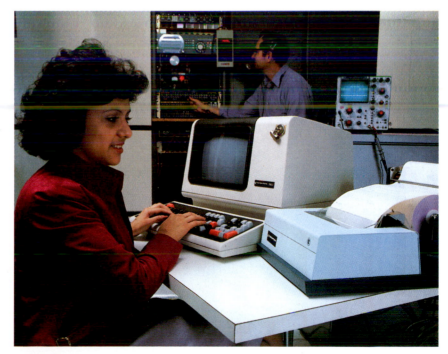

▼ A telex switching center where messages can be received and transmitted via a system similar to the telephone network. To send a message, the operator first dials the receiving subscriber's number. The receiving telex confirms its code number, and the message can then be typed directly to its destination or into the computer memory and transmitted when complete. The advent of electronic mail systems has now made telex largely redundant in the developed world.

SEE ALSO:	BINARY SYSTEM • COMPUTER • ELECTRICITY • ELECTROMAGNETISM • INTERNET • TELECOMMUNICATIONS • TELEPHONE SYSTEM • TYPEWRITER • WORD PROCESSOR

Telemetry

Telemetry, or telemetering, is the measurement of a physical quantity, such as a voltage, pressure, or temperature, and the transmission of the measured quantity over a distance to receiving apparatus, which displays or records it. The link between the primary detector and the receiver may be a direct cable connection or a radio or microwave link.

The first telemetry systems were used by the electricity supply industry for monitoring the voltages and currents throughout their supply networks. Before World War II, direct landline connections (pilot wires) were used, and later, signals superimposed on the power lines themselves. The earliest known patent for telemetry was issued in the United States in 1885.

The basic telemetry system consists of the primary detector or pickup, a transmission system, a receiving system, and an output device for the display or recording of the data.

Electric telemetry

Electric telemetry, such as that used for the supervision of power supply networks, in its simplest form consists of a remote metering system. In a substation, voltage transformers and current transformers are used to drive voltmeters and ammeters. By using pilot wires to connect them to instruments in a central control room, duplicate readings can be obtained. This system works well over short distances where the number of

◀ The Payload Operations Center for the International Space Station is where all the scientific data from the experiments onboard is received by telemetry. The data is then fed into computers for analysis by ground-based scientists.

individual sets of readings is small. Because each set of information requires its own circuit, it is not practical to provide a large number of channels over any great distance.

A variation of this system uses instruments that produce electric pulses at a rate proportional

◀ Astronaut Robert Crippen prepares to key data into the cabin computer of the space shuttle *Columbia*. The shuttle is equipped with sensors that gather information on conditions in space, and monitor the physiological conditions of the astronauts. Telemetry is used to transmit this information to Earth.

to the value of the quantity they are measuring, and these pulses are transmitted to the receiving instruments, which translate them back into voltages, currents, or power levels. This system is known as pulse-rate telemetry. In pulse-length telemetry, however, the lengths of the pulses, and not the rates at which they are transmitted, are proportional to the measured values.

Multiplex telemetry

To enable telemeter links to be transmitted over a single channel, some means of keeping them separated from each other must be provided. This goal is achieved by using various forms of multiplexing, such as time-division multiplexing. The time-division multiplexing (TDM) system scans each transmitting element in turn and transmits the signal pulses in sequence to the receiving station. The receiver scans the incoming signals and directs each set of pulses to its respective indicating or recording instrument.

The transmitting and receiving ends of the system are kept in synchronization by means of a synchronizing pulse transmitted at the beginning of each frame or scanning cycle. Time-division multiplexing may use either a pulse-rate system or a pulse-length system (also called a pulse-width or pulse-duration system) to control the signal pulses.

Radio telemetry

Radio telemetry, the transmission of data between the two stations by means of a radio link, employs a radio signal that is modulated by a subcarrier signal carrying the data. The subcarrier may contain a single data channel or may itself be time-division multiplexed (commutated). Frequency modulation is the main form of modulation used, and the carrier signal may be modulated by a group of subcarriers, each of a different frequency.

Pulse modulation is often used instead of frequency modulation, and in this case, the transmitted signal is represented by changes in the phase angle of the carrier wave as opposed to frequency or amplitude modulation.

The different types of multiplexing methods and the various forms of modulation are combined in several ways to produce telemetry links best suited to particular requirements. Many missile control systems use FM-FM telemetry, in which the carrier wave is frequency modulated by a group of subcarriers that are themselves frequency-modulated by the data signals they carry. FM-PM is similar to FM-FM, but in this case, the carrier is phase modulated by frequency-modulated subcarriers.

Uses

In addition to its usefulness in electricity supply networks, telemetry has many applications in other distribution systems such as gas, oil or water pipelines. It enables the flow rates and pressures along a pipeline to be continuously monitored from a small number of control stations.

One of the most important uses of telemetry is the transmission of data to and from satellites, space probes, and crewed space vehicles. The telemetry systems used by crewed space vehicles handle data concerning the course, position and engineering systems of the vehicle, and also physiological data such as the temperature, respiration, and pulse rates of the astronauts.

Satellites and crewless vehicles transmit data covering a wide range of subjects, depending on the particular application of the vehicle concerned. Apart from the sensors that monitor the onboard systems of the vehicle, satellites and probes carry instruments that collect data—for example, on cosmic radiation, magnetic fields, and Earth resources. All this data is transmitted back over radio telemetry links to tracking stations on the ground or to tracking ships at sea, which convert the signals into readable form for analysis.

◄ A power supply control room where system data are displayed on color monitors. Telemetry allows utility companies to monitor the status of the supply network even in remote locations.

SEE ALSO: ANALOG AND DIGITAL SYSTEMS • CABLE NETWORK • PIPELINE • POWER SUPPLY • RADIO • TRANSFORMER • WATER SUPPLY

Telephone-Answering Machine

▲ The introduction of digital exchanges allows messages to be stored at the exchange and accessed by dialing a retrieval code.

built up across the capacitor to trigger an electronic switch, which activates the set. Microelectronics were built into the design of the later machines, making them cheaper to manufacture. Consequently, many private homes can now afford answering machines; they are no longer used purely in business.

Transmit-only machines

The message for transmission is prerecorded on a closed loop of tape normally enclosed in a compact cassette-type case. It is recorded by conventional recording techniques that include an erase head for eliminating any message previously recorded on the loop.

When the set is activated by a caller, the message is replayed, and the tape stops automatically when it has gone through one cycle. There are several techniques for detecting when the tape has completed one cycle. In one system, a small hole is punched in the tape. As the hole passes a light beam, it permits the light to activate a photoelectric cell. This cell in turn controls a circuit that stops the drive motor. Another technique involves placing a small strip of conductive metal in the tape loop. When the metal strip passes over two adjacent contacts, an electric circuit is established, causing a switch or relay to stop the drive motor. In some machines, the tape is thickened at the stop position.

Once the drive circuit has been disengaged, the inertia of the system carries the tape on slightly before it stops so that the machine can be activated by the next caller.

A telephone-answering machine is a device for transmitting a message to a subscriber who calls an unattended telephone. Most machines will also record any message that the caller wishes to leave. In analog systems, both the prerecorded message and the callers' messages are recorded on magnetic tape. Analog systems have now been mostly superseded by digital systems that use microcontrollers to digitize, store, and play messages.

Analog systems

Various analog systems have been marketed, but the techniques involved are similar. The answering set is powered from the main electricity supply and linked to the wires that would normally lead to a conventional telephone. The set is activated by the alternating current (AC) from the exchange that, with a normal telephone, operates the bell or tone caller. The AC current is rectified, producing a direct current (DC) that charges a capacitor. Charging continues for about 10 seconds or for a preset delay (usually set according to a number of rings) before a sufficient voltage has

▼ Many telephone systems have a built-in answering machine that records messages digitally. On some models, messages can be picked up from another telephone on a command or signal from the owner of the telephone.

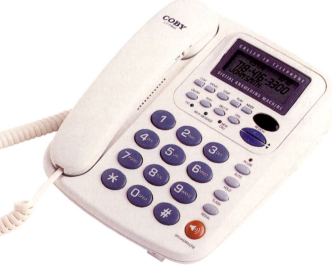

Message-record facility

When a message-record facility is provided, the circuit that stops the tape at the end of one cycle also initiates the record operation. Messages are sometimes recorded on a separate tape. For most purposes, this tape need be no more than a simple cassette or special tape cartridge, but when a large number of messages must be recorded, reel-to-reel recording is sometimes used.

To make sure that a caller does not use all the available tape for recording messages, some machines incorporate a time switch that limits the length of a message. In more sophisticated machines, the speech signals from the caller are monitored, and a pause in speech of greater than about 15 seconds causes the machine to stop recording. The machine will be ready for reuse only when the caller has replaced the handset.

Digital systems

Digital systems contain a microcontroller that takes input from the answering machine it is controlling and controls the machine by sending signals to different components. Microcontrollers are tiny, low-power computers that are embedded inside another device (they are also called embedded controllers). Unlike personal or mainframe computers, they are dedicated to one task and run one specific program, which is stored in read-only memory (ROM). Like analog systems, digital systems also run off the main electricity supply and usually have a battery to back up the supply. There is also a small liquid crystal display (LCD) or light-emitting diode (LED) display that shows the number of messages on the machine and usually also the date and time.

When a caller leaves a message, the microcontroller digitizes the caller's voice using an analog-to-digital converter. As its name suggests, this device converts the analog sound wave of the caller's voice into a stream of bytes and records the bytes, not the wave. The microcontroller then stores the digitized message in low-power random-access memory (RAM). When the message is played back, the microcontroller reads the bytes from RAM and converts them back into an analog wave by a digital-to-analog converter (DAC). Because RAM is a high-speed memory device, the microcontroller can easily erase one of the messages and move the other messages forward into the free space.

Cell phone and exchange services

Cell phone networks supply an answering service for subscribers. Callers who call a cell phone that is unattended, busy, or switched off can record a message that is then stored by the network. The

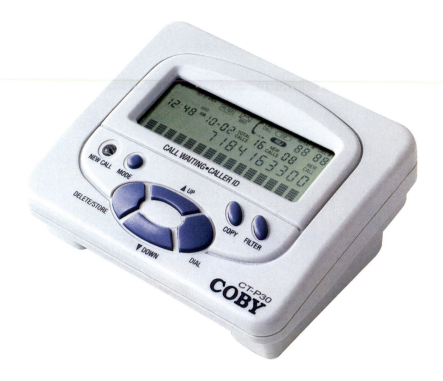

display on the cell phone immediately alerts the subscriber that there is a message waiting, and the subscriber can call a network number to listen to, save, or delete the waiting voice mail. The subscriber normally pays for this service.

Telephone-exchange systems also provide answering services when the phone is busy or unattended. In businesses, this service can take the form of an internal voice mail, in which callers can leave messages on a particular extension number that are later retrieved by the subscriber. Such systems allow employees to leave a personalized recorded message on their phones and reduce the need for paper messages to be taken.

Alternatively, the exchange system may provide a free network-based service to private householders that enables subscribers to access messages from the central exchange. The system can be set up to record messages from callers when the phone is busy or unattended. A special dial tone alerts the subscriber that messages are waiting; they are replayed when the subscriber dials the answering-service number. A finite number of messages can be stored for a limited period of time, after which they will be automatically deleted. A recording tells the subscriber when the mailbox is almost full. Usually, the answering message cannot be personalized, but the received messages can be edited (deleted or saved). Such a telephone-answering system is useful in households in which there is only one phone line that is used regularly for Internet access.

▲ Digital answering machines have many functions beyond the recording of messages. Most can identify the caller to the receiver, filter out unwanted calls, indicate if another caller is trying to get through, and forward calls to a different number.

SEE ALSO: ANALOG AND DIGITAL SYSTEMS • CELLULAR TELEPHONE • MAGNETIC TAPE AND FILM • TELEPHONE SYSTEM

Telephone System

A modern telephone system may serve millions of customers through lines that extend to their homes and workplaces from local telephone exchanges, which are switching centers for routing calls. These lines support connections with telephones, facsimile machines, and computer modems. Each local exchange has trunk connections with other nearby local exchanges and with long-distance exchanges that handle telephone traffic between different regions and countries.

Invention

The principal means of access to a telephone network is the telephone handset, which has evolved from a device invented by Alexander Graham Bell, a British-born teacher of the deaf in Boston, Massachusetts. Bell's invention emerged from his efforts to find a means of simultaneously transmitting separate messages to different telegraph receivers through a common wire.

His first experiments centered around reed relays attached to tuning forks in such a way that their tuned oscillations produced electrical signals that oscillated at the frequency of the fork. In this way, he hoped to stimulate the oscillation of a similar tuned reed relay connected electrically to the first but without disturbing other relays in the circuit tuned to different frequencies. During the preparation for one experiment, Bell had his ear pressed against one of the relays at the moment when his assistant, Watson, plucked another relay that had become stuck. Bell then heard the pitch of the plucked relay with that of another relay in the circuit—a sound he would not have heard were his ear not pressed to the relay.

Watson later suggested that this lucky observation had set Bell on course for inventing the telephone. Bell himself said, "If I could make a current of electricity vary in intensity precisely as the air varies in density during the production of sound, I should be able to transmit speech telegraphically." In fact, all analog parts of telephone systems convey sound in just such a way.

Telephony became possible with the invention of devices that could effect the changes from sound waves to electrical signals and from electrical signals to sound waves: the microphone and the speaker. Bell's first breakthrough came in June 1875, when he and Watson made and connected two devices called diaphragm receivers. These devices consisted of taut metal foil mounted next to electromagnetic coils. Such apparatuses were effective as speakers, but their performance as

microphones was poor. Nevertheless, the sound produced at one receiver in response to speech at the other resembled speech sufficiently to encourage Bell to develop the idea further.

The next development focused on the receiver. One of the problems with the metal diaphragm had been that its oscillations produced only minute variations in voltage to drive the receiving diaphragm. The solution to the problem was to use an external power source and a microphone whose resistance varied in response

▲ British Telecom's new line in public telephones includes provisions for sending e-mails and also for sending text messages to mobile telephones. In addition to the normal numerical buttons for dialing, it has a full QWERTY keyboard for composing such messages.

to sound waves impinging on it. The current flow between the microphone and the receiver would then oscillate in time with variations in resistance and hence with pressure variations in the sound.

The arrangement that brought success for Bell consisted of two electrodes immersed in acidified water—in effect, an electrochemical cell. The resistance of this cell increased in proportion to the separation between its electrodes, so the attachment of a diaphragm to one could connect its resistance to the variation of sound waves. Using such a microphone, Bell spoke the first words ever carried by telephone on March 10, 1876: "Mr Watson—come here—I want to see you."

Handset developments

Although the shape of the telephone instrument has varied greatly over the years, its principal features have remained constant. Apart from the microphone and speaker, a telephone must have some means of connecting with the exchange, indicating the number required, and attracting the subscriber's attention to incoming calls.

Transmitter. The first practical telephones replaced Bell's acid-filled transmitter (microphone) with a device based on a bed of carbon granules sandwiched between two metal electrodes. Carbon (in the form of graphite) conducts electricity moderately well in bulk, but the conductivity of its granular form depends on the amount of contact between the granules and hence how tightly they are packed together.

One of the electrodes in a carbon microphone is a foil diaphragm. When a user speaks into the microphone, the vibrations of the diaphragm cause oscillations in the packing density of the carbon granules. The changing resistance governs the flow of a current whose variations mimic the pressure variations in the sound waves. The granules in such microphones were prone to clogging together, causing muffled sound and crackling at the receiver, a problem that could be resolved by shaking or hitting the microphone.

Modern telephones have compact electret microphones, sometime called condenser microphones. They have a diaphragm of electret—a plastic that has a permanent charge separation between its two faces—parallel to a conducting plate connected to the output. Oscillations of the electret cause variations in the charge that accumulates on the conducting plate, variations that translate into an oscillating output current.

Amplification. The output from the above types of microphones is too weak to drive a current to the exchange and requires amplification. The U.S. inventor Thomas Edison developed a matching network for this purpose. It is essen-

tially a transformer that functions by raising the oscillating component of the microphone output to higher voltage. In the case of carbon-granule microphones, that output is superimposed on a direct current, which is necessary for the function of the microphone. The transformer is entirely insensitive to the direct-current component.

Receiver. The receiver is the loudspeaker of a telephone. In one type of modern receiver, the signal passes through a coil attached to a flexible cone. A permanent magnet is situated behind the cone. Variations in the signal create an oscillating magnetic field in the coil, which causes the coil to vibrate in the manner necessary to reproduce the sound picked up by the remote microphone.

In another type, the electrostatic speaker, the signal is fed to a conducting diaphragm made of metal foil or metal-coated plastic film. The diaphragm is sandwiched between two grids that carry opposite charges, so electrostatic forces cause it to vibrate as the signal oscillates between positive and negative voltage peaks.

Housings. Early telephones were of the candlestick variety: their transmitters were mounted on wooden or metal column stands that could be handheld for conversation, and their receivers were attached by flexible cords so they could be held to the ear. There was no dialing mechanism—a caller would crank a generator that rang an electromagnetically operated bell to alert the operator. The operator would answer this call by connecting to the caller's line and then take the details of the destination for the call. The operator would signal an incoming call by ringing a bell in the subscriber's telephone.

▼ This "smart" telephone enables its user to send instructions to household appliances, as well as functioning as a cordless and mobile handset.

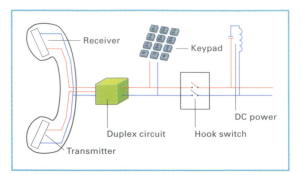

► The components of a basic telephone apparatus. The duplex circuitry directs signals from the inward line to the receiver and those from the transmitter to the outward line. This system prevents feedback howl.

Later models incorporated the bell and a rotary dial in a molded casing made first of Bakelite—a hard brown-to-black thermoset—then in more modern plastics. The transmitter and receiver were combined in a second molding—the handset—shaped to present them to the mouth and ear, respectively. When not in use, the handset would rest in a cradle on the main part of the telephone, depressing a so-called hook switch as it did so. (The name derives from the fact that later candlestick models had a hook on which the earpiece rested, and this hook moved a switch that connected and disconnected the line.)

Modern telephone formats reflect the possibilities created by the miniaturization of components and the change in dialing systems. Keypads have replaced rotary dials, and they are often included in the handset. Similarly, silicon-chip signal generators and electrostatic loudspeakers have replaced electromagnetic bells, and they can also fit into a small, lightweight handset. In effect, what was the main part of the telephone has now been demoted to being a simple cradle.

Cordless telephones have a base set that communicates with one or more handsets by radio. In most cases, the communication between handset and base station is in digital form and encrypted so that only those handsets associated with a given base set may use it. Such systems normally have a choice of around 10 frequency channels available, and the base set automatically selects the channel that is suffering from least atmospheric interference at a given time.

Headsets that contain miniature headphone speakers and an electret microphone have become popular in the workplace, since they leave the hands free to operate a computer keyboard. The same devices are also popular for IP (Internet protocol) telephony, where two callers link their computers to local Internet service providers through the telephone network, and communication then proceeds via the Internet.

Signaling the exchange

When the handset is lifted from its cradle, a hook switch automatically makes the connection between the telephone and the exchange. At the same time, it breaks the circuit by which the exchange energizes the telephone's ringer.

Direct-current electricity, supplied by the exchange, is used for signaling between the subscriber and the exchange. The first signal is the dial tone, which emanates from the exchange and indicates that the connection is ready to receive a dialed number. The number is then signaled to the exchange as a series of pulses or tones.

Older telephones have a rotary dial with finger holes for the digits 1 through 9 and then 0, cut in a counterclockwise series near its circumference. The subscriber dials a digit by inserting a finger in the appropriate hole, turning the dial clockwise to a bar that prevents further turning, and then releasing the dial. The dial then returns to its

► Videoconferencing is one of the benefits brought by IP (Internet protocol) telephony. A high-speed Internet connection, together with the appropriate software and hardware, makes it possible to converse with and see moving images of an equally equipped person in any part of the world—all for the cost of a local telephone call.

original position under the force of a spring. As the dial returns, contacts in the back of the dial behind each number hole connect and then disconnect with the loop contacts (the loop is the circuit between the telephone and the exchange). This process sends a series of pulses along the loop that corresponds to the number dialed; it is called loop-disconnect (LD) dialing.

Modern telephones have keypads with the digits 0 through 9 and function keys, such as ∗ (star) and # (pound). Each key causes a tone of a different frequency to be sent down the line, and the exchange interprets these tones as digits of a telephone number or, if preceded by ∗ or #, as part of an instruction code. This system is called multifrequency tone (MFT) dialing. Many MFT telephones can also be switched to send simulated LD pulses, so they can be used with older exchanges not geared for MFT.

Local distribution

The local distribution network is that part of the system that connects subscribers' telephones to their local exchanges. Originally, all telephones were connected to the exchange by bare copper, bronze, or galvanized iron wires carried on insulators fixed to poles. The drawbacks of this system are numerous: overhead wires must be thicker than their current demands in order to withstand wind and the settlement of ice and are nevertheless prone to be brought down in extreme weather; they are susceptible to lightning strikes and interference from nearby high-voltage equipment; and they are unsightly.

A common modern practice is to lay thick, multipair cables in underground conduits that fan out from exchanges. A large cable of this type might consist of up to 4,800 pairs of aluminum or copper wires; each wire is insulated in paper or polyethylene, and a tough polyethylene sheath holds the whole bundle held together.

The large cables split into successively smaller cables, culminating in distribution points. From these points, single-pair cables run to the subscribers' telephones. In some areas, the distribution points are poles fed by an underground cable carrying usually 10 to 15 pairs of wires. Overhead wires radiate from the top of the pole. These wires may be either a bare cadmium–copper alloy or drop wires—pairs of copper-plated steel conductors insulated by a PVC sheath. In other areas, each telephone is served directly by a one-pair underground cable from the distribution point.

Fiber-optic cable systems offer many thousands of times more capacity than similar-sized wire bundles and are increasingly being used to replace conventional cables. Optical fibers carry digitized signals as pulses of laser-generated light, so this type of system requires equipment that converts analog signals into digital form to drive lasers and further equipment that reads the light pulses and converts them into pulsed electrical signals that can be reverted to analog form. Some modern exchanges handle digital signals directly. More rarely, the fiber-optic system connects directly with the subscriber's equipment. Some large companies have this type of connection.

Exchanges

At the exchange, local-distribution cables split into individual pairs of wires that terminate on distribution frames for connection to the exchange equipment. Each telephone system varies in the exact details of its exchanges compared with others, and some systems use more than one type of exchange. Practically all exchanges in developed countries are fully automatic.

Manual exchanges. In manual exchanges, now almost extinct, the telephone wires terminate on switchboards. A warning light illuminates when a caller picks up the receiver and completes the circuit. The operator then connects his or her headset to the caller's line and requests the desired number. Connections are then made to local telephones and other exchanges by means of cords with plugs at each end. Inserting the plugs in the sockets of two lines links those lines together.

Strowger selector. Automated exchanges were made possible by an electromechanical switch invented in 1889 by Almon B. Strowger, a Kansas City mortician. The Strowger selector was an exchange switch operated remotely by the subscriber's loop-disconnect dialing pulses: each pulse advanced the switch one position.

The Strowger selector consisted of a movable contacting arm, called a wiper assembly, and cir-

▲ Hundreds of thousands of wires converge at a typical exchange. Color coding helps ensure that the correct connections are made when installing a new subscriber's line.

cular banks of fixed contacts arranged along an axis to form a cylinder. The first number dialed selected the bank of contacts, and the second number selected the position of the wiper within a bank. A selector of 10 banks with 10 positions each therefore had 100 connection options.

Crossbar exchanges. The next step in the evolution of the automatic exchange was the crossbar type, which consisted of arrays of horizontal and vertical conductors. Incoming calls would arrive at one of the vertical bars, while the horizontal bars led to outward connections. The two sets of bars were closely spaced, and any pair of horizontal and vertical bars could be brought into contact by an electromagnetic actuator. The most advanced of these systems, developed in the mid-1970s, could make connections between 35,000 lines.

Digital electronic exchanges. Most modern exchanges use a different logic to make connections. Each subscriber line and each long-distance route to another exchange is logged in a computer register of equipment "locations." When a subscriber makes a call, a central computer reads the dialed pulses or tones as a number and finds the matching entry in the location register. If that location is free to receive a call, the computer identifies the most efficient connection route through the exchange and makes the physical connection; otherwise, it returns a busy signal to the caller.

Electronic exchanges use semiconductor switches that allow more rapid connections than their electromechanical predecessors, which had to move physically to register each number. They also have the benefit of allowing additional services to be offered to subscribers, some of which are accessed using star and pound keys followed by an appropriate code. These services include the facilities for the subscriber to forward incoming calls to another number (call forwarding), to partake in multiple-subscriber (or conference) calls, to automatically keep trying a busy number until a connection can be made, and to receive a warning signal when another caller is trying to make contact (call waiting).

Some systems allow subscribers to dial a code to interrogate the exchange on the last number that called; callers may conceal their identity by dialing another code. Other services include exchange-based answering services that take calls after a predetermined number of rings or when the line is busy. These systems issue an outgoing message that can be personalized by the subscriber, and they keep messages in memory until deleted by the subscriber.

PBX. Many companies now access the telephone network through a PBX (*private branch exchange*) on their own premises. Such systems connect calls made between extensions within the company, offering many or all of the features of an advanced public exchange, as well as connecting outgoing calls to the public network. Incoming calls to a central number can be connected by operator, while key extensions have direct lines that bypass operator connection.

Long-distance calls

From the point of view of an exchange, incoming calls fall into two categories: those that require connection with other subscribers connected to the same exchange and those that must be routed via other exchanges. The difference between the two is signalled by whether or not the number is preceded by a local-area or international code. Calls to remote exchanges proceed via a hierarchy of primary, sectional, regional, and national centers. High-volume routes frequently have direct connections that bypass the general network.

Signals are carried between centers by wire and fiber-optic cables (with amplifiers inserted at intervals to maintain signal strength) or by microwave links and satellite circuits. Digital multiplexing expands the capacity of such links by allowing several thousands of calls to occupy interlaced time slots on a single connection.

▼ Technicians at British Telecom's Worldwide Network Management Centre monitor the health of inland and international connections. This system allows them to pinpoint impending failures and, in many cases, take remedial action before service to customers is affected.

SEE ALSO: Amplifier • Cellular telephone • Electromagnetism • Electronics • Fiber optics • Loudspeaker • Microphone • Oscillator • Satellite, artificial • Semiconductor • Sound • Telecommunications • Transformer

Teleprompter

Although actors can be expected to learn their parts word perfect for plays, few presenters on live television can be expected to do the same. Their scripts would have to be learned at short notice, and each script is often the equivalent of a long monolog in the theater—a notoriously difficult proposition, even for an experienced actor. TV presenters and newscasters, then, have to rely on methods other than memory to perfect their delivery. Even the most experienced and well rehearsed are liable to deviate from the script or, at worst, dry (forget their lines) or cut (leave lines out). TV production has evolved a range of prompts and cues, some borrowed from the theater and film and some that have been designed to overcome the particular problems of TV presenters.

Prompting

It is possible to use a quiet verbal prompt to help presenters in difficulty, but this method can lead to problems. Unless the prompt is made extremely quietly, steps have to be taken to render it inaudible—the usual method is to depress a muting key to kill the microphone (or microphones) momentarily. More subtle prompting methods are generally employed.

There are two main kinds of prompt: reminder notes (sometimes called *aides-mémoires*) and continual references. Reminder notes are used to outline the show format, to show subject headings, or to give pieces of important information and data. Continual references give the complete script.

Many TV presenters carry small hand notes or a clipboard containing notes, questions to be used in interviews, and perhaps research material. Less obvious to the viewer are cue cards, often less kindly known as goof sheets or idiot cards. They are generally handwritten and held by members of the floor crew. The biggest problem with handheld reminders is that the eye lines are wrong, causing viewers to question why the presenter is staring out into space. Wrong eye lines are a sign that all is not going right for the presenter.

The solution to the eye-line problem is to mount the reminders on the camera, near the lens axis—exactly where the viewer would expect the presenter to be looking. Reminders are written on flip cards or flippers hung beneath the lens. A member of the floor staff flips the cards over.

Continual references

More detailed script information is needed for news bulletins and for more complex programming. It was realized in the very early days of TV that seeing the top of a newscaster's head while he or she reads from a script on the desk does not make for interesting viewing. The answer to the

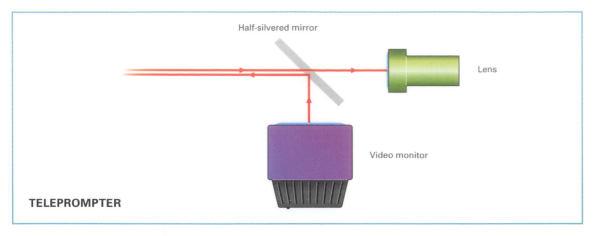

TELEPROMPTER

Half-silvered mirror

Lens

Video monitor

◀ A teleprompter works by reflecting an image of the words to be spoken on a mirror mounted at a 45-degree angle in front of the camera lens. The image of the text as seen by the prompter camera is electronically reversed left-to-right so that the mirror image will appear correct. As the mirror is only half silvered, it acts as a two-way mirror.

problem is to use a teleprompter, which can be attached, like flip cards, to the camera below the lens or stood on the floor on the camera lens axis—whichever the newscaster prefers.

Teleprompters are either mechanically or electronically driven and may advance at a fixed rate or be remotely controlled—either by the newscaster or by one of the floor crew. A typical teleprompter has approximately 20 words visible at any one time; the frame usually has eight lines.

In addition to simple teleprompters, there are a number of types of video prompters. Video prompters solve the problem of the slight difference in position between the flip cards and the true lens axis. One version of the video prompter, called the hard copy prompter, is still sometimes used. A paper roll with large print is placed under high illumination. The image from the paper roll reflects off the glass in the same way as the image on the display tube. Using a paper roll does have the added complication that the writing on the paper has to be reversed if the presenter is going to be able to read the script. As well as reversing the printing on the roll, the image could be reflected twice, or the script could be printed on a clear acetate roll. The acetate roll can then be turned over and lit from either above or below.

Hard-copy prompters have now mostly been replaced in TV studios by soft-copy prompters, which use computers and monitors. A sheet of glass is mounted at 45 degrees to the camera lens. Mounted at 90 degrees to the bottom of the lens (so that its image reflects off the glass) is a video monitor. The script is displayed in one of two ways—a camera may be pointed at a teleprompter, or computer-generated lettering may be used. The camera's image is reversed to counteract the effect of any reflections coming off the glass.

The advantages of computerized prompters are that the text is sharp and easy to read because it is an electronically generated image, revisions are easy to make without compromising legibility,

◀ Teleprompters can be self-standing, enabling them to be placed at various points around a room or set or mounted on a camera. Camera mountings enable the broadcaster to look straight into the camera, effectively making eye contact with the viewer.

◄ Modern teleprompter machines use computer-generated lettering that is sharp and easy to read and can be replaced rapidly if a news story changes on air.

and once the script has been keyed into the computer, the text can be formatted in the standard way with narrow lines and large, bold letters.

There is an art to reading this kind of device. If the presenter keeps his or her head in the same position, it becomes obvious that he or she is reading the script. Experienced presenters change their head position casually, to break the fixed gaze. The second difficulty with prompters is that they can restrict the shots that are available to the director. Prompters must be close to the presenter so that they can be easily read. If more than one camera with a prompter is being used, the prompters have to be synchronized so that the presenter can easily and correctly follow the script. If more than one camera is being used, it is also normal to incorporate camera cues into the script so that the presenter knows where to look next.

In addition, having the prompter close to the presenter makes the script easy to read, but the constant left-to-right movement of the presenter's eyes can be distracting to the audience. On the other hand, moving the prompter farther away reduces this problem but makes it more difficult for the presenter to read the script.

Software is now available that enables personal computers, including laptops, to be turned into teleprompters. Once the script has been keyed in or downloaded from disk, the monitor can be placed next to the camera for the presenter to read. The scrolling of the script is remotely controlled with a mouse and keypad. Laptop computers are sometimes used for this purpose by presenters for short field takes, although many still rely simply on a notebook or clipboard.

Production timing

As well as making life easier for the presenter, teleprompters have an important role to play in the production process. Timing is vital in TV; programs must start and finish as scheduled, and commercials have to be inserted at the correct time. The script has the breaks inserted in it, and the pace of the program can be regulated within certain limits by altering the progress of the script through the prompter; the presenter simply adjusts his or her reading speed accordingly.

If one part of the program overruns the allotted time, and the presenter is reading from a prompter, it is relatively simple to get back on schedule. Parts of the script can be removed, and the viewer need never be aware of the alterations. Timing remains in the hands of the director and the production team, rather than being an extra worry to the already overburdened presenter.

SEE ALSO: MICROPHONE • TELEVISION CAMERA • TELEVISION PRODUCTION

Telescope, Optical

▲ The Anglo-Australian reflecting telescope at Siding Spring, New South Wales, is ideally located away from the glare of city lights and polluted air-conditions that obscure faint astronomical objects. The main mirror is protected by a shutter of steel petals, and the main tube swings on the horseshoe bearing mounted in the base.

Devices for enlarging the apparent size of distant objects to make the details more easily visible were first made around the start of the 17th century, when several people independently discovered the principle of the telescope. By 1609, telescopes could be bought on the open market, and in the following year, the Italian scientist Galileo Galilei turned one to the sky and thereby inaugurated a revolution in astronomy. In addition to their use in astronomy, modern telescopes are used as gunsights and for other military purposes, in surveying instruments, and in laboratory spectroscopes.

Telescopes collect more light than the human eye, so in addition to magnifying objects, they can show objects that are too faint to be seen directly. For most astronomical purposes, the ability to gather light is more important than magnification. All telescopes have essentially two parts: the objective, which may be a curved mirror (in reflecting telescopes, used only for astronomy) or a lens (in refracting telescopes, which can be used for all purposes), and the eyepiece, consisting of a lens or a group of lenses. The objective forms an image of the distant object at its focal point, and this image is then magnified by the eyepiece, which acts as a simple magnifying glass. For many astronomical purposes, a photograph of the object is required, and in this case, the eyepiece is dispensed with. The film is placed at the focal point of the objective, where the image is focused, so that the arrangement is exactly the same as that of an ordinary camera.

Magnification

When the telescope is in normal adjustment, the focal point of the eyepiece coincides with the intermediate image produced by the objective, and the final image seen by the eye is apparently at a very great distance (at infinity). The magnification of the telescope is the ratio of the apparent size of the final image to the apparent size of the object itself, and for normal adjustment, this ratio is equal to the focal length of the objective divided by that of the eyepiece. Different magnifications can be achieved with the same objective by using eyepieces of various focal lengths; for example, a small astronomical telescope with an objective of focal length 48 in. (1.2 m) would give a magnification of 48 with a 1 in. (2.5 cm) focal length eyepiece and a magnification of 96 with a 0.5 in. (1.3 cm) eyepiece.

With any particular eyepiece, the magnification can be increased by moving it nearer the objective, but as doing so brings the final image closer to the eye, eye strain can result when viewing for a length of time. The size, or aperture, of the objective determines the maximum magnification that can be usefully employed in a telescope. A small objective does not give as much detail in the intermediate image as a larger objective, because of the diffraction of light at the edge of the objective; thus, a high-powered eyepiece will not show any more detail in the final image than a moderate-powered one. A magnification of 200, for example, is perfectly adequate for a 6 in. (15 cm) aperture telescope, and the use of a higher power may magnify the image to such an extent that its dimness makes the details hard to see.

The brightness of the final image also depends on the intermediate image, which decreases as the square of the focal ratio (the focal ratio is the focal length of the objective divided by its aperture). The reason for this phenomenon is that a longer focal length increases the size of the intermediate image and hence makes it dimmer, while a larger aperture collects more light and hence produces a brighter image. For observing stars, which appear more or less as points of light even in the largest telescopes, the focal length is not important; the faintest star that can be seen depends only on the aperture. A large aperture means that a telescope collects a large quantity of light. It is for this reason that astronomers have built successively larger telescopes that can reach fainter and thus more distant objects.

Refracting telescopes

The earliest telescopes used a lens as the objective, but it was soon found that the images suffered from aberrations or imperfections. The most serious aberration of these refracting telescopes was the production of false color around the images, caused by the fact that a lens brings light of different wavelengths to a different focus. The resulting spread of colors that degrades an image is termed chromatic aberration. Thin lenses with long focal length minimize chromatic aberration, but telescopes that employ such large lenses are immensely long and cumbersome, measuring 150 ft. (46 m) or more in length. Suspended by a complex arrangement of poles and pulleys, these aerial telescopes were used to make important discoveries about the Solar System, including Saturn's rings and several of its satellites.

The size of these telescopes, however, limited their usefulness, and until the introduction of the achromatic lens by the British inventor John Dollond in 1758, chromatic aberration was a serious hindrance to astronomical research. An achromatic lens has two components of different kinds of glass so that the chromatic aberration of one lens cancels out that of the other, overcoming much of the false color. The invention of the achromatic lens led to the development of the 18.5 in. (47 cm) refractor used to discover the tiny, faint, white dwarf star that accompanies Sirius. The two largest refractors ever built—and still in use in 2002—are the 36 in. (0.91 m) of Lick Observatory in California and the 40 in. (1.01 m) of Yerkes Observatory in Wisconsin.

There is an upper limit to the size of a refractor, and the Yerkes telescope approaches that

▼ The eyepiece of a terrestrial telescope. The power is varied by altering the gap between the lenses. Astronomical and Galilean designs (bottom) show how the image is formed by passing the light through a variety of concave and convex lenses.

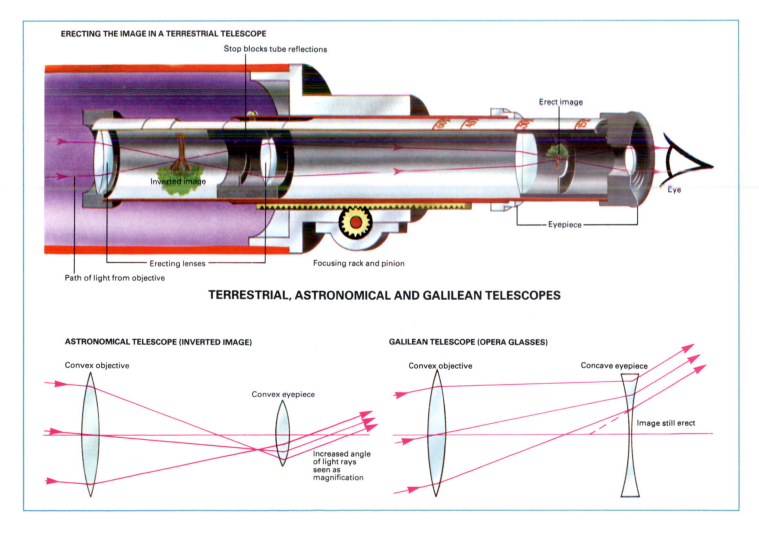

ERECTING THE IMAGE IN A TERRESTRIAL TELESCOPE

Stop blocks tube reflections

Erect image

Inverted image

Eye

Eyepiece

Erecting lenses

Focusing rack and pinion

Path of light from objective

TERRESTRIAL, ASTRONOMICAL AND GALILEAN TELESCOPES

ASTRONOMICAL TELESCOPE (INVERTED IMAGE)

Convex objective

Convex eyepiece

Increased angle of light rays seen as magnification

GALILEAN TELESCOPE (OPERA GLASSES)

Convex objective

Concave eyepiece

Image still erect

limit. The reason for a limit is that large lenses tend to sag because they are supported only around the edges. If a lens is made thicker to give it more strength, the glass absorbs some of the light passing through it, thereby canceling out the advantage of a larger aperture.

Image inversion

Simple refracting telescopes produce an inverted image of the object. When this image is magnified by the eyepiece, it remains inverted, and so this type of telescope is not convenient for viewing terrestrial objects. One way of erecting the image (turning it right way up) is to incorporate a pair of lenses just behind the intermediate image to erect it without producing any magnification; this arrangement leads to a longer and hence heavier tube. Alternatively, a pair of prisms can be used, as in prismatic binoculars. Both these arrangements, however, lead to an appreciable loss of light by reflection at the extra glass faces, and so are used only for terrestrial purposes and not for astronomy.

Reflecting telescopes

Before the advent of achromatic refractors, the possibility of using a curved mirror as an objective had been investigated by the Scottish scientist James Gregory and the English scientist Sir Isaac Newton. A major problem with reflecting telescopes is that the image is formed in front of the mirror in the path of the incoming light. Only in the largest astronomical telescopes can an observer actually sit at the prime focus without blocking off a large proportion of the incident light. Newton's solution was to place a small flat mirror in the tube at 45 degrees to reflect the light from the objective, or primary mirror, out of the side of the tube before it forms an image. This image is then studied with an eyepiece in the usual way. The Newtonian reflector is popular with amateur astronomers because the flat secondary mirror is cheap and this design does not require a hole to be cut in the primary. A later development, the Cassegrain reflector, uses a convex secondary mirror to reflect the light back down the tube and through a hole in the center of the primary mirror.

Unlike a normal looking glass, in which the back surface is coated with a reflecting layer, a telescope mirror is coated on its front surface, usually with a thin layer of metal such as aluminum to avoid the problem of double reflections. Coating also means that the glass does not have to be optically perfect because light does not pass through it and that only one surface needs to be shaped and polished. The glass does, however,

need to have a low coefficient of expansion to ensure that its shape fluctuates little with changing temperature. In addition, exposing the reflective surface makes it liable to tarnish. A further problem with reflecting telescopes is that the two mirrors can get out of alignment much more easily than one lens, so these telescopes are rather delicate and are used only for astronomy.

The first large telescope using a glass mirror was the 60 in. (1.5 m) reflector set up in 1908 on Mount Wilson, California, by George Ellery Hale. Hale also planned a giant 200 in. (5 m) reflector, which eventually opened on Mt. Palomar in 1948, ten years after his death.

For many years, the Hale reflector was the world's largest and most powerful optical telescope. It can provide magnified images at either a Cassegrain focus or at a Coudé focus (which lies adjacent to the main mirror). Conversion from one optical system to the other is simple and quick, making the telescope extremely versatile and adaptable.

Often, even the huge reflector of the Hale telescope might not collect sufficient light to give a clear, magnified image at either of these two focuses. A faint image becomes fainter as it is magnified, so the design of the Hale reflector enables an observer to sit near the principal focus (which lies opposite the main mirror in the path of the incident light) and observe the unmagnified image. The disadvantage of placing the observer in the light path is greatly outweighed by the advantage of being able to observe a clearer image.

▲ An image of the galaxy NGC 628 in Pisces taken by the Gemini Multi-Object Spectrograph on Hawaii's Mauna Kea. This instrument uses an array of more than 28 million ultra-sensitive pixels combined with the main 27 ft. (8.1 m) mirror to produce high-resolution images.

Large reflecting mirrors must have extremely smooth surfaces, making them prohibitively expensive. One solution is to assemble a number of smaller mirrors, which are cheaper to make. The collecting area of a much larger telescope can then be mimicked. The largest telescope of this type is at the Keck observatory on Mauna Kea in Hawaii. It has thirty-six 6 ft. (1.8 m) wide hexagonal mirrors with a combined collecting area of 818 sq. ft. (76 m^2). Electronic image intensifiers are used to boost the faint light received from the most distant objects, and computers are used to bring out otherwise imperceptible detail—a technique that is already bringing useful results.

Plans for even bigger reflector telescopes composed of many mirrors include the California Extremely Large Telescope (CELT), a 100 ft. (30 m) telescope proposed by the University of California and the California Institute of Technology, and the OverWhelmingly Large telescope (OWL), a 300 ft. (100 m) reflector telescope being developed by the European Southern Observatory. Reflecting telescopes are also used in the study of astronomical objects emitting wavelengths in the infrared part of the electromagnetic spectrum.

Galileo's telescope

The telescope used by Galileo was of a somewhat different design from those described so far. The light from the objective lens is intercepted by the eyepiece, in this case a concave lens, before it forms an image, and this arrangement gives an upright final image. The field of view of a Galilean telescope is, however, small. Its principal use is in opera glasses, where the relatively short tube and erect image are important assets.

Schmidt camera

Schmidt cameras and telescopes are probably the most sensitive optical systems that it is possible to devise for high-quality photography. They are used when good images over a wide field of view are required at low light levels. In astronomy, the wide field of view has made the Schmidt telescope the principal instrument for carrying out photographic surveys of the night sky.

A spherical mirror forms good images on its axis from light striking its central regions. However, light striking the outer regions of such a mirror is focused at a different point on the mirror's axis. This problem, known as spherical aberration, gets worse as mirrors with faster f-ratios are used, that is, as the diameter becomes large compared with the focal length, giving brighter images.

A simple solution is to alter the spherical surface to a paraboloid, a figure slightly deeper in the center than a sphere, thus eliminating spherical aberration entirely. The penalty is that off-axis images suffer badly from another type of distortion, or aberration, known as coma. A more satisfactory solution consists of combining a spherical mirror with a correcting lens of some sort.

An Estonian optician, Bernhard Schmidt, realized in 1932 that, if the correcting lens was placed at the center of curvature of the mirror, off-axis rays would be able to produce almost as good images as on-axis rays and that such a system could have a wide-angle field of view. This system, with a corrector at the center of curvature, is called a Schmidt camera.

The focal plane in a Schmidt camera lies midway between the corrector and the mirror but is curved with its center at the center of curvature of the mirror, that is, at the corrector. The photographic emulsion recording the image in the camera must be bent accurately to this surface. Two of the largest Schmidt cameras in present use, both of focal ratio f/2.5 with mirrors 72 in. (1.8 m) in diameter and corrector plates 48 in. (1.2 m) in diameter, are located at Mt. Palomar in California and at Siding Spring Observatory in New South Wales, Australia. A smaller version, with a corrector plate 39 in. (1 m) in diameter, is at the European Southern Observatory in Chile. In all these cameras, the center of the photographic plates protrudes almost 0.4 in. (10 mm) in

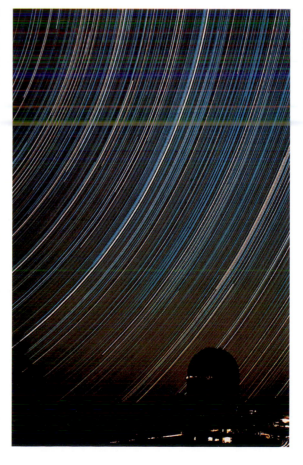

◀ A photographic tracing showing star trails as Earth turns on its axis and rotates around the Sun.

front of the corners. The bending, handling, and uniform manufacture of such large, thin, plates are not trivial problems.

These three large Schmidt cameras have fields of 6 degrees in diameter (12 times that of the Moon). They have been used to survey vast areas of the sky in great detail, enabling interesting objects to be located for study with large telescopes. Their wide fields are suitable for finding the relative positions of a number of objects in a single picture; the entire Northern Hemisphere was recorded on photographic plates by the 48 in. (1.2 m) Schmidt at Mt. Palomar in California. Plates of the Mt. Palomar Sky Survey, as it was known, are now standard references for astronomers the world over.

The correcting lens in a Schmidt camera is usually a thin, nonspherical corrector plate (3.9 in., or 10 cm, thick for the 48 in. Schmidt camera), but a solid Schmidt camera can be made, whose corrector and mirror consists of one piece of glass, with the corrector surface figured on one end and the spherical mirror figured and aluminized (coated to make it reflective) on the other. A slot is cut out in the middle to accept the film. The speed of such a camera is phenomenal; it can be made as fast as the theoretical limit of f/0.5 without unacceptable degradation of image quality. A solid Schmidt camera can be made only in small sizes because of the difficulty of manufacturing a large flawless piece of glass; it also suffers severely from chromatic aberration. It has found application as the camera in spectrographs where single-color images of lines are formed and chromatic aberration is no disadvantage.

Mercury mirrors

Another development in the design of optical telescopes has been the use of revolving pools of mercury as mirrors. When a liquid is made to rotate in a uniform gravitational field, its surface naturally forms a parabola that may be adjusted by varying the rate of rotation. These reflecting telescopes are relatively inexpensive and can be made very large. In 2002, an array of eighteen 33 ft. (10 m) mercury mirrors was being planned for a site in Chile; it would provide the equivalent light-collecting power of a 138 ft. (42 m) telescope.

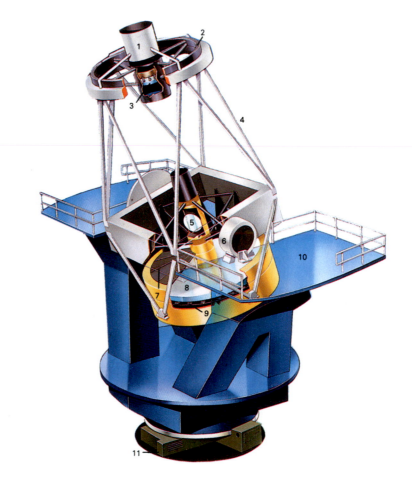

▼ The 13.8 ft. (4.2 m) Herschel Telescope built on La Palma, Canary Islands. The remote location of the telescope provides favorable conditions for observing faint details in deep space—there are no glaring city lights to make focusing difficult, and there is little air pollution on the islands. Key: (1) observer's cage, (2) pivoted support, (3) secondary mirror, (4) steel framework, (5) first Coudé mirror, (6) pivot, (7) mirror cover, (8) main mirror, (9) mirror support, (10) observing floor, (11) turning mechanism.

FACT FILE

- The first telescopes to be produced and sold commercially were made by Hans Lippershey at the beginning of the 17th century and sold to the Dutch Army for use in military reconnaissance. Early telescopes were limited by size to a magnification no greater than x20.

- In 1845, William Parsons, Earl of Rosse, built in Ireland what was then the world's largest telescope. He made two mirrors, each 72 in. (1.82 m) across and weighing 4 tons, to be used in rotation in the telescope. Known as the Leviathan of Parsonstown, the telescope was mounted between two 56 ft. (17 m) walls and consisted of a tube 58 ft. (17.5 m) long. With tremendous light-gathering power, this telescope was the first to show that some nebulas are spirals.

- In Atacama, Chile, the European Southern Observatory is linking four of its 27 ft. (8.2 m) reflecting telescopes to produce a Very Large Telescope (VLT). It will possess the light-collecting power of a 52 ft. (16 m) optical telescope, making it the largest in the world.

SEE ALSO: ASTRONOMY • CAMERA • DIFFRACTION • LENS • LIGHT AND OPTICS • PHOTOGRAPHIC FILM AND PROCESSING • PRISM • SOLAR SYSTEM • SPACE PHOTOGRAPHY • TELESCOPE, SPACE

Telescope, Space

◀ This proposed design for the Next Generation Space Telescope (NGST) uses four separated sunshields to reduce the temperature of the sensitive infrared instruments.

Telescopes on Earth are limited in their ability to view astronomical objects owing to the obscuring effect of Earth's atmosphere and the increasing problem of light pollution. These problems may be solved by placing telescopes in orbit around Earth and transmitting the information they receive back to bases at ground level.

For many years satellites have been used as space observatories. One of the best known and most successful is the Hubble Space Telescope (HST), launched in 1990. This telescope is designed to observe the infrared, visible, and ultraviolet wavelengths of the electromagnetic spectrum, a goal that is achieved using a variety of instruments that have constantly been upgraded since the telescope's launch. The telescope orbits Earth once every 97 minutes at an altitude of 380 miles (612 km) and at a speed of 17,500 mile per hour (28,000 km/h). Power is provided by two solar arrays that provide the satellite with 2,400 watts.

The largest optical instrument on HST is the primary mirror, which is around 8 ft. (2.4 m) in diameter. Soon after HST was launched, scientists realized that there was a problem with this mirror, as the images produced were blurred. It became clear that manufacturing errors had caused the mirror to be ground incorrectly, and so a method for correcting the problem was devised. This correction consisted of the addition to the telescope of 10 mirrors, installed by astronauts during a space shuttle mission, that adjusted the light paths from the mirror to the receiving instruments and so solved the problem of blurring.

HST also contains several scientific instruments, including the Wide Field Camera II, which takes images in the visible spectrum; the

▼ Since the Hubble Space Telescope was launched in 1990, astronauts on space shuttle missions have regularly serviced and replaced its instruments to improve the telescope's capabilities.

Faint Object Camera (FOC), which takes detailed images within a small field; and the Near Infrared Camera and Multi-Object Spectrometer (NIC-MOS), which takes images in the infrared region and is therefore able to see through the interstellar gas and dust that obscures visible light.

The Hubble Space Telescope has vastly widened understanding of the Universe by providing images of objects that would be impossible to see from Earth-based observatories, including greater knowledge of the development of supernovas, increased understanding of the evolution of galaxies, and an improved estimate for the age of the Universe—12 to 14 billion years old.

In 1999, the National Aeronautics and Space Administration (NASA) launched another telescope, Chandra, which observes X rays from quasars, black holes, and the remnants of exploding stars. This 45 ft. (13.7 m) long telescope travels in an elliptical orbit that at its apogee is a third of the distance to the Moon. Mirrors inside the telescope focus the X rays onto instruments that record the information received and allow it to be transmitted to Earth, where it is analyzed.

The Solar and Heliospheric Observatory (SOHO) is a joint project funded by the European Space Agency (ESA) and NASA. This observatory, launched in 1995, contains a variety

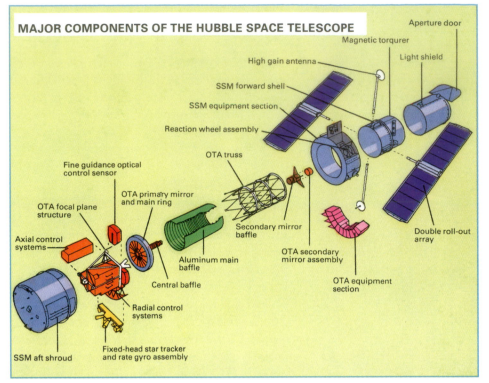

MAJOR COMPONENTS OF THE HUBBLE SPACE TELESCOPE

Aperture door
Magnetic torquer
Light shield
High gain antenna
SSM forward shell
SSM equipment section
Reaction wheel assembly
OTA truss
Fine guidance optical control sensor
OTA primary mirror and main ring
OTA focal plane structure
Secondary mirror baffle
Axial control systems
Aluminum main baffle
OTA secondary mirror assembly
Double roll-out array
Central baffle
Radial control systems
OTA equipment section
SSM aft shroud
Fixed-head star tracker and rate gyro assembly

of instruments that enable scientists to learn about the internal structure of the Sun, its outer atmosphere, and the solar wind. SOHO has provided a wealth of new data on solar behavior, such as evidence to suggest an upward transfer of magnetic energy from the Sun's surface to the corona and information on the dynamic nature of the Sun's solar atmosphere.

Origins

NASA has been building on its successes with the Hubble under a program called Origins, which aims to answer two important questions—where do we come from, and are we alone? NASA hopes to answer these questions using a series of ground- and space-based telescopes of increasing technological sophistication. Precursor space missions in this program include HST and the Far Ultraviolet Spectroscopic Explorer (FUSE), which was launched in 1999 and provides information in the ultraviolet range of the spectrum, which is blocked by Earth's atmosphere. The first-generation missions are planned to begin in September 2005 with the launch of the Starlight mission. It consists of two spacecraft that will move in formation and work as an interferometer. An interferometer is formed from two or more telescopes that combine the information they obtain to produce a single image. The telescopes are located some distance apart and are capable of producing images with the resolving power of a single, much larger telescope. In this way, highly detailed images can be produced without having to build single, very large telescopes.

▲ In addition to these components, the Hubble telescope includes the Wide Field Camera II, and the Advanced Camera for Surveys (ACS).

▼ A new image of the Horsehead nebula taken by the Hubble telescope.

The two telescopes in Starlight will have to move in formation with a high degree of precision to be able to produce images showing a high level of detail and will have to do this over separations of 130 to 1,970 ft. (40–600 m). This mission will test and improve the technology necessary for a much larger array of telescopes called the Terrestrial Planet Finder (TPF), due to be launched around 2012, which will be used to capture images of distant planets.

Another first-generation mission is the Space Interferometry Mission (SIM). This space telescope, due to be launched around 2009, will use interferometry to take images in the visible spectrum and will seek to identify any stars that show a distinctive wobble that indicates the gravitational pull of orbiting planets. This information will then be used by the TPF in its search for planets.

The Next Generation Space Telescope (NGST), planned for launch some time around 2009, will look at the formation of stars and galaxies near the beginning of the Universe. This telescope will observe wavelengths in the infrared range of the electromagnetic spectrum and will be able to see objects 400 times fainter than is possible with any other infrared telescope currently deployed. The NGST will also have a primary mirror 26 ft. (8 m) in diameter and will require a sunshade the size of a tennis court to shield the telescope from the heat of the Sun.

SEE ALSO: ASTRONOMY • ELECTROMAGNETIC RADIATION • RADIO ASTRONOMY • SATELLITE, ARTIFICIAL • SOLAR SYSTEM • SPACE PROBE • SPACE SHUTTLE • TELESCOPE, OPTICAL

Television Camera

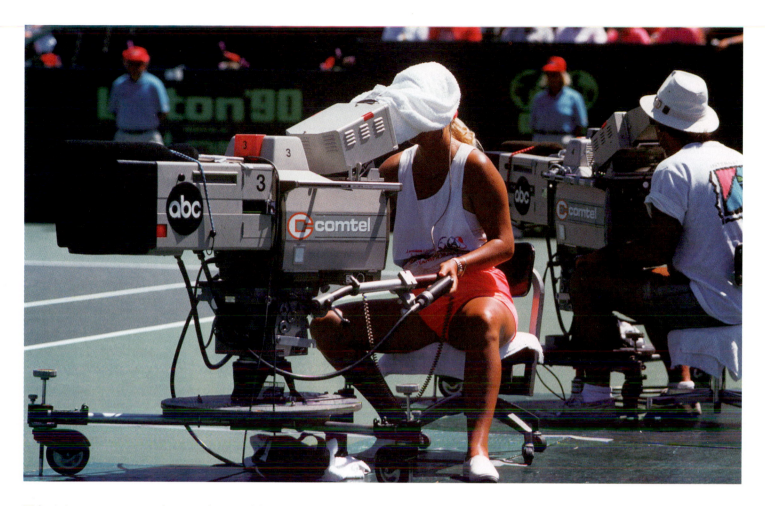

Television cameras are devices that enable moving pictures to be converted into electronic signals that are then transmitted using radio waves or along cables to television receivers. The earliest television cameras used a mechanical system in which a rotating disk containing a series of holes was used to scan the image to be transmitted. The light that passed through the holes stimulated a photosensitive cell, which converted the light into an electric signal. Early designs, such as those by the Scottish inventor John Logie Baird, produced poor quality images and were ultimately superseded by electronic systems.

This new television system, invented in 1933 by the Russian-born U.S. electronics engineer, Vladimir Zworykin, used a cathode ray and was the first practical system to be entirely electronic. The iconoscope camera consisted of an evacuated glass envelope containing a sheet of mica covered with tiny globules of silver, called a mosaic, treated with cesium and oxygen. When photons struck these globules, electrons were realized as a result of the photoelectric effect, the number of electrons being proportional to the number of photons. The release of the electrons caused the plate to have a particular distribution of positive and negative charge corresponding to the brightness or dimness of the different parts of the image. A beam of electrons produced by an electron gun was then used to scan the surface of the silver. As each globule was struck by the beam of electrons, a change of electrical potential would occur, the amount depending on the charge on the particular globule. This change in potential then passed to a signal plate behind the mica sheet so that, as the beam of electrons passed over the silver globules, a fluctuating voltage was created in the signal plate. This voltage was then amplified to produce the picture signal. This system, however, was prone to problems, such as uneven shading, and was soon improved upon with the development of the orthicon.

The orthicon also consisted of an evacuated tube and had much in common with the iconoscope, but the mosaic in this instance was made of small squares of a photosensitive material, and the scanning beam of electrons was slowed down before striking the photosensitive surface to reduce the numbers of electrons liberated from the surface by high-velocity impacts.

The orthicon was in turn superseded in the early 1940s by another camera, developed by

▲ Mobile cameras enable television makers to follow live action at a variety of different outdoor events. Pictures are sent by a cable to an outside broadcast truck from where they are beamed by satellite to a central television network.

RCA, called the image orthicon. In this camera, the image was focused onto a photocathode, which is a continuous photosensitive coating that releases electrons in response to light in such a way that the brightest parts of an image cause the largest release of electrons. These electrons are then attracted to a target electrode made of thin glass. A beam of electrons then scans the surface of the target, and the electrons are absorbed or deflected according to the charge on a particular area. The deflected electrons then bounce back to the rear of the tube, where their number is increased several thousand times by an electron multiplier. The output from this multiplier then becomes the television signal.

During the 1950s, another form of camera tube was developed called the vidicon. This camera used the effect of photoconductivity rather than photoemission. In the vidicon, a thin photoconductive layer is coated on the signal plate. The image is focused on this surface, and the resistance of a particular area, which is high at low light levels, decreases as the level of light increases so that the distribution of varying conductivity corresponds to the light and dark areas of the image. As with the other systems, an electron beam scans the surface of the photoconductive layer and thus neutralizes the voltage. The change in electrical potential transfers to the signal plate by capacitive action and is then used to produce the television signal.

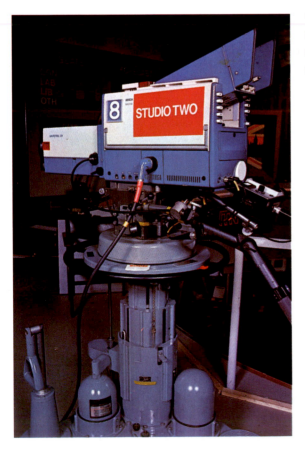

◀ A color television camera. Each picture is scanned twice, in alternate stripes, to reduce flicker.

A further development is the flying-spot scanner, which is used for transmitting images of still transparencies or motion picture film. A beam of electrons is made to scan a fluorescent phosphor surface, producing a moving spot of light that is then focused onto the surface of the film. The amount of light that passes through the film depends on the transparency of the film at the point being scanned. This light is then received by a photoelectric cell, creating a current that increases or decreases with respect to the lightness or darkness of the film image. The television signal is then derived from this current.

The scanning beam

In the iconoscope, the electron beam scans the upper surface of the mosaic but in the systems that followed, such as the orthicon and vidicon, the scanning occurs on the rear surface. The beam moves over the rear surface of the target in exactly the same way as the eye moves over a printed page in reading. The beam moves from left to right across the image, returns rapidly to the left again, and scans a second line immediately under the previous line, continuing in this manner until the bottom of the image is reached. The beam then returns to the top of the image and begins the process again. The movement of the electrons is controlled by magnetic fields produced by pairs of metal plates.

In most European countries, 625 scanning lines are used, and each complete scan of the target is accomplished in $\frac{1}{25}$ second, so 25 complete pictures are transmitted every second. In the United States, the picture is composed of 525 lines, and 30 pictures are transmitted per second.

As the target is scanned, the varying voltage of the picture signal is interrupted for a brief interval every time the beam returns to the left-hand side of the image and, for a longer interval, every time it returns to the top of the image.

Color images

To produce color television images, more than one camera tube must be used. In one system, two color-selective (dichroic) mirrors separate the incoming light into the wavelengths corresponding to blue, green, and red. Mirrors are then used to direct the respective colors to different camera tubes. The scanning of the three color images occurs in unison so that when the resulting combined signal is reproduced by the television set, it creates a precise full-color copy of the scene viewed by the camera. A fourth tube may also be added to receive a full-color image, and this information is used to produce a luminance signal, the result being a higher-quality final image.

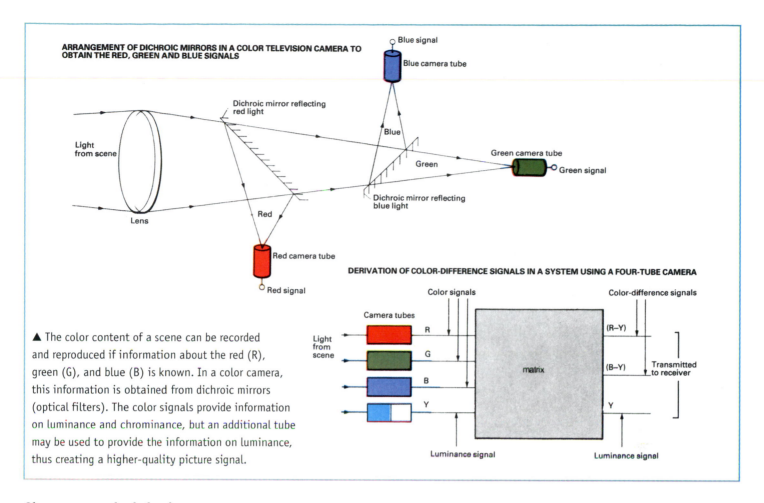

ARRANGEMENT OF DICHROIC MIRRORS IN A COLOR TELEVISION CAMERA TO OBTAIN THE RED, GREEN AND BLUE SIGNALS

Blue signal
Blue camera tube
Dichroic mirror reflecting red light
Blue
Light from scene
Green camera tube
Green signal
Green
Dichroic mirror reflecting blue light
Lens
Red
Red camera tube
Red signal

▲ The color content of a scene can be recorded and reproduced if information about the red (R), green (G), and blue (B) is known. In a color camera, this information is obtained from dichroic mirrors (optical filters). The color signals provide information on luminance and chrominance, but an additional tube may be used to provide the information on luminance, thus creating a higher-quality picture signal.

DERIVATION OF COLOR-DIFFERENCE SIGNALS IN A SYSTEM USING A FOUR-TUBE CAMERA

Color signals
Color-difference signals
Camera tubes
Light from scene
R
G
B
Y
matrix
(R–Y)
(B–Y)
Y
Transmitted to receiver
Luminance signal
Luminance signal

Charge-coupled devices

Instead of using vidicons or image-orthicons, new cameras that use charge-coupled devices (CCDs) have been developed. Charge-coupled devices use a light-sensitive material on a silicon chip to produce a current from which the television signal is derived. CCDs store charge when light falls onto a device called a transistor gate, or capacitor, also known as a pixel. CCDs are more sensitive to light than other photosensitive devices and can be used to produce camera imaging systems that have a combined power of around 10 million pixels. CCDs are also more durable than conventional camera tubes and can be made much smaller, enabling CCD cameras to be lighter and therefore more flexible in their range of uses.

The development of high-definition television (HDTV) requires television cameras that can produce images suitable for the new number of scanning lines, either 720 or 1,080, depending on the system. CCDs are ideal for these requirements and, when combined with digital methods of transmission, produce much clearer television images than conventional analog systems.

Transmission of color information

The three outputs of the color camera tubes or from charge-coupled devices must be transmitted to the receiving end, because a color picture tube requires red (R), green (G), and blue (B) inputs to recreate the original image. The picture tube thus requires three separate signals. These signals need not, however, be the R, G, and B picture signals themselves. Any three signals that contain R, G, and B will do because from these signals the R, G, and B signals can be obtained by algebraic operations in a circuit known as a matrix.

The operation of the matrix is similar to that of the algebra used in solving simultaneous equations. One signal involving R, G, and B already exists as the luminance signal, usually represented by Y. Two other signals are therefore required, and the two selected are the (R-Y) and (B-Y) signals, known as color-difference signals. A subcarrier is used to transmit the two color-difference signals, and a number of methods have been devised for recovering them at the receiver. To keep the color transmission within the channel, the color subcarrier is located in the frequency band of the video signal, and its frequency is carefully chosen to prevent it—and the modulating signals—from causing interference with the luminance signal.

SEE ALSO: Cathode-ray tube • Charge-coupled device • Photoelectric cell and photometry • Television production • Television receiver

Television Production

Television production is the process that leads from an outline concept to a program that is broadcast live or recorded for subsequent transmission. The exact details of the process vary greatly, depending on the type of program—period drama series or live news broadcast, for example—but certain techniques and technologies are common to many types of programs. This article will confine itself largely to describing technical aspects of television production.

Cameras and lights

The most fundamental pieces of equipment in television production are television cameras. These cameras view the action through optical systems that focus images onto arrays of CCDs (charge-coupled devices). CCDs are light-sensitive semiconductor devices that produce output voltages that vary in response to changes in the light intensity that falls on them. The output from the CCD arrays is the basis from which a signal is constructed to drive television monitors.

Cameras respond to light reflected by the subjects in their view, so these subjects—actors, props, and scenery—must be well illuminated to

ensure good picture quality. Television studios are equipped with powerful floodlights that fulfill this task. The lighting is so arranged as to avoid the casting of unnatural shadows, which would cause a distraction and detract from the viewers' illusion of reality for dramatic programs.

When filming in outdoor locations, natural light is often supplemented by some form of artificial lighting. For many sports events, arena floodlighting is sufficient for this purpose. Some outdoor events, such as motor racing, are shot using natural light alone, since the physical area in which the event takes place would make comprehensive artificial lighting impractical.

Sets, props, and wardrobe

Sets are the surroundings of the action in a television production and thus play a key role in creating a suitable atmosphere for the program. Dramatic productions often use real locations, particularly for outdoors scenes. Some long-running series, such as soap operas, have specially built sets whose buildings appear realistic but might be mere facades or conceal functional areas, such as canteen facilities and props stores.

▲ Television programs can be filmed live before an audience or on a closed set. Great effort is made to make the scenes look as realistic as possible, whether it be the interior of a house or on location.

Indoor sequences tend to be shot in studios using sets whose walls and doors are crafted from hardwood and paint, for example. For dramatic productions, these sets tend to resemble rooms, but one wall is missing to allow access for cameras. In some cases, part of the ceiling is left open so that mirrors can be used to film overhead shots from floor-based cameras. In all cases, sets are designed around the placement and movement of cameras, and tracks for camera dollies (wheeled platforms) must sometimes be included in the set.

Props (short for "properties") are the artifacts placed in sets or worn by actors. They include watches, furniture, and wall decorations—in fact, all the noncostume articles except the scenery. Wardrobe comprises the costumes of actors in dramatic productions and the outfits of presenters of factual programs. The combination of props and wardrobe provides visual information that contributes to the audience's appreciation of the program. Particular attention must be paid to the choice of props and wardrobe for period dramas, since a modern watch worn in an old-time drama would damage the illusion of a long-gone era. Many production teams also include continuity experts, who are responsible for ensuring that actors' hairstyles, costumes, and accessories remain the same for a series of linked sequences even if circumstances or scheduling require those sequences to be filmed out of order.

Programs such as news broadcasts and interview programs use abstract sets whose characteristics suit the intended tone of the program. Cool shades, such as blues and grays, reinforce the formal nature of a serious news broadcast, as does clean-lined furniture. Warmer tones suggest less formality and are suitable for broadcasting movie reviews. Interview-based programs often use more homely sets and softer furnishings to emphasize the informality of interviews with stars, for example, whereas bold primary colors and oversized furniture might be used to appeal to an audience of preschool children. The specific type of camera must be taken into consideration when choosing set colors, since each type of camera has its own color characteristics.

Blocking and rehearsals

Blocking is the production stage in which the actors or presenters read through the script and the director decides on how the performance should be paced and which words and lines should receive emphasis. It is also the stage when the positions of actors are established for the various parts of a scene and when the sets might be fine tuned and furniture repositioned accordingly. Once these parameters have been set, the cast or presenters can start rehearsing so that the final presentation is as natural as possible. The precise positions of actors can be determined in the final shoot by floor marks, which also help the camera, lighting, and sound crews to prepare for shooting using stand-ins in place of the actors.

Second unit

While actors or presenters—the "talent"—are preparing their contributions, a second unit can be gathering material that does not require their participation. These might include outdoor shots of buildings or landscapes, hand-drawn or computer-generated graphics, library footage of famous events or locations, and outside-broadcast footage to support a studio-based news report. The production team that provides this material is usually entirely separate from the crew that work in studios with the talent.

Studio effects

The final production can be influenced by effects created during filming, as opposed to those that are introduced at the editing stage. Some of them, such as lighting and meteorological effects, are borrowed from stage trickery; others are exclusive to movies and television.

Lighting. Televisual-effect lighting can influence the final output in a great many ways. The impressions of the shapes, textures, colors, and sizes of objects can all be molded by careful manipulation of lighting, as can the impression of distance. Aside from these essentially static lighting effects, environmental and illusory effects can be used to create impressions of sunsets, water ripples, and flickering flames, for example.

Projection. Television uses three kinds of projection to create effects—front, back, and reflex projection. Front projection is the simplest of the

▼ Shooting on location. The smooth track between the crew and the actor allows a wheeled camera dolly to follow the moving actor without being jolted by cracks in the sidewalk.

▶ This picture shows a typical television studio. Large overhead lights provide the strong and even illumination needed by the cameras. The horizontal rods are counterbalanced booms, from which microphones hang over the heads of actors or presenters, just out of shot of the cameras.

three. The camera films a subject in front of a screen onto which either still or moving images are projected. Most common is the use of front projection in television to project abstract or geometric patterns through metal stencils—a frequently used effect in the staging of variety shows. Back projection is more complex: cameras film the action against a translucent screen onto which moving or still images are projected from behind.

In modern practice, reflex projection—also called front-axial projection—has almost replaced back projection. With reflex projection, an image is projected onto a half-silvered mirror that reflects it along the camera lens axis while the camera films through the mirror. The projection reflects off a background screen made from millions of tiny glass beads. The process is highly directional, reflecting more than 90 percent of the projected light directly back along the camera axis. The advantage of this technique is that the quality of the projected image is almost unaffected by studio lights—only light that originates on or near the projection axis will degrade it.

Filters. Many types of filters can be used with television cameras. Those used in creating particular effects include star filters that create pointed haloes around bright spots of light, diffusion disks that reduce image sharpness, low-contrast filters that desaturate and mute colors, fog filters, night filters, color filters, and multiple-image prisms.

Electronic effects

Many of the above-mentioned effects are falling into disuse as the variety and sophistication of electronic effects increases. These effects can be superimposed on recorded video footage in an editing suite, and the version that includes effects is then recorded for subsequent editing stages and eventually for transmission.

Superimposed images. Superimpositions are achieved by fading up two picture sources. The pictures often intermix with little difficulty. Problems can occur where black appears in one picture: the coinciding detail from the other picture then appears to be solid. Conversely, peak white from one picture can completely bleach detail from the other. Combinations of hues may also mix together to produce another hue.

Black-level adjustment. Black-level adjustment is achieved by electronically darkening the lowest tones in a scene. This process hides wrinkles in black backdrops, for example, and can disguise tonal variations to some extent. The technique is especially useful in conjunction with some animation effects and particularly for blending puppeteers' black-gloved hands with black backdrops in certain types of puppet shows.

Tone and color reversal. Tone- and color-reversal effects are popular devices for creating title sequences. In monochrome footage, dark tones replace light tones, and vice versa. In color footage, each color can be replaced by its complementary color, so red, green, and blue interchange with cyan, magenta, and yellow, for example. This effect can also be used to produce positive video recordings from film negatives without making a positive print.

Blue-screen effects. Blue-screen effects are an example of color-separation overlay—a technique whereby two images are intermeshed to form a composite image on screen. They are widely used in news reports and weather forecasts, when a studio-based presenter appears in front of a backdrop that shows the scene of an event or a weather map, for example. In fact, the presenter is filmed against a plain blue screen, and the backdrop is added from a different source.

Blue screen works by switching between image sources at the appropriate point in the scan of each line of an image (television pictures consist of hundreds of horizontal lines that are scanned from side to side and from top to bottom on the screen). The switching signal is the output from the blue tube of the camera that is shooting the main image—the presenter, in the above example. When the scan reaches the blue screen, the output of the blue tube increases and switches the output to the second image—the backdrop.

The blue-screen technique also has applications beyond news and weather broadcasts. Actors can be dwarfed by blown-up images of everyday surroundings, set at the rim of an erupting volcano, or even placed inside a computer-generated

ELECTRONIC NEWS GATHERING

Electronic news gathering (ENG)—also called electronic journalism—is a method of on-location news reporting that uses video cameras to capture images. The images and sound from an ENG session can be transmitted directly to the news studio for inclusion in a live news report, or they can be recorded on tape for subsequent editing. The introduction of ENG enabled news journalists to get their reports onto viewers' screens much more swiftly than was possible with earlier technology.

Live coverage of events—from sporting occasions to embassy sieges—has long been possible using outside broadcast (OB) units. These units, comprising truck-loads of crew and equipment, are slow to reach the scene of action and not very mobile when they arrive. Thus, OB units rarely make contributions to news programs. A faster, more flexible response to breaking news is possible using a film crew of two people. However, film has to be taken to the studio and developed before it can be shown—a slow process.

An ENG team combines the mobility of a film crew with the speed to screen of an OB unit. Its camera and microphone can be operated by a single person, and they can provide signals for recording on separate image and sound channels of video tape. However, the advantage of ENG is that those signals can be transmitted directly to the television center by a UHF radio link. The equipment for this link is carried by a support truck and comprises modulating equipment, a UHF transmitter, a rooftop antenna, and a power generator. Transmission requires a clear line of sight to the receiving antenna at the base or a relay station, so the antenna is usually raised on a telescopic mount to help obtain a line of sight to the receiver.

In the United States, transmission was initially in analog form on seven channels between 1,990 MHz and 2,110 MHz. A change to digital transmission on narrower bands between 2,025 MHz and 2,100 MHz is expected to have been completed within the first decade of the 21st century.

▲ Before electronic news gathering, outside-broadcast teams, such as this one, were the only means of transmitting live signals to central news studios. The amount of equipment and number of people involved limited the speed of response and flexibility of such crews.

▼ Electronic news gathering is indispensable for the new generation of news channels, of which CNN is an example. The race to get rating-winning footage of breaking news on screen before rival companies is fierce.

landscape. There are certain limitations to the blue-screen technique, however. Persons shot against a blue screen cannot wear blue clothing: if they did, parts of the backdrop would appear through them. Also, blue light reflected off the screen onto other objects can cause blurred fringes between the two components of an image. Furthermore, it is a challenge for actors and presenters to interact with a background that is invisible to them at the time of shooting. A monitor that shows the final image can help, but it takes skill for presenters to learn how to point to symbols on maps, for example, guided by the view in their monitor.

Temporal effects. Temporal effects can be achieved in a variety of ways once the action has been recorded in real time. Fast motion speeds up subject movement and cuts the time taken for an event or series of events; slow motion does exactly the opposite. Freeze-frame stops the action dead, while reverse motion plays the action backwards. For example, a sequence in which a pile of rubble assembles itself as a building can be produced by reversing a recording of a demolition.

Edited productions

Editing is the process that combines images, sounds, and effects to form a product suitable for broadcasting. The nature of the editing process varies greatly between different program formats, but its aim in all cases is to produce a well-paced program that holds its viewers' attention by using techniques such as cuts between different camera angles. At the same time, the use of editorial tools must be judged wisely so as not to overwhelm the content. Fast and frequent cuts might be suitable for a short sequence of intense action but would be tiring and intrusive if used throughout.

Some programs, in common with most movies, are shot by recording each scene many times over using a single camera in a variety of positions. The job of the editor is then to construct a smoothly flowing sequence of images from the various recorded takes of each scene.

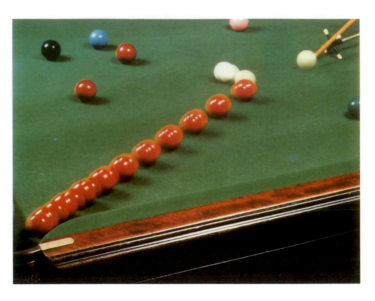

▲ In this image, several freeze-frame shots are superimposed to show the path of the red ball to the pocket. All the intervals between consecutive shots are the same, so the images of the ball get closer together as the ball slows near the pocket.

▼ This video-mixing desk is used to combine the inputs from various video sources in the recording of a master tape. The desk can manipulate images to produce special effects.

There are various means by which cuts between camera angles can be made without jarring. Most work by relating the cut to an audible or visible cue. The sound of a telephone ringing might be closely followed by a cut from a group shot to a close-up of the telephone, for example, and then by a cut to a shot of the person who goes to answer the call. Similarly, an actor casting a glance off screen could be used as a cue for a cut to the object of his or her attention. In essence, these cuts seem natural because they match the expectations of the viewers: the view goes where the attention of a viewer is drawn by the associated cues.

This type of editing requires actors to perform each scene uniformly in each take. They must repeat their performances in synchronization with the dialog so that subsequent cuts do not cause inexplicable changes in their positions, expressions, and postures. Continuity experts also check for consistency of details, such as hairstyles, between takes. It then remains for the editor to fix any inconsistencies that occur despite the efforts of the acting and continuity teams.

Each recording starts with a view of color bars and a slate. The color bars are used in the color-correcting process that occurs when the master tape is recorded. The slate carries information that identifies the program, episode, and scene to which the recording belongs, as well as details of the sound format and other comments that might be needed in the subsequent editing stages.

Once the material has been recorded, the tape is ready for the actual editing process. Unlike film, which can be cut and spliced to make edits, recorded footage must be rerecorded in its edited form. In the offline editing stage, the editor plays through all the tapes to produce an edit decision list, or EDL. This list identifies the sequences of shots that will constitute each scene in a production by referring to the time code recorded on each tape. The list also specifies how one shot should change into the next—by a sharp cut or a slow dissolve, for example.

The next stage is online editing, when the various contributions are rerecorded on a master tape. Title graphics, captions, and subtitles are introduced using a character-generating (CG) computer, and the transitions between shots are effected using equipment that manipulates signals from various video inputs.

In addition to the basic effects, such as fades and cuts, sophisticated video-editing equipment can ripple an image to signal the start of a flashback sequence, it can produce split-screen effects by dividing the screen between two or more video inputs, or it can produce an effect such as "wrapping" one image around a virtual cylinder or globe to reveal a different background or unpeeling the image from one video input to reveal the start of the next shot. In addition to the video editing that occurs at this stage, the color balance of the recording is corrected if necessary, and sound effects and dubbed dialog are added to the mix and their quality enhanced for recording onto the master tape.

"Live" productions

Many programs are produced live or at least live on tape ("live on tape" means the program is recorded as if it were being broadcast live and only stopped if a major problem occurs). This type of program includes broadcast sports events, news broadcasts, and studio-based chat shows.

In live broadcasts, the person responsible for the composition of the output is the director. Numerous camera operators and sound engineers provide the raw material for the broadcast according to rehearsed maneuvers and live instructions delivered to them from the director by headphones. The director chooses the camera whose output will be televised at any given time, while also giving instructions for repositioning inactive cameras between shots. In some cases, cameras are manipulated by robots in response to remote-control signals from the director's suite.

In interactive television, several output options are broadcast simultaneously, and viewers select their preferred formats from what is available. Typical options include the normal view as chosen by the director, specific camera views, and split screens occupied by simultaneous views from different camera angles or combinations of camera views, fact-filled boxes, and captions.

▲ Shooting television programs on location means that all the equipment found in a studio has to be transported and set up on site. Location teams, or units, have to be highly organized and use modified equipment that can be maneuvered over a variety of terrains. Outdoor locations suffer from problems not found on a set, such as unexpected background noises, poor lighting, and inclement weather.

SEE ALSO:	Charge-coupled device • Movie camera • Sound mixing • Television camera • Video camera • Video recorder

Television Receiver

Television is essentially a system that transmits images and sound as electronic signals from a transmitter source to receivers in the home via a receiving aerial designed to pick up the signals, which are then decoded and projected once again as images and sound on a picture tube or screen.

The very earliest ideas of how television would work assumed that every picture element would be transmitted simultaneously over separate circuits, as in a system proposed by George Carey of Boston in 1875. Around 1880, the key principle used in all forms of television, that of rapidly scanning each element successively, line by line and frame after frame, relying on the persistence of human vision to interpret the picture, was proposed by both W. E. Sawyer in the United States and Maurice Leblanc in France.

Early mechanical systems were proposed by Paul Nipkow in Germany in 1884 and Boris Rosing of Russia in 1907. However, the first television pictures were made possible by the development of the neon gas-discharge lamp in 1917, which enabled the light intensity at the receiver to be varied by changing the electrical current going into the lamp. This technology was adopted by John Logie Baird, a Scottish inventor, who began experimenting with mechanical television in 1923 using the Nipkow principle.

In 1926, Baird gave the first demonstration of television by transmitting moving pictures in half tones. These pictures were made up of only 30 lines, repeated about 10 times per second. The results, though basic and transmitted on a tiny screen a few inches high, were the humble beginnings of television and sparked further research. Baird's system, alongside Giuglielmo Marconi's ultimately successful electronic system, were tried out in an early experiment in broadcasting in England between 1929 and 1935.

Picture reception

Modern electronic televisions reproduce the picture at the receiver—the television set— by using a cathode-ray tube, or CRT. The tube contains an electron beam, focused on a screen, which scans it in exactly the same pattern as the camera tube beam. The picture tube's screen has a uniform coating of a material that emits light when struck by the beam, and if the beam density is controlled by the picture signal from the camera, a reproduction of the original scene is built up on the picture tube screen. Because complete pictures are received at the rate of 25 per second, movement in the original scene is portrayed as effec-

tively as it would have been in the original transmitted movie or program.

To obtain a satisfactory image at the receiver, it is essential that the beam in the picture tube should be exactly in step with that at the camera tube—at every moment it should be exactly at the same point of the same line as the camera tube beam. This precision of movement is achieved by the use of synchronizing signals. A signal known as the line synchronizing signal (or line sync signal) is sent every time the scanning beam in the camera tube reaches the right-hand side of the image. The signal is used at the receiver to deflect the picture tube beam to the left-hand side of the screen. Similarly, a signal known as the field synchronizing signal (or field sync signal) is sent every time the scanning beam in the camera tube reaches the bottom of the image. This signal is used at the receiver to deflect the picture tube beam to the top of the screen.

To avoid the need to send the sync signals separately to the receiving end, they are combined with the picture signal but have no visible effect on the receiver screen. Because the field sync sig-

▲ Television receivers have had to be adapted to keep up with the development of digital technology and new methods of projecting the image onto the screen. High-definition models make use of high-resolution electron guns and masks and precision tuners.

nal occupies the time of several lines, not all the 625 lines appear on the picture tube screen. Also, the line sync signals must be kept going throughout the duration of the field sync signal so that the receiver line deflection circuits are not interrupted. The combined picture and sync signal is known as a video signal, and this is the signal that is sent from the camera to the picture tube, either directly by line, as in closed-circuit television, or via radio waves, as in the more usual television broadcasting.

Sound accompaniment

Sound is radiated from a separate transmitter that commonly uses the same transmitting antenna as the vision transmitter. Frequency modulation (FM) is used for the sound accompaniment. The sound carrier frequency is placed near that of the vision so that both signals can be amplified simultaneously in the early stages of receivers, and the two signals are together regarded as constituting a television channel. The frequency band occupied by a channel depends on the spacing of the sound and vision carriers and on the frequency band of the vision signal.

Signal decoding

The video signal has to undergo several processes in the receiver using integrated circuits or, in older TV sets, tubes or transistors.

Television receivers operate on the superheterodyne principle, that is, most of the amplification and selectivity of the receiver is provided by an amplifier known as the intermediate frequency (IF) amplifier. The carrier frequency of every signal selected by the tuner is changed to the IF value and applied to the IF amplifier. The tuner contains a frequency changer stage and a preceding carrier frequency amplifier known as a radio frequency (RF) amplifier.

The video and sound signals for the selected channel are amplified together in the early stages of the receiver but are divided later and handled by separate circuits. The video signal is abstracted from the modulated carrier by the vision detector and, after further amplification, is applied to the picture tube. The sync signals are removed from the video signal in the sync-separator stage, and the line sync signals are applied to the line oscillator to lock it at the correct frequency. The output of the line oscillator is fed to deflection coils clamped around the neck of the picture tube, and these coils are responsible for horizontal scanning. The frequency of the line oscillator can be adjusted by a control (called line hold or horizontal hold) to bring it into the range in which locking occurs. The field oscillator (responsible for

vertical deflection) is similarly locked, the frequency control being labeled field (or frame) hold or vertical hold. The sound signal (assumed amplitude modulated) is abstracted from the modulated carrier by the sound detector and, after amplification, is applied to the loudspeaker.

Color television

To enable a receiver to reproduce the correct color for each colored area of the image, it must be given two items of information: the basic color (or hue) and its strength (or saturation). The hue (whether red, yellow, green, or whatever) is determined by the position of the color in the spectrum. Saturation is a measure of the strength or weakness of the color. If the hue is red, the color may be crimson, pink, or some intermediate shade. Thus, the hue is determined by the extent to which the color is diluted by white. Crimson is a saturated color and pink unsaturated.

Information about the hue and saturation of every colored area of the picture must be sent to the receiving end. By using only three primary colors, it is possible, by varying the proportions of each, to produce practically all known colors. The colors chosen for television are red, green, and blue (generally abbreviated to R, G, and B). It is necessary to analyze the image of the original colored scene and to measure what fraction of each area's color is contributed by red, green, and blue.

▼ A color television tube works by deflecting the beams from three electron guns through holes in the mask behind the screen. The beams strike phosphor dots on the screen, which glow either red, green, or blue.

TELEVISION TUBE

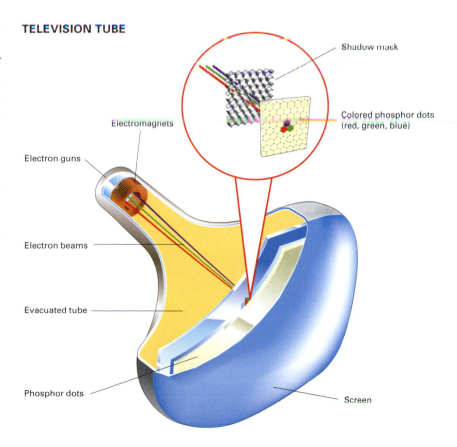

Shadow mask

Colored phosphor dots (red, green, blue)

Electromagnets

Electron guns

Electron beams

Evacuated tube

Phosphor dots

Screen

◄ Advances in television receivers are gradually reducing the need for bulky tubes. This model uses plasma technology, which reduces the screen to only 4 in. (10 cm) deep, enabling it to be hung on a wall. The plasma is a mixture of rare gases trapped between two glass plates and electronically controlled to activate the phosphors. A grid of colored microfilters positioned on the screen help to deliver realistic color rendering.

This analysis is carried out in the color television camera. The image is split into its red, green, and blue components using dichroic mirrors. These mirrors can reflect light belonging to particular regions of the spectrum but permit the remainder to pass through unhindered. The red, green, and blue images so obtained are focused on the targets of three identical camera tubes, each containing an electron beam, as in the black and white system. The three beams are focused on their targets and scan them in exact synchronization. From the tubes, three picture signals are obtained, one representing the red content of the picture, another the green content, and the third the blue content. By combining these outputs, a signal representing the black and white content of the picture is obtained. This combined signal, known as the luminance signal, is the basic signal transmitted in a color television system.

NTSC system

The first color television system was the NTSC (National Television System Committee), introduced in the United States in 1954 and also used in Japan, Canada, and Mexico. In this system, the color subcarrier is amplitude modulated by the two color-difference signals by quadrature modulation. The method involves resolving the carrier wave into two components with a 90 degree phase difference between them. Each component is then separately amplitude modulated by a color-difference signal.

After modulation, the two color-difference signals are combined to form the chrominance signal. The color-difference signals can be recovered at the receiver in a circuit known as a quad-rature detector. This requires for its operation a reference signal very accurately locked to the subcarrier frequency. A few cycles of the subcarrier are therefore transmitted immediately after each line sync signal, known as the color burst.

During transmissions, the chrominance signal is superimposed on the luminance signal. The effect of quadrature modulation and the subsequent combination of the two color-difference signals is to produce a new signal at the subcarrier frequency, the amplitude and phase of which convey the color information. The NTSC system has one disadvantage—any variations in the phase of chrominance signal are interpreted by the receivers as changes in hue; NTSC receivers must therefore have an overriding phase control, which can be manually adjusted.

PAL (phase alternating line) system

To overcome the effects on reproduced hue of unwanted phase changes in the chrominance signal, the Telefunken Laboratories in Hannover, Germany, developed a system of automatic compensation, and thus, PAL receivers do not need a hue control. This is the system used in Britain, Australia, and most of Europe.

The method used reverses the polarity of the (R-Y) signal on alternate lines at the transmitting end. The reversal is achieved by an electronic switch. A similar switch is required at the receiver to restore the original polarity. The two line signals are then averaged to remove phase errors.

SEE ALSO: Cable network • Cathode-ray tube • Digital display • Television camera • Television production

Temperature

The idea of temperature is natural to human beings—its perception is a fundamental sense—but it was realized as early as 1610 (the time of Galileo) that for scientific purposes human skin is not sufficiently accurate as a thermometer. One of skin's drawbacks is that it requires a certain amount of heat energy to be transferred before a sensation is felt, so that a spark from a firework sparkler does not feel hot, in spite of its very high temperature, because its mass is very low and contains only a minute amount of heat.

This example demonstrates the difference between temperature and heat: any point in a body is at a particular temperature, whereas heat is meaningful only when a definite amount of substance is being considered. When matter is viewed on a very small scale, the molecules of which it is composed are all moving—either vibrating about their average position in a solid or traveling about between collisions with other molecules in a liquid or gas. Each molecule has some kinetic energy as a result of this motion, and the heat energy of a body is the total random kinetic energy of all its molecules. The temperature of the body is a measure of the average kinetic energy of the molecules.

This view of temperature has arisen only in the last century as a result of thermodynamics and the related subject statistical mechanics, which allows the definition of a purely theoretical temperature scale, known as the absolute, or Kelvin, scale, which does not depend on the use of any particular type of thermometer. All practical thermometers, measuring temperature by, for

◀ Quartz-sheathed profiling thermocouples ensure that this furnace remains at the correct temperature while silicon wafers are being processed. At the high temperatures involved here, the thermocouple is virtually the only type of accurate temperature-measuring device available.

▼ A comparison of the Fahrenheit, Celsius, Kelvin, and Rankine temperature scales.

example, the length of mercury in a glass tube or the resistance of a platinum wire, give slightly different readings for any temperature other than that at which they have been calibrated. An ideal gas, one that obeys the gas laws, can be used in a thermometer, which gives a temperature scale identical to the theoretical temperature scale. Any ordinary gas at very low pressure behaves like a nearly ideal gas; thus, a gas thermometer can be used to measure temperature on the absolute scale. This type of thermometer is not easy to use, however, so in practice, a number of fixed points have been measured with a gas thermometer, and other more convenient thermometers are calibrated in terms of their temperatures.

Absolute zero

Temperatures on the Kelvin scale, named for the Scottish physicist Baron Kelvin (William Thomson), are measured from absolute zero, the lowest temperature that is theoretically possible, and the standard fixed point, defined as 273.16 kelvins (abbreviated 273.16 K) is the triple point of water, the temperature at which ice, water, and steam can all exist in equilibrium. (This temperature is slightly different from the melting point at atmospheric pressure and is more fundamental.) This interval defines the size of the degree. Some of the other fixed points, measured with the constant-volume gas thermometer, are the boiling points of hydrogen (20.28 K) and water (373.15 K) at one atmosphere pressure.

Temperature scale	°F	°C	K	°R
Water boils	212	100	373	672
Blood temperature	98.6	37	310	559
Water freezes	32	0	273	492
CO_2 freezes	−109	−78	195	351
Oxygen freezes	−297	−183	90	162
Absolute zero	−460	−273	0	0

Historically a number of different temperature scales were used before the Kelvin scale was adopted. One was that devised by the French scientist René-Antoine Ferchault de Réamur (1731), on whose scale the freezing point of water was 0° and the boiling point 80°; this scale is now very little used—one occasionally sees it on old French wall thermometers. The first accurate thermometers were made in 1714 by the German physicist G. D. Fahrenheit, who set his lower fixed point, 32°F, as the melting point of pure ice; on this scale, the lowest temperature he could reach, by mixing ice and salt, was 0°. The purpose for so doing was that all normal meteorological temperatures would be positive. The upper fixed point was body temperature, which he took as 96°, because early thermometers had eight degrees of heat and cold. Dividing each of them up into a further eight degrees gave 64°, which is the difference between 32° and 96°. Later and more accurate measurement of the scale, using steam (212°F) as the upper fixed point, placed body temperature at 98.6°F.

The Fahrenheit scale is still in popular use in many countries, although it is gradually being replaced by the Celsius (or centigrade) scale, on which the freezing and boiling points of water are 0° and 100°, respectively. The original scale of Swedish astronomer Anders Celsius was the opposite of this one—large numbers corresponded to low temperatures—but it was soon reversed. This scale is in everyday use in most countries, as well as for general scientific purposes. (The Celsius degree is exactly the same size as the kelvin—no longer called the Kelvin degree—and temperature in °C can be converted to K by adding 273.15.) The Rankine scale, named for the Scottish physicist William John Macquorn Rankine, which has been used in engineering, starts at absolute zero and uses degrees equal in size to a Fahrenheit.

The absolute zero of temperature cannot actually be reached according to the third law of thermodynamics, and the lowest achieved to date is 0.5 millionths of a kelvin. This temperature was reached in four stages: first by cooling a suitable crystal to a few degrees absolute by the expansion of helium gas and then to 1 K by rapidly evaporating liquid helium. The atoms of the crystal were cooled to a thousandth of a degree by slowly reducing a very strong magnetic field without allowing heat to flow into the crystal, a process commonly referred to as adiabatic demagnetization.

At the other end of the temperature scale, the surfaces of stars range from 3000 to 100,000 K. These temperatures can be deduced either by spectroscopy—observing the spectral lines of the star, giving the kinetic temperature, or by studying how much electromagnetic radiation is emitted at different wavelengths, giving the radiation temperature. If the star's matter is dense enough for the radiation to be scattered by many atoms before emerging from the surface, the distribution of energy with wavelength is given by a mathematical relationship formulated by the German physicist Max Planck, which depends only on the temperature. A hot star, for example, emits proportionally more radiation at shorter wavelengths as compared with a cooler star, and so it appears bluer. The total amount of radiation also depends on the temperature and increases as temperature to the fourth power.

The interpretation of radiation from a hot body can be misleading, however, if the radiation is not scattered enough to be in equilibrium with the ions. The outer parts of the Sun's atmosphere (the corona) appear much fainter than its surface, which is 6000 K, only because it is very rarefied. The kinetic temperature of the corona, corresponding to the actual speed of the ions, is in fact about a million kelvins. Even higher temperatures than this can occur in astrophysics: the center of the Sun is thought to be at 15 million kelvins.

◄ A probe for testing deep-sea temperatures. The temperature on the deepest parts of the ocean floor is only slightly above freezing.

SEE ALSO: Electromagnetic radiation • Gas laws • Spectroscopy • Thermodynamics • Thermometry

Tensile Structure

One of the features of modern architecture has been the great interest in the development of new concepts and techniques. Obvious examples are specialized structures designed to give large clear spans for such applications as exhibition halls and sports arenas. A number of unconventional approaches have been used to achieve this aim, including the geodesic dome, pneumatic buildings, and tensile structures, which can be thought of as engineered versions of the tent.

A tensile structure is light with a curved surface and supporting elements in tension. In most cases, the double curvature of the surface gives a high degree of rigidity to the load-bearing surface. Because the supporting elements are in tension, efficient use is made of the supporting material. The ability to span wide areas with comparatively small amounts of material is one of the main attractions of tensile structures.

Tensile structures are generally easy to build and can be permanent or temporary. A building can be dismantled as easily as it was erected and moved elsewhere according to need. If designed to be permanent or long-standing, the main structural elements—such as membranes, struts, and guys—can be replaced easily whenever needed, continuously renewing the building rather than patching it up. Speed of erection is another feature, and the components can be prefabricated off site. Owing to these features—and the relatively modest use of materials—tensile structures are much cheaper than conventional buildings. Running costs such as lighting, heating (or cooling), and maintenance are also reduced.

Cablenets

There are two main forms of tensile structure. In membrane structures the covering is usually a plastic material that acts as its own support. Alternatively, the covering can be essentially unstressed and supported by a separate load-bearing structure. Typically such supporting structures consist of a cable network, or cablenet, with the individual cables interlinked to form a mesh. The cablenets are held in position and stressed by means of poles, arches, masts, guys, and a variety of other supports to give the required shape. When loaded in tension, flexible networks of this type automatically take up a shape that is in balance and evenly transmits the stresses from the supports. The structural form of the cablenet is very important. Nets made of squares, hexagons, and rhomboidal diagonals are the most satisfactory because they can be stretched easily in virtu-

◀ The swimming stadium at the 1972 Munich Olympics consisted of an interlocking system of saddle-curved nets edged with steel cables.

ally any frame without losing their balanced tension. Triangularly formed nets, though, become elongated under tension. This elongation unloads some of the cables, disrupting surface tension and causing unequal distortion.

The surface covering can be laid over the cablenet or suspended from it. A range of lightweight materials can be used, including fabrics and plastic films as well as sheet metal and wood.

Another arrangement proposed for some very large structures involves the use of a double cable system—an upper one of thick cables and a lower one, forming the roof, of small mesh. The upper system would be attached to the lower one at a number of points; snow loads on the roof would thus be transmitted to the upper cable support system. The lower system, made up of steel nets with 16 in. (40 cm) meshes, would be infilled with thin panels.

Membranes

Fabrics and plastic films can be used to carry the structural loads in a tensile structure as well as acting as a covering, resulting in a membrane structure. The fabrics used for the membranes are constantly being developed and improved upon and vary according to final use. The commonest

There are, however, disadvantages to vinyl-coated polyester that make it unsuitable for more permanent structures. In a fire, it gives off a thick black smoke that would prohibit its long-term use in many areas for safety reasons. Under tension, polyester fabrics continue to stretch so that, after a period of time, the necessary tensile properties for this kind of architecture are lost. Finally, when exposed to the elements, vinyl-coated polyester ages. The plasticizers in the vinyl tend to rise to the surface of the fabric, creating a sticky layer that traps dirt and encourages mildew.

The final argument in favor of vinyl-coated polyester for temporary structures is its cost. Even if a structure is to be used for several years, it may be cheaper to renew the polyester membrane a couple of times rather than spend five times as much on a more durable fabric.

◄ The supporting masts of one of the Florida Festival structures. Cables radiating from the cone cap provide additional support to the membrane material.

material for shorter-term projects, such as exhibition halls, is a woven polyester coated with PVC.

This fabric is light and flexible and has a stretchability factor of around 12 percent, which allows it to absorb minor inaccuracies in pattern cutting without distortion or wrinkling. It is particularly suitable for structures that may be put up, dismantled, folded up, stored, transported, and then reused. It is also ideal for collapsible roofs operating on the fan principle, which can be raised into tension or lowered into a storage position depending on the weather. A wide range of brilliant colors can also be built into the fabric.

◄ An architect's scale model of a computer-designed structure, made from photoelastic material, is being exposed to polarized light. The light clearly shows up the stress points in the tensioned fabric as interference lines of bright color.

For permanent tensile structures, the most common membrane fabric is woven glass fiber coated with Teflon (PTFE). This material is much stiffer than polyester, with a warp elongation under stress of less than 2 percent. The resistance to stretch eradicates the danger of long-term distortion, but the designing, patterning, and assembling must be carried out with extreme accuracy.

Teflon-coated glass fiber is noncombustible, radiant, heat and water resistant, and chemically inert. Because dust and dirt cannot penetrate the weave, they are either blown away by wind or washed away by rain, making the fabric virtually self-cleaning. The fabric's strength comes from the glass fibers, and its durability from the fluorocarbon resins in the Teflon coating.

In most projects, the Teflon-coated glass fiber fabric proposed for the membrane is as much a part of the original design as the shape and tension engineering of the building. Teflon is applied by passing the woven fabric through a Teflon bath, thereby filling the "windows" formed between intersecting filaments. The size of the windows varies according to the tension applied to the fabric as it is passed through the bath. Increased tension elongates the windows and makes them narrower.

Each successive layer of Teflon reduces the fabric's translucency, and opacifiers can be added to the Teflon to increase both opacity and reflectiveness. Usually about 75 percent of the Sun's heat and light is reflected by a coated glass fiber membrane, while a further 20 percent is absorbed by the fabric itself. Translucency, however, can vary up to 20 percent. By using more than one layer, an effective thermal insulation is created in the roof, making it functional in both hot and cold climates. Sufficient light can still penetrate Teflon-coated glass-fiber fabrics to allow plants to grow normally.

Cables are usually made from steel, because it has a low cost, availablility, and long life. Kevlar and glass fiber cables are stronger and stiffer but are more expensive and degrade when exposed to ultraviolet light.

Design

Much of the development of tensile structures is due to the work of the German structural designer Otto Frei, who has been responsible for a number of notable buildings. One of the techniques used by Frei in the development of his designs was the study of curves and shapes formed by soap films in model conditions approximating the design he had in mind. Photographed against squared grids, the soap films provide minimal surface models—ones with the least area within a closed curve and so in balanced tension. The shapes taken by soap films are ideal for tensile structures because they do not contain uneven stresses that would require extra external support.

To develop the design, special water-soluble foaming agents, capable of forming very thin and highly stressed films, are stretched over model framing. The grids are either superimposed or projected by light onto the film surface, enabling

▲ The Teflon-coated glass-fiber membrane of the Florida Festival structure, which is supported by one large mast of 106 ft. and three smaller ones of 62 ft., covers a huge area of 90,000 sq. ft.

the designer to make accurate measurements, which he or she can use when working to full scale in designing and assembling the membrane. Thin rubber films are used in the same way. Using soap films, Otto Frei was able, over several years of tests and measurements, to develop a dependable mathematics of tensile structural designing and engineering.

The contemporary tensile architect-designer uses computer programs, which add ease and speed to the design process and enable the derivation of optimum designs. Working with an interactive graphics computer, the operator keys in coded information about the shape and strength of the proposed fabric, the spacing and qualities of supports and guys, and any special features—such as peaks and wells—to be included in the design.

Applications

Two important structures in the development of tensile architecture were built in the United States in the 1950s, both making use of cablenets. The Raleigh Arena in North Carolina, built in 1953 to Matthew Nowicki's design, uses a saddle-shaped cablenet stretched between two inclined and overlapping parabolic arches. The average width of the cablenet mesh is 70 in. (1.8 m), and the roof skin is built up from corrugated metal sheet, with heat insulation and a bitumen coating.

The Ice Hockey Rink of Yale University in Connecticut, built between 1956 and 1958, consists of a very rigid vertical concrete arch supporting two cablenets, one on either side. The cablenets are anchored at their outer edges by two curved concrete walls overlaid with a 2 in. (5 cm) thick wooden deck and weatherproofed with neoprene. The whole structure covers an area of about 200 ft. (61 m) by 180 ft. (55 m).

More recent applications of tensile structures in the United States include the Florida Festival structure, which contains many tropical plants, including palm trees. Supported by a large mast

▼ The Hajj Terminal at Jeddah International Airport in Saudi Arabia is effectively a series of 210 connected tents, made from 4.5 million sq. ft. (425,000 m²) of Teflon-coated glass fiber.

of 106 ft. (33 m) and three smaller ones of 62 ft. (19 m), the dramatic swooping shape consists of four peaks and one chasm that plunges down into the interior of the structure like a whirlpool. Rainwater cascades down this funneling shape to form a spectacular waterfall. The whole edifice covers an area of 90,000 sq. ft. (8,360 m²) and contains 40 shops amongst shrubs and palms.

Another application is the tensile roof over the Franklin Park Zoo in Massachusetts, covering an area of some 410,000 sq. ft. (38,000 m²). Providing a winter environment for the animals, it also contains many plants necessary to simulate natural habitats. Where insufficient light penetrates the fabric for certain plants, special plastic panels of greater translucency are built into the structure.

Cablenets and membranes can also be supported by cables strung between masts. The Sidney Myer Music Bowl in Melbourne, Australia, was built using a main support cable 558 ft. (170 m) long leading over two 70 ft. (21 m) masts. They supported a triangular net that, once in place, was paneled with plywood covered in aluminum foil. This structure not only protected the orchestra and audience but also acted as an acoustic reflector.

The 1972 Olympic Games in Munich, Germany, introduced tensile structures to a wider audience. The arenas and grandstands were covered by an interlinking system of saddle-curved nets edged with cables. In all, they covered an area of 237,000 sq. ft. (22,000 m²), with maximum spans of 443 ft. (135 m). Calculations for the flowing, wavelike roof nets were made purely mathematically on the basis of model analyses of earlier developments.

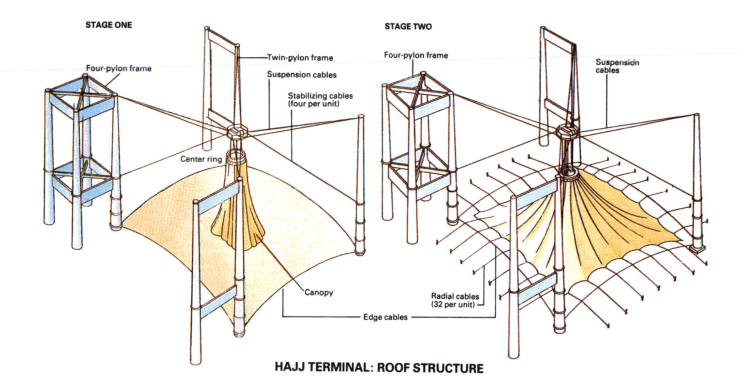

STAGE ONE

Four-pylon frame

Twin-pylon frame

Suspension cables

Stabilizing cables
(four per unit)

Center ring

Canopy

Edge cables

STAGE TWO

Four-pylon frame

Suspension
cables

Radial cables
(32 per unit)

HAJJ TERMINAL: ROOF STRUCTURE

Some of the earliest tensile structures were little more than sun awnings to shade small groups of people, but one fairly recent structure—the Hajj Terminal at Jeddah International Airport, Saudi Arabia—covers no less than 105 acres (42.4 ha). Its purpose, too, is to provide shade for people—in this case, the hundreds of thousands of devout pilgrims flying in and out of Jeddah each year en route to Mecca.

The Hajj Terminal is not one big tent but a series of 210 connected tents divided into ten closely spaced groups. To ensure that the 4.5 million sq. ft. (425,000 m²) of fabric was securely guyed and tensioned on the rows of steel pylons that are the main supports, preconstruction testing and calculation included computer analysis and wind-tunnel tests. The Teflon-coated glass fiber of the terminal's 10-acre (4 ha) roof is stronger than steel, requires a minimum of maintenance, and is bleached by the strong sunlight to a heat-reflecting white that helps to control the internal temperature.

More recent projects include the Millennium Dome in London, England, which was erected to celebrate the new millennium. The foundation, main supports, and Teflon-coated roof of the dome, which were completed in mid-1998, create an interior floor area of more than 861,000 sq. ft. (80,000 m²). The roof measures 1,050 ft. (320 m) in diameter, with a total extension of some 969,000 sq. ft. (90,000 m²), and reaches a maximum height of approximately 165 ft. (50 m). The roof assembly is supported by a web of 2,600 cables suspended from a circle of 12 bright yellow

▲ Prototypes of the Hajj Terminal tent units were tested in the United States before construction began. Strain gauges and sensors were fixed to the fabric, cables, and rings to detect design faults.

▶ The open structure of the terminal is ideal for Saudi Arabia's hot climate. The roof reflects the Sun's glare but lets plenty of light into the interior.

▲ Construction of the Hajj Terminal began with the erection of the support columns—four braced together for the corners and two for the perimeters of each 21-tent module. For stage two, the round collars forming the apex were hoisted up, and then the fabric was spread out, fixed with cables, and tensioned.

◀ Tensioned steel bars are embedded in the concrete of this bridge; without them, the concrete would crack under the tensile forces.

▶ The steel tensioners embedded in a concrete beam bridge.

FACT FILE

■ Early tensile architecture was based on the suspension bridge. A Bohemian engineer and bridge builder, Bedrich Schnirch, designed and built fireproof roofs for theaters, churches, and warehouses in which heavy timber framing was replaced by chain rafters suspended from walls. Completed in the 1820s, these were the first European tensile buildings.

■ Buckminster Fuller, the inventor of the geodesic dome, designed a ten-story building in which the floors were suspended from a central mast. Projected for construction at the North Pole, the building was never begun. Fuller incorporated the same idea into his Dymaxion House, in which the central mast supported both roof and first floor, as well as being used as a service core.

■ Centerpiece of the 1951 Festival of Britain was the Skylon sculpture, a 328 ft. (100 m) high aluminum cigar-shaped mast supported 43 ft. (13 m) above the ground by means of cables and three latticework girders that jutted outward from a central point beneath the mast.

■ In 1958 the Sidney Myer Music Bowl was built in Melbourne, Australia. It was designed as an open canopy so that part of the audience could sit on the grass during performances. It was refurbished in 2001 to include six hydraulic scissor lifts that elevate the orchestra pit in sections as required.

steel masts, inclined slightly from the vertical, which rise nearly 330 ft. (100 m).

The somewhat eccentric design of the dome has been both praised and heavily criticized. It is, however, undoubtedly a superb example of tensile structural engineering and in close-up is awe inspiring. In shape, it is a space age, flattened semicircle with scalloped edges, punctuated by raked supporting masts and a hole to one side that accommodates one of the ventilation shafts for the Blackwall Tunnel under the Thames River, which runs beneath. During 2000, when the Dome exhibition took place, a nightly light show lit up its white surface.

Another recent tensile structure, finished in 1993, is the Denver International Airport (DIA). A Denver architectural firm, Fentress Bradburn Architects and Associates, designed the Jeppesen Terminal, which has approximately 1.5 million sq. ft. (140,000 m²) of space, including a central atrium that is walled by glass and covered by a translucent tensile membrane roof.

DIA's atrium, or Great Hall, is 900 ft. by 210 ft. (300 by 70 m). The roof's outer waterproof shell is made of Teflon-coated woven fiberglass; the inner membrane is made of uncoated woven fiberglass. Inner and outer roof membranes comprise 15 acres of material. Ten percent of visible light passes through roof fabric for daylighting; the fiberglass has little mass, since it does not conduct heat or store it. The white Teflon-coated surface reflects 90 percent of sunlight.

Other notable recent tensile structures include the San Diego Convention Center, completed in 1990; the 1990 Cynthia Woods Mitchell Pavilion; and the Vancouver Conference Center.

SEE ALSO: ▷ BUILDING TECHNIQUES • GEODESIC STRUCTURES • GLASS FIBER • POLYTETRAFLUOROETHYLENE (TEFLON)

Tesla Coil

Invented in 1892 by the Croatian-born U.S. physicist Nikola Tesla, the Tesla coil is a source of high voltage and high frequency currents. An induction coil is used to step up a low-voltage source to a high one. The high-voltage terminals of the secondary winding of the induction coil are connected to a spark gap, and this circuit is completed through the primary winding of the Tesla coil and a capacitor.

The voltage in the primary is increased, by the same inductive process as in the induction coil, to a much higher voltage in the secondary. Moreover, the spark gap in the primary circuit causes the current in the primary to oscillate at frequencies of several million hertz, and this oscillation is recreated in the secondary, hence the output of the secondary is of both high voltage and high frequency; its principal use is in experimental work.

A variable capacitor may be incorporated in the secondary circuit to make it resonate with the primary, thus creating the highest frequency possible in the secondary. An alternative to the induction coil in the primary is a transformer.

The frequency of the secondary current is so high that points of high and low potential are set up around the secondary circuit. If the potentials are fed to two parallel wires and the terminals of a Geissler tube (a tube containing a gas at low pressure that glows when subject to an electric voltage) are placed across them, then the tube will glow or remain dark at equally spaced positions as the Geissler tube is moved along the wires.

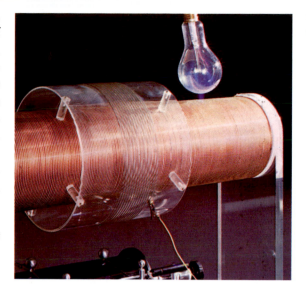

◀ A reconstruction of Tesla's original coil.

The Geissler tube test is put to use to detect breaks in high-vacuum equipment made of glass. The output of the secondary is used as a probe unit, applied to the outside of the glass. If there is a leak in the system and the pressure is about ten torr (a torr is a unit in expressing very low pressures; one torr equals 1/760th of a standard atmosphere), then the nitrogen present in the air leaking into the system will give a characteristic pink glow. If the pressure is 1.5 torr, striations appear, growing larger as the pressure reaches 0.05 torr, whereupon there is a green fluorescent glow on the glass walls of the equipment. This glow then fades until at the limit of accuracy of the method, 0.01 torr, there is blackout in normal ambient light.

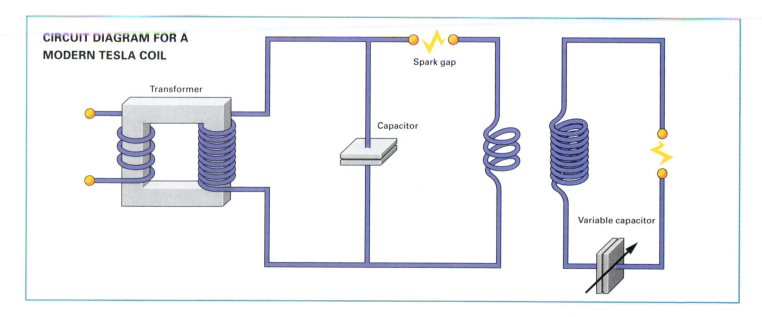

CIRCUIT DIAGRAM FOR A MODERN TESLA COIL

Spark gap

Transformer

Capacitor

Variable capacitor

▲ The Tesla coil circuit is used to produce a high voltage and high frequency current from a lower voltage and lower frequency current.

SEE ALSO: CAPACITOR • INDUCTION

Textile

There are three main types of fabric: woven, knitted, and fiber. The term *fiber* is used to describe the nonwoven fabrics—those not formed by weaving, which is the interlacement of two threads (warp threads, which run lengthwise, and weft threads, which run across). Such fabrics are manufactured from a sheet, web, or batt of either aligned or randomly orientated fibers that are held together usually by a combination of mechanical, chemical, and solvent processes.

In one mechanical method, for example, barbed needles punch into the web of fibers to entangle them thoroughly. A felt is produced by the ability of certain fibers to mat together under the action of moisture, heat, and pressure. The term *nonwoven* is also used for fabrics in which a web of fibers is held together by stitching threads or in which one set of fibers is laid, noninterlaced, across another set and they are bound by a third set of threads knitted into them.

Many of the soft synthetic fibers, as well as woolen yarn, lend themselves to knits and similar fabrics. They are produced by a continuous thread interlacing or looping with itself as it traverses to and fro or by a series of threads interlooping with adjacent threads.

Types of textile fibers

Textiles are classified according to the fibers of which they are composed, whether natural fibers—such as silk, wool, linen, or cotton—or synthetic fibers—such as rayon, nylon, and polyesters. They are also classified according to their structure or weave—the manner in which warp and weft cross each other in the loom.

Linen is made from flax and was first used by the ancient Egyptians, who made clothing and household articles from it. They also used linen, a symbol of purity, in religious practices.

Sheep have been raised for wool since biblical times. Wool is elastic, resilient, and absorbent and is also an excellent insulator because of its bulk.

Cotton is the most common textile fiber now in use. After the invention of the cotton gin by the American inventor Eli Whitney in 1793, cotton became the most important fiber in the world for quantity, economy, and utility. Several species of the cotton plant are cultivated for the whitish outer fibers of the seeds. It forms a light, durable cloth that is used in a variety of garments, furnishings, and other products.

Silk may have been woven by the Chinese as long ago as the 27th century B.C.E. The thread is produced by the caterpillar of the silkworm moth.

The filaments from several unraveled cocoons are twisted together to make strands, which are combined together. The sticky seracin secretion is washed away, and sometimes metallic salts are added for weight. Silk is lustrous, elastic, and very strong, and its quality and beauty inspired many early scientists to attempt to develop synethtic fibers to resemble it.

The commercial production of synthetic fibers started in the late 19th century. The early synthetic fibers, called rayons, were derived from natural cellulose, made from wood pulp. Later, acetates and triacetates were developed, derived from cellulose acetate. Today most synthetic fibers are derived from organic polymers, materials consisting of large organic molecules.

Nylon was introduced in the 1930s. It is used widely in the production of clothing, hosiery, parachute fabric, and rope. After 1940, many other synthetic fibers were developed, including dacrons, polyvinyls, polyethylenes, acrylics, aramid, olefins, polyester, and spandex.

To make synthetic fibers, a molten polymer or polymer solution is extruded as filaments through tiny holes in a spinneret. The fibers are then

▲ A patchwork quilt stitched together by hand from pieces of woven, printed fabric—a task that would have taken many hours. Different fabric textures and patterns may be mixed together to produce particular effects. Quiltmaking skills have been developed over thousands of years.

solidified by a chemical process. Treatments to the fibers after spinning include drawing, annealing, finishing, and coating. The advantage of synthetic fibers is that the physical characteristics can be adjusted to suit specific requirements. Properties such as weight, abrasion, heat resistance, moisture resistance, and elasticity, among other things, can be optimized.

High-strength materials

High-strength materials such as carbon and graphite are used to reinforce composite fabrics. Heat is used to chemically change rayon or acrylic fibers to carbon fibers, and carbon fibers convert to graphite fibers at temperatures above 4532°F (2500°C). Heat-shielding materials, aircraft fuselages, spacecraft, yacht hulls, and sports equipment all use carbon fibers.

Fibers such as aramid (aromatic polyamide) and polyethylene are used to provide protection from bullets and shrapnel in car bodywork and clothing and for crew seats in military aircraft. Kevlar, for instance, an aramid, is five times stronger—weight for weight—than steel. Kevlar is also flame and bullet resistant, and it does not rust, freeze, or boil. It can be woven into ropes and is virtually indestructible. Unlike other synthetics, however, Kevlar retains its mechanical properties over a wide temperature range and is like steel in that it stretches only slightly as it approaches breaking limits. Its other properties include high resistance to abrasion, great stiffness, and good damping abilities that enable it to resist shock. If the material does fail, it does so progressively, rather than in a catastrophic way.

▼ Left: Brocade (top), pile and looped (middle), and leno type (bottom) are different weaves that can be employed to give a fabric a specific textural identity. Right: Nylon fibers being given a special durable coating in a finishing machine.

Textile production

The number of different processes involved in textile production varies with the type of product. Raw cotton is processed in a cotton gin, which removes seeds and other flaws before being transported in bales for spinning. Wool is sorted, graded, and scoured before being processed into yarn. Flax is converted into spinnable linen fiber by various mechanical and chemical processes. Silk cocoons are softened in warm water before the filaments are unwound. They are then twisted together to form multifilament yarns, a process known as throwing.

Almost all synthetic fibers are produced as filaments, which are processed into yarn—as for silk—and then cut into short lengths of fiber that are processed like raw cotton or wool.

Yarn is produced by spinning. Filament fiber, such as silk, can be simply twisted into yarn. Staple fibers must be carded to form a length of ropelike fibers, then combed to straighten them, and finally pulled out into continous strands that are twisted. The degree of twist determines certain characteristics: light twisting creates soft-surfaced fabrics, while hard twisting produces hard-surfaced fabrics, which are more likely to shrink but are more dirt and wrinkle resistant.

Knitted fabrics are formed by interlocking yarn in a series of connected loops, either by hand or by machine.

Origins of woven fabrics

Although there are no records regarding the origin of weaving, there is no doubt that Paleolithic people had acquired the arts of twisting cords,

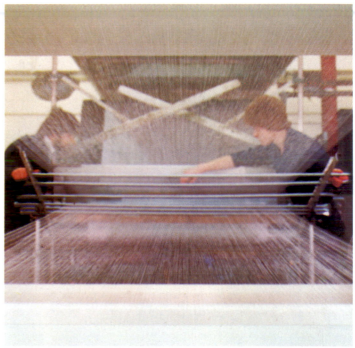

◄ These Samburu Moran warriors from Kenya still follow the traditional tribal lifestyle, but they are clothed in printed cotton fabric that they import from the city.

braiding, and sewing, while Neolithic people cultivated and used flax for woven structures.

Remains of flax threads, spinning whorls, and weaver's weights and remnants of woven cloths (some of them twilled) have been found in ancient Swiss lake dwellings. These findings indicate that during the later Stone Age, humans selected textile fibers and acquired the skills of spinning and weaving. The art of weaving was further developed by the early Egyptians.

Simple woven fabric structures

Simple weaves are formed by the over and under interlacement of one series of threads (the weft) with another series of threads (the warp). In plain weaves, the two series are at right angles.

The simplest weaves are plain, twill (diagonal lines on the face of the fabric), and satin. The mat weaves are a derivation of plain weave: groups of threads are interlaced rather than a single one.

Forty-five-degree twill weaves are formed by interlacing each warp thread over and under a group of weft threads, but they differ from mat weaves in that each interlacing moves one weft thread off compared with its neighbor, resulting in a diagonal pattern. This diagonal pattern can be upward from right to left (S twill) or upward from left to right (Z twill). Twill weaves may obviously be over or under to varying extents.

By moving the interlacings more than one thread off, the angle of twill can be varied. For

example, 5-1-1-2-1-1 interlacings moved two off give the well-known whipcord weave, with a bold five-float steep twill and the 1-1-2-1-1 part of the interlacings forming a sunken line between the bold twills. With simple twill weaves, however, variation of twill angle is achieved simply by spacing the thread closer together in one direction than the other, such as in gaberdine.

Simple weaves in which either the warp or the weft predominates on the fabric face include satin (warp dominated) and sateen (weft dominated). This pattern is generally accentuated by the closer spacing of warp or weft, respectively.

There are, however, two variations from the simple over-and-under interlacement of threads. In the first, gauze or leno weaves, certain warp threads move alternately to right and left of adjacent threads between interlacements with the weft. The second is used in pile structures such as velvet, velveteens, corduroys, and carpets.

Deep textures and compound structures

The interlacing of weft with warp can be varied to an almost unlimited extent, allowing deep texture effects. In a honeycomb weave, for example, the more tightly interlacing threads sink to a lower level in the woven fabric, with the long floats of the more loosely interlacing threads rising to give the ridges a cellular effect. Texture may also be introduced by varying the yarn thickness.

Patterns and color

Woven stripes, checks, and patterned designs are developed by combining two or more weave elements, either single or compound, in the total pattern of interlacing. Probably the best-known stripe weave is the herringbone that alternates S and Z twill across the width of the fabric.

By introducing different-colored yarns throughout the warp and weft, other design effects may be achieved. If the groups of colored threads are large, the emphasis is for colored stripes and checks, such as in the various tartans. If the thread groups are small, however, neither the color pattern effect nor the weave is as apparent as the resulting effect of the different color floats of warp and weft combining to give color-and-weave effects.

Fabrics

Many different varieties of fabrics exist. Brocade is a patterned fabric, usually of single texture, in which the figure is developed by floating the warp threads, the weft threads, or both, the threads being bound in a more or less irregular order. The ground is usually formed by a weave of simple elements. Many upholstery brocades are made with a satin ground and a weft figure.

Calico is plain cotton cloth heavier than muslin. Chiffon was originally a very light, sheer, open-mesh fabric made from silk yarns in plain weave. The present-day fabric is also made from synthetic fiber yarns. The term *chiffon* is also used to describe the lightest types of particular cloths, such as chiffon velvets and chiffon taffeta.

Chintz is a glazed, printed, plain-weave fabric, originally and usually of cotton and lighter than cretonne. Crepe is a fabric characterized by a crinkled or puckered surface. The effect may be produced in a variety of ways—for example, by the use of S and Z hard-twisted yarns, by the use of a crepe weave, or by chemical treatment in finishing to produce differential shrinkage.

Crepon is a crepe fabric that is more rugged than the average crepe, with a fluted or crinkled effect in the warp direction. Cretonne is a printed upholstery fabric originally and usually of cotton and of heavier weight than chintz.

Damask is patterned fabric made with one warp and one weft in which, generally, warp satin and weft sateen weaves interchange. Twill or other binding weaves may sometimes be introduced. Denim is a cotton cloth in warp-faced twill made from yarn-dyed warp and undyed weft yarn. Drill is a twill fabric of similar construction to a denim but usually piece-dyed.

Dimity is a fabric, usually cotton, that is checked or striped by corded effects that are made by weaving two or more threads as one.

Flannel is an all-wool fabric of plain or twill weave that feels soft. It may be slightly milled

▶ Synthetic materials are used extensively for the carpets and upholstery in today's automobiles—they are harder wearing and easier to clean than natural fibers and often cheaper to manufacture.

(processed so that the felting properties of the wool fibers make it impossible to see the weave) or raised (brushed to raise the nap). Flannelette is a cloth made from cotton warp and soft-spun cotton weft, subsequently raised on both sides to give an imitation of the true flannel.

Georgette is a fine, lightweight, open-texture fabric, usually in plain weave, made from crepe yarns, usually two S twisted and two Z twisted in both warp and weft.

Jean is a 2-1 warp-faced twill fabric used chiefly for overalls. The term *jeanette* is sometimes used to describe the lighter-weight cloths, and these may be used for linings.

Muslin is a general term for a lightweight, open cloth of plain weave or simple leno weave.

Seersucker is a fabric characterized by the presence of puckered and relatively flat sections, particularly in stripes but also in checks. The effect may be produced in a variety of ways—for example, by weaving so that ground warp threads are tensioned more than the puckered stripe threads or by chemical treatment so that certain parts of the fabric contract more than others.

Serge is a piece-dyed fabric, of simple twill weave of square or nearly square construction, with a clear finish.

Shantung is a plain-weave, silk dress fabric exhibiting random yarn irregularities resulting from the use of yarn spun from wild (Tussah) silk.

Taffeta is a plain-weave, closely woven, smooth, and crisp fabric with a faint weft-way rib, produced from filament yarns. The warp-thread spacing is closer than the weft-thread spacing.

Tapestry is a closely woven, patterned fabric of compound structure in which the pattern is developed by the use of colored yarns in the warp, weft, or both; a fine binder warp may also be present.

Zephyr is a fine cloth of plain weave used for dresses, blouses, and shirts and made in various

◀ Rolls of yarn (spun thread) on a loom used for making plain or striped toweling material; these yarns form the warp threads of the loom.

qualities. A typical cotton zephyr has colored stripes on a white ground and a cord effect made by the introduction of coarse threads at intervals.

Nonwoven textiles

Nonwoven fabrics are produced by bonding or interlocking the fibers. A number of different methods are used, including mechanical, thermal, chemical, and solvent, or a combination of these. Resin bonding and thermoplastic (heat-setting) bonding are the main bonding methods. Resin is applied to the fibers, which are then dried, heat cured, and sometimes pressed. For thermoplastic bonding, a thermoplastic fiber, which has a lower melting point than a base fiber, is blended with the base fiber. The mix of fibers is pressed between heated rollers, a process that causes the plastic fibers to bond to the base fibers. Mechanical means to produce nonwoven textiles include a needle-punch machine that interlaces and interlocks the fibers.

FACT FILE

- The famous Irish linen industry had its beginnings in the ninth century B.C.E., when Phoenician traders introduced flax. Modern Irish linen originated with French Huguenot exiles who immigrated late in the 17th century.

- Geotextiles are woven synthetic fibers used in the construction industry to stabilize foundation materials. They can weigh up to 30 oz. per sq. yd. (1,000 g per m²) and are found in road systems and embankments, where they are used for erosion control. Their three main functions are separation, reinforcement, and filtration.

- Woolen cloth was so important to the Roman army that Julius Caesar employed an expert in sheep breeding to get the best materials for his soldiers' cloaks and tunics. Lucius Julius Columella crossbred the best breeds from various parts of the Roman Empire.

- The techniques of silk production were once a closely guarded secret, which the Chinese kept from the time of the invention of the fabric, around 2640 B.C.E., until almost 2,000 years later, when silkworm eggs were smuggled out of the country and taken to India, Turkey, and Greece.

Finishing processes

Dyeing and printing are the two main finishing processes for textiles. Textiles can be dyed after weaving or knitting (piece dyed), loose fibers can be dyed in a vat (stock dyed), or the yarn or filament can be dyed before weaving or knitting (yarn dyed). Printing techniques include intaglio roller printing (the most common method), relief roller printing (also called surface, peg, or block printing), and screen printing.

There are a number of other finishes that may be applied to textiles before they are acceptable to the consumer. Unfinished textiles, called gray goods, are usually dirty, harsh, and unattractive. Finishes can also be applied to improve the durability and performance of the textile, such as crease resistance or shrink control.

Napping, which creates a soft, velvety surface and increases the warmth of the fabric, can be applied to woolens, cottons, and spun silks and rayons. Fine wires on cylinders lift the short fibers to the surface, forming a nap. Shearing, which has the same purpose, is used on pile fabrics to cut the raised nap to a uniform length.

The process of beetling may be applied to linen and cotton made to resemble linen. It produces a hard, flat surface that has high luster and is less porous. The dampened fabric is wound around a cylinder and pounded with heavy mallets.

Tentering is a process that removes creases and wrinkles, straightens the weave, and dries the fabric to its final size. The fabric passes through a heated chamber on a frame of chains fitted with pins or clips. When applied to wet wools, it is called crabbing; applied to synthetics, it is called heat setting. The latter term may also be used to refer to the permanent setting of pleats or creases.

Calendering, which is not usually permanent, uses heat and pressure to impart a flat, glossy surface. Moiré (a wavy effect), embossing (a raised design), glazing (a polished surface), and ciré (high gloss on rayons and silks) are all variations.

Creping, which produces a puckered effect, is achieved either by passing the fabric between hot, indented rollers or by rolling caustic soda onto the fabric in a pattern.

Crease resistance is achieved by applying a synthetic resin, such as epoxy.

▲ Packing underpants made from nylon, which was developed in 1935 and first used to make clothes in 1939. Synthetic fibers are widely used by the textile industry, often in conjunction with natural fibers, to produce fabrics with particular qualities, such as crease resistance and stretch.

SEE ALSO: COTTON • DYEING PROCESS • FABRIC PRINTING • FIBER, NATURAL, • FIBER, SYNTHETIC • LOOM • WATER-REPELLENT FINISH

Theatrical Lighting

In a live performance, lighting needs to do much more than just illuminate the performers—it must accentuate their physical presence and focus the attention of the audience. At the same time, it must establish the appropriate environment. It can also conceal the paraphernalia of production.

The basic qualities of light are direction, color, and intensity. In everyday use, only intensity and, to a limited extent, color can be remotely controlled during rehearsal and subsequent performances. However, developments in the lighting of rock-music shows have produced equipment of greater sophistication and ability.

Direction of light

The main acting light needs to come from an angle of about 45 degrees above the performer's eye level. Above this angle, shadows are created on the face; below it, there may be too much light on the scenery. To accentuate the three-dimensional form requires the same area to be lit from at least two sources about 90 degrees apart.

Sidelighting adds emphasis and texture and predominates where movement rather than facial expression is important. The sources for this type of lighting should be relatively high so as to pass over the heads of performers who are near and strike the performers on the opposite side of the acting area. A variation of this technique is used in ballet productions, where the sidelight is horizontal to the stage floor.

To help the audience focus on the most important aspect of the production, the stage is divided into small areas, each being served by a few sources. By adjusting relative intensities of the sources, selected areas can be emphasized.

▲ Rock concerts make much use of special lighting effects to add drama to the proceedings.

▶ The more than 300 lights in use on this set can be programmed to produce sequences of changes that can match the tempo and mood of the music.

Beam quality

Most of the lighting on a stage needs to be selective, so the majority of the light sources are spotlights rather than floodlights. There are basically two different types of spotlights—the Fresnel spot and the profile (ellipsoid) spot.

The Fresnel spot employs a large-diameter, short-focus Fresnel lens to provide a circular, soft-edge beam. The beam of light may be spread to flood or contracted to spot by moving the position of the tungsten–halogen lamp and anodized aluminum reflector relative to the lens. The advantage of Fresnel spots is that the soft edges of the beams merge with one another. This feature is particularly useful for creating washes of color. The disadvantage is that soft edge, together with its high degree of spill, tends to illuminate the more immediate surroundings. The beam may be contained and roughly shaped by the addition of a barn-door attachment (four hinged flaps that can be mounted and rotated around the lens of the spotlight). The intensity of a Fresnel light is determined by the lamp wattage (typically 300, 500, 650, 750, 1,000, and 2,000 watts) and the lens diameter.

The par, or beamlight, has come into common use in the theater from the rock-music business. This unit is simply a lamp that contains its own

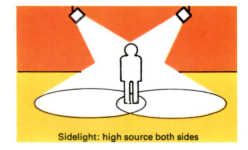

The BP4 HMI Pani scenic projector has a 15 kW output and produces dazzlingly bright backdrop pictures that are clearly visible over almost any level of stage lighting.

parabolic reflector and lens. The beam, which is intense and therefore ideal for pure color washes or shafts of sunlight, is not variable. It is elliptic in shape and closely resembles that of the Fresnel—it may be contained by the addition of barn doors.

PC, or plano-convex, spots resemble the Fresnel, but their tighter soft-edged beam with less spill is useful where control is important.

For really close control of beam shape and edge, the profile (ellipsoid) spot is ideal. In this optical system, the light from the lamp is collected by an ellipsoid anodized aluminum reflector and directed through a gate with four built-in shutters that shape the light beam. This aperture is then hard or soft focused by a lens. Even when soft

▼ Strategically placed spotlights are used to throw scenic shadows over actors to enhance the staging of a production.

focused, the beam has a diffused rather than a soft edge, so the light can be precisely directed. Profile spots may also be used with patterns (cutout masks) designed to produce special effects, such as leaves, prison bars, windows, and so on.

The profile spotlight was originally designed to produce a fixed beam angle, unlike those of the Fresnel or PC spotlights, which are variable. However, some profile spotlights now have two lenses. In addition, most profile spotlights offer control over the position of the bulb relative to the reflector so that the beam may peak in the center or be more even or flat. Profile spotlights produce the least spill, so they are usually located in the auditorium rather than on stage.

Another optical system used for theatrical lighting is the simple floodlight that provides a wash of light over a large area. Floods may be found in individual units or together in strips and are usually placed at the front of the stage.

Spotlights are often referred to as instruments, lanterns, or luminaires. Follow spots are narrow-beam focusing instruments that are manually operated. They are usually operated from an adjustable stand, and the powerful beam follows the performer on a stage, surrounding him or her in a large pool of light. New models allow iris and color changes to be preprogrammed, allowing the operator to concentrate on moving the beam to follow the performer.

House lights are the general lighting provided for the audience area (usually dimmed while the production is in progress). Working, or backstage, lights illuminate the area behind the stage.

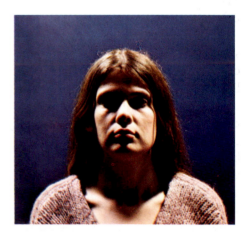

Top light: straight down

Front: direct horizontal fill

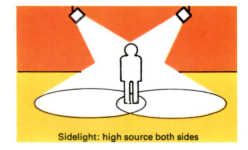

Sidelight: high source both sides

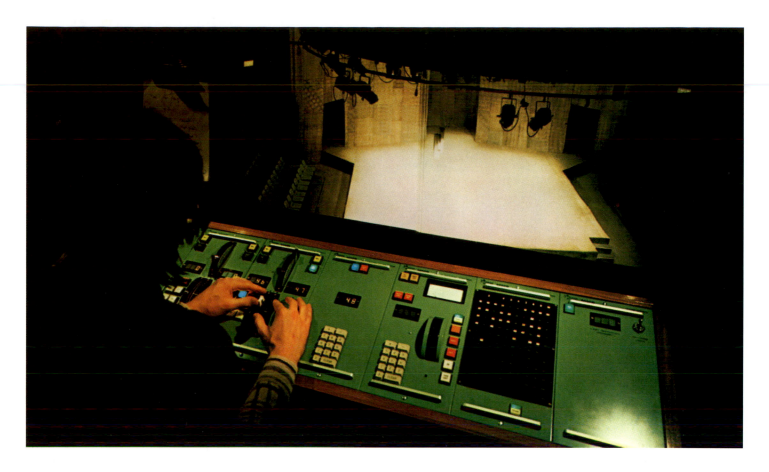

Strobe lights are designed to create a strobe effect, usually using an arc lamp as the light source. Strobes turn on and off repeatedly at a relatively fast rate and are usually used in an area where there is no other illumination to create a flickering, slow-motion effect.

Color

Manufacturers produce hundreds of different color filters, called gels, in nonflammable material. The color gel, in its frame, is slipped into slots on the front of the lamp housing. The choice of colors for a particular production is closely linked to the style of the production. For drama, no colors (pale tints) are appropriate, because they can bias the general ambience without distorting the actors' features. Stronger colors can be used for special effects in music shows. If very strong colors are used simultaneously, the result approaches white. Using strong-colored light on strong pigments of a different hue can create either a completely different color or even black.

A range of uncolored diffusion filters is available that can soften the edge of the beam. Although primarily intended for use in profile spotlights, diffusion can be useful in any light source.

Intensity control

All lighting systems have a central panel wherein the relative intensities of the spotlights can be adjusted. During the course of a production, the operator may make several changes, or cues, some more visible to the audience than others. The dimmers in use today are virtually the same for an opera house as for a local community hall; it is the facilities provided by the control desk that differ.

The most desirable situation is to to provide each spotlight with its own dimmer. Alternatively, control of the fixtures can be grouped according to angle or color or both. Traditionally, dimming includes a centralized dimmer rack that feeds the distribution equipment (the set of electrical boxes containing the individual receptacles into which the fixtures plug).

The required intensity levels can be preset in advance, even for only 10 or 12 dimmers. The operator sits at a lighting console overlooking the stage rather than operating handles of a large switchboard. Further freedom for the operator to concentrate on the performance is provided by the computer-controlled memory systems that can record the precise intensity levels of the lighting required and recall them as and when they need to be faded in by the operator on cue. These memory consoles consist of a computer with a keypad and potentiometers that control electric potentials (the voltage at a given point in an electric circuit relative to a reference point).

▲ A dimmer board in the control room of a theater. The operator initiates a cross fade from one recorded preset to another to match the change of scene on the stage.

SEE ALSO: FILTER, OPTICAL • LENS • LIGHT AND OPTICS • LIGHTBULB • PROJECTOR, MOVIE AND SLIDE • STAGE EFFECT

Thermic Lance

A thermic lance is a cutting tools that uses the heat released by a substance burning in pure oxygen to cut through a material by melting it. Most thermic lances use metallic iron as fuel; the reaction then produces a molten slag of iron (III) oxide (Fe_2O_3), and the heat of that slag is sufficient to bore holes through concrete and metals.

The most common type of thermic lance consists of a long steel tube, usually ⅜ or ½ in. (9.5 or 12.7 mm) in diameter, that has one open end and an oxygen inlet at the other. The tube contains a core of iron or steel wires as fuel for the lance. Pure oxygen enters the tube at around 8 to 12 atmospheres pressure (116–174 psi) and flows between the core of wires and the outer tube. The core wires and the outer steel tube gradually burn away during the operation of the lance.

◄ Oxygen–fuel thermic lances cut through sheet steel. The fuel and oxygen are supplied separately through color-coded pipes.

Operation

Iron in bulk reacts only slowly with pure oxygen at room temperature, and the rate of release of heat is insufficient to start a thermic lance burning spontaneously. Hence, a blowtorch is used to heat the open end of the lance to the ignition point, above which iron burns spontaneously in the oxygen stream. From this point, the lance will continue to burn until the oxygen supply is disconnected. The open end of the lance is then pushed against the object to be pierced—the workpiece—and gradually bores through it by melting and blowing away successive layers.

Concrete blocks and walls can be split by boring a row of cylindrical holes in them using a thermic lance and then joining the holes by use of a jackhammer or other mechanical means. This technique requires around 15 holes cut by a ⅜ in. (9.5 mm) lance for every yard (meter) of cut width. Steel reinforcement of the concrete helps the cutting process, since the steel burns in the flame, providing additional heat.

Thermic lances are also useful in clearing the tap holes of blast furnaces during operation. After each withdrawal (tapping) of molten metal, the tap hole becomes blocked by solidified metal. Once enough molten metal has accumulated in the furnace to merit another tapping, a small hole is made by the thermic lance and the molten metal flowing through it clears the rest of the opening.

Powder lance

An important alternative type of thermic lance is the powder lance. Rather than having core wires, a powder lance uses powdered iron carried on a stream of compressed air. The iron and oxygen then burn beyond the mouth of the lance, in a similar manner to gas and air burning beyond the mouth of a Bunsen burner. Powder lances cut without coming into contact with the workpiece, and they can be mounted on a carriage to perform continuous-slit cuts, saving the noise and vibration associated with cutting between bore holes cut by standard thermic lances. A further advantage of the powder lance is a smooth surface finish on the cut edge of the material.

Oxygen–fuel lance

Some thermic lances burn fuel gas or oil rather than iron. These fuels burn in oxygen beyond the end of the lance, giving the advantage that the tip does not come into contact with the workpiece. Oxygen–fuel lances are particularly useful for melting scrap metal and igniting furnaces.

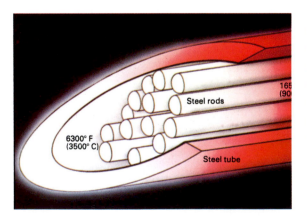

Steel rods

6300° F (3500° C)

Steel tube

165 (90

◄ This cutaway shows the structure of a thermic lance that burns iron from the steel casing and core wires in a stream of pure oxygen. This type of lance gradually burns away during cutting operations.

SEE ALSO: CONCRETE • FLAME AND IGNITION • FURNACE • IRON AND STEEL • JACKHAMMER • METAL CUTTING AND JOINING • OXYGEN

Thermodynamics

Thermodynamics is the study of transformations of energy and the useful work that can emerge as energy changes from one form to another. The term *thermodynamics* derives from the Greek words *therme* (heat) and *dynamikos* (powerful). This etymology reflects the origin of thermodynamics in the early 19th century, when it was largely concerned with the efficiency with which the heat content of steam could be made to perform work in steam engines. While the efficiency of engines remains an important application of thermodynamics, its scope has expanded to encompass such subjects as the course of chemical reactions and the absolute temperature scale.

Internal energy

Internal energy is one of the key concepts of thermodynamics: it is the amount of energy possessed by an object or collection of objects by virtue of parameters such as physical state (solid, liquid, or gas), pressure, temperature, and chemical composition. The total energy of a body is thus divided into kinetic energy, associated with its motion as a whole, potential energy, associated with its position energy in an external force field (such as the gravitation field), and internal energy.

When considering internal energy, thermodynamicists start by defining systems, which are arbitrary collections of matter. The choice of system definition is steered by function, so the thermodynamics of a rocket might be calculated for a system that comprises the propellant, the oxidant, and possibly the materials of which the combustion chamber is composed. Changes in the parameters of the chosen system—those caused by combustion in this example—lead to changes in its internal energy that determine the amount of work available from the system.

Heat energy

Heat is a fundamental form of energy, yet a precise and accurate definition of its nature proved elusive to early physical scientists. An early theory described heat in terms of caloric, a fluid that was believed to permeate all substances. Scientists observed that a hot object and a cold object in contact tend to reach a uniform temperature, and that phenomenon was explained by the flow of caloric from the hotter body to the colder body.

The notion of caloric was first challenged by Count Rumford, who noted that when a cannon was bored, the outflow of heat continued for as long as the boring process lasted. Calculating that the heat released by boring would be sufficient to

▲ This picture illustrates the second law of thermodynamics in action: as the chemical energy of burning coal is converted into high-grade kinetic energy, large amounts of low-grade heat must also be released, hence the huge clouds of steam. In total, around one-tenth of the chemical energy of the coal does useful work.

melt the cannon, Rumford concluded that the heat released by boring could not be attributed to the original caloric content of the cannon and that the work done during the process of boring must somehow be converted into heat.

In the 1840s, the British physicist James Prescot Joule contributed to the modern understanding of heat as a form of energy with experiments in which he measured the heat produced by mechanical work. Joule showed that the relationship between work done and heat generated was constant regardless of how the conversion was effected and that one calorie—the amount of heat required to raise the temperature of one gram (0.035 oz.) of water by one degree Celsius (0.56°F)—is equivalent to 4.18 joules of mechanical energy. (1 joule is the amount of work done when a force of 1 newton acts over a distance of 1 meter.) This is the mechanical equivalent of heat.

Temperature and heat capacity

Temperature is clearly related to heat but is even more directly related to the notion of hotness. No net transfer of heat occurs when two bodies at the same temperature are in contact, but when a body comes into contact with another at lower temperature, heat will be transferred from the hotter to the cooler body until the two reach the same temperature or until they are separated.

In some cases, a cooler body may contain more heat than a hotter body, yet the flow of heat will still occur from hotter to cooler if the two are in contact. The amount of heat required to increase the temperature of a body by one degree Celsius is called the heat capacity of the body. The heat capacity of a body depends upon its mass (the amount of matter present) as well as its composition and physical state. Hence, a cold body that has a great heat capacity may hold more heat than a hot body that has a lower heat capacity.

First law—conservation of energy

Joule's demonstrations of the mechanical equivalence of heat were examples of interconversions of two types of energy: heat and mechanical (kinetic and potential). Many other energy

CARNOT CYCLE

Various types of engines for converting heat into more mechanical energy were invented even before the basic laws of thermodynamics had been posited. The earliest examples were first used in the early 18th century for pumping water out of mines; later designs turned drive shafts in factories and provided the traction of steam locomotives. All these engines were highly inefficient, converting less than 10 percent of the heat energy into useful work, and many engineers sought ways of improving their efficiency.

One such person was Sadi Carnot, a French engineer. In 1824, Carnot started to calculate the efficiency of an ideal heat engine, one that would be completely insulated and frictionless. According to this model, heat would be supplied to an ideal working fluid at one temperature and absorbed from the same fluid at a lower temperature. Between these stages, the fluid would perform work in expanding against a piston in a cylinder.

To calculate the efficiency of such a model, Carnot divided its action into a repeating series of four steps, called the Carnot cycle. The first step in this cycle is the heating of the working fluid, at a fixed volume, to the temperature of the hot reservoir. The second stage is the expansion of the fluid in the cylinder with no transfer of heat energy. The fluid becomes cooler as a consequence of the expansion, and the expanding fluid does work on the piston. In the third stage, the fluid gives up heat energy as it cools to the temperature of the cold reservoir; once again, the volume of the fluid is

fixed. In the fourth stage, the piston does work on the fluid to compress it without a transfer of heat occurring. The cycle then repeats indefinitely.

The efficiency of this model engine is the amount of useful work done divided by the amount of heat taken from the hot reservoir. Dividing the action into the four steps of the Carnot cycle simplifies the calculation of these quantities and reveals that even the ideal engine is less than 100 percent efficient. This idea fits with the first law of thermodynamics, since the amount of energy transferred to the cold reservoir must be greater than zero. Hence, the amount of heat energy that becomes useful work must be less than the heat energy transferred from the hot reservoir in the first stage of the cycle.

In fact, the efficiency of the Carnot engine would be equal to the difference in absolute temperature between the hot reservoir and the cold reservoir divided by the temperature of the hot reservoir. (Absolute temperature is measured on the

Kelvin scale, whose intervals are identical to those of the Celsius scale and whose zero is at −273°C, −460°F.) Applying this formula to an ideal heat engine working with a hot reservoir at the boiling point of water (373 K, 212°F, 100°C) and a cold reservoir at 283 K (50°F, 10°C), the result is 24 percent efficiency. In fact, the real efficiency of such an engine would be lower owing to losses of energy caused by friction and heat loss in the cylinder. Nevertheless, the formula reveals that greater efficiency is obtained by having the greatest possible temperature gap between the hot and cold reservoirs.

Lord Kelvin realized in 1884 that the Carnot engine could be used to define an absolute temperature scale. This, the Kelvin scale, is still the fundamental temperature scale in physics. Temperatures below absolute zero are impossible to obtain, since they would make the Carnot engine more than 100 percent efficient and would imply the creation of energy and thus contravene the first law.

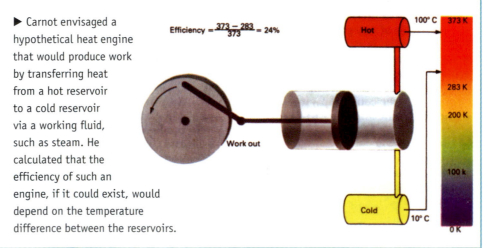

▶ Carnot envisaged a hypothetical heat engine that would produce work by transferring heat from a hot reservoir to a cold reservoir via a working fluid, such as steam. He calculated that the efficiency of such an engine, if it could exist, would depend on the temperature difference between the reservoirs.

$$\text{Efficiency} = \frac{373 - 283}{373} = 24\%$$

► This eruption of Mount St. Helens, Washington, is a dramatic example of an increase in entropy.

changes also occur routinely. Consider a falling brick. While being held aloft, the brick has potential energy owing to its existence as mass in a gravitational field. When the brick is released, its potential energy starts to decrease as it falls, and its kinetic energy increases as it starts to fall faster. If the effects of air resistance are neglected, the rate of increase of kinetic energy matches the rate of decrease in potential energy, so the overall energy of the brick remains the same. On impact with the ground, some of that energy is released in the form of sound waves, some may go into breaking chemical bonds if the brick shatters, but most of it becomes heat.

In another example, a motor converts electrical energy into mechanical energy and heat that is generated by the passage of current through the resistance of its coils. When the amounts of mechanical and heat energy produced are measured, their sum is found to be equal to the amount of electrical energy consumed by the motor.

The important conclusion that follows from Joule's experiments and others is that the total amount of energy of a system remains constant provided the system exchanges no energy with its environment. This phenomenon is called conservation of energy, and the statement of its existence is the first law of thermodynamics.

When radioactivity was first discovered near the end of the 19th century, some scientists thought it resulted from nuclear reactions that violated conservation of energy. A few years later, the German-born physicist Albert Einstein calculated the equivalence between mass (m) and energy (E) to produce the famous equation $E = mc^2$, in which c is the speed of light in a vacuum. The impact of this discovery was similar to that of Joule proving the equivalence of heat and mechanical energy: Einstein proposed the existence of mass–energy—a single entity of which one facet is mass and the other energy. Hence, the revised first law of thermodynamics states that mass–energy is always conserved.

Second law—increasing disorder

The flow of heat from hot bodies to cooler ones is a familiar observation from everyday life and one that was confirmed by Sadi Carnot's analysis of the ideal heat engine. In fact, all the steps in the Carnot cycle are reversible, so the ideal heat engine can be made to run backwards, functioning as a heat pump. Calculations reveal that work must be done on a heat engine in order to pump heat from a cold reservoir to a warmer one. This fact is the basis of heat pumps that supply heating systems with energy from the cold ground as well as air-conditioning units that pump heat from cool buildings into the warmer environment.

Carnot's hypothetical device works within the confines of conservation of energy whether functioning as a heat engine or a heat pump, yet it seems that nature lends a hand when the machine runs as an engine. This is one of many examples that can be cited in support of a proposal that natural processes tend to result in the transfer of heat energy from a place where it is concentrated to a place where it is more dilute. Carnot's cycle shows that low-temperature heat energy is less useful for doing work than high-temperature energy, so the natural process has the result of converting high-grade energy—high grade in terms of its potential for doing work—into lower-grade energy.

In 1850, the German physicist Rudolf Clausius postulated that heat could never flow spontaneously from a cold body to a hotter one, and by 1865, he had coined the term *entropy* for a measure of the unavailable energy in a system. This postulate led to the second law of thermodynamics: in a spontaneous process, the entropy of a system must always increase.

Entropy has since become associated with disorder, since processes that increase entropy also increase the amount of chaos in a system. In the case of a brick that falls to the ground and smashes, low-entropy potential energy is converted into high-entropy sound and heat, and energy is put into breaking chemical bonds. No energy is lost, but the reverse process—one in which the dispersed fragments of the brick would somehow reunite as a solid brick and rise to an elevated position—is impossible: it would imply a reduction of entropy in the system.

Some processes seem to defy the second law—the fabrication of a brick from clay would be a good candidate. In such cases, it is invariably true that some entropy-generating factor has been overlooked: the burning of fuel in the excavators that extract the clay and in the kilns that fire the brick in this example. In fact, the law that entropy must increase is so inviolable that entropy is sometimes called time's arrow—it is the factor that determines which way an apparently reversible process will proceed as time passes.

Thermodynamics and the Universe

It is the difference in temperature between Earth and the Sun that fuels Earth's energy resources, with the exceptions of tidal and nuclear power. The transfer of radiated heat from the Sun stirs up Earth's atmosphere to create air currents and the fall of rain and snow, which can be harnessed to produce wind power and hydroelectric power, respectively. More important for humans, light energy from the Sun drives the photosynthesis reactions that build plants. In their turn, plants pass on energy from the Sun in the form of chemical energy when consumed as food, and they are the ultimate origin of fossil fuels.

Earth also radiates heat to its colder environment. If it did not, it would eventually match the Sun's temperature of around 11,000°F (6000°C). These are two stages in a process that physicists predict will ultimately lead to a state of maximum entropy in the Universe, where all matter will be at a uniform temperature only fractionally above absolute zero. This state is called heat death.

Statistical mechanics

Early thermodynamics concerned itself purely with macroscopic phenomena—the properties of matter in bulk, such as temperature, pressure, and volume—and it was at first difficult to see the origins of these phenomena in the behavior of individual atoms and molecules. The first step toward linking macroscopic and molecular properties was made with the kinetic theory of gases, which succeeded in describing the properties of gases—in particular the relationship between the pressure, temperature, and volume of a sample of gas—and the movements of gas molecules. The understanding of the molecular level of matter flourished with the development of quantum theory, however, and a means of explaining macroscopic thermodynamics in terms of molecular properties became possible after all.

Quantum mechanics described the various energy states that matter can occupy. Any given molecule has various forms of energy, including the kinetic energy of its translational and rotational motions and the combined kinetic and potential energies of its vibrational motions. Added to these are the electrostatic potential energies and kinetic energies of its constituent nuclei and of the electrons that reside near the nuclei and those that form the chemical bonds in the molecule. Quantization allows each type of energy to have a range of discrete values, and the total energy of a molecule is the sum of the allowed values for each type of energy.

When several molecules form an assembly, the individual molecules have different energies within the allowed ranges of values. For any given state of the assembly, the individual molecules distribute themselves among the allowed energy levels according to a statistical distribution. This distribution pattern is named the Boltzmann distribution for the Austrian physicist who applied it to the speeds of molecules in a sample of gas. The Boltzmann distribution varies with temperature, and ever more molecules exist in higher energy levels as temperature increases. This condition requires an input of energy, and the rate at which energy must be supplied as temperature increases is the origin of heat capacity. Entropy is related to the number of energy-state combinations that could correspond to a given total energy—the greater this number, the greater the entropy.

Translational energy levels tend to be more closely spaced than other energy levels. Consequently, liquids, dissolved substances, and gases have more possible energy-state combinations and greater entropy than similar solids, which are not as free to move. As a result, chemical reactions that release gases and dissolutions of solids proceed even if they absorb low-grade heat energy and convert it into high-grade chemical energy. The increase in entropy that results from matter becoming less ordered more than makes up for the conversion of energy to a more ordered form.

▼ When water falls over the edge of a waterfall, its potential energy decreases and its kinetic energy increases. At the foot of the waterfall, the extra kinetic energy becomes sound and heat energy, the latter producing a measurable increase in the temperature of the water.

SEE ALSO: GAS LAWS • MATTER, PROPERTIES OF • NEWTON'S LAWS

Thermoelectric Device

The term *thermoelectricity* traditionally refers to three closely related effects—the Seebeck, Peltier, and Thomson effects—that cause the interconversion of electrical energy and heat energy. These effects are the basis of the operation of a number of thermoelectric devices, including certain types of thermometers, refrigerators, and small power generators. The scope of the term excludes other relationships between heat and electricity. One such relationship is the Joule heating effect, whereby the passage of a current through a resistance produces heat.

The Seebeck effect occurs when two different metals are joined to make a circuit. If the two junctions are maintained at different temperatures, a net voltage arises in the circuit and drives a current around the circuit. The converse of this effect, called the Peltier effect, occurs when a current is driven around such a circuit. This current causes one junction to become warmer and the other to become cooler. The Thomson effect occurs in a conducting bar where there is a temperature gradient along the line of current flow. When a current flows along the bar, heat is either emitted or absorbed; the direction of heat flow depends on the composition of the conductor and the direction of the temperature gradient.

Conduction

In order to understand how thermoelectric effects work, it is first necessary to have some understanding of the structures of metals and the factors that allow them to conduct. The nuclei of metal atoms vibrate around fixed positions in regular structures called lattices. Most of the electrons of each atom are tightly bound to nuclei by the attraction that exists between positive and negative charges, and these electrons rarely stray far from their associated nuclei.

A few electrons are screened from the nuclei by other electrons nearer the nuclei, so they experience a much weaker pull. In fact, the attraction is so weak that these electrons are relatively free to drift through the lattice. In general, the motion of electrons is random, and their charge is evenly spread through a sample of metal. In the presence of an electrical field, however, electrons experience a force in the direction from high to low

◀ This power source for marine navigational aids uses thermocouples to produce electricity from the heat of radioactive decay of strontium-90.

▼ This thermopile, once calibrated, can measure the temperature of objects from the heat energy they emit as infrared radiation.

electrical potential. This force causes a net drift of electrons and is the origin of electrical currents. The number of free electrons per unit volume of a metal depends on its composition, as does the ease with which those electrons move.

Temperature has an influence on average speed of electrons, making them move faster at a high temperature. The electrons move randomly in the absence of an electrical field or temperature gradient, however, and no net current flows.

Thermoelectric effects

Some thermoelectric effects arise from changes in the distribution of electrons in conductors caused by variations in temperature. Others arise because electrical effects impose changes in the thermal energy of electrons, which is manifested in the temperature of the conductor as a whole.

Seebeck effect. In 1822, the German physicist Thomas J. Seebeck observed signs of an effect that would later form the basis of devices such as thermocouples. Seebeck was working with a circuit that consisted of a copper wire joined in two places to a plate of bismuth. When he heated one copper–bismuth joint but kept the other cool, he detected a magnetic field near the circuit.

Thinking that the heat had magnetized the metals, Seebeck named this the thermomagnetic effect. In fact, the magnetic field arose because of current flowing in the circuit, not because of any

permanent magnetization of the metals by heat, and the phenomenon was later more properly ascribed to a thermoelectric effect.

If a bismuth plate is connected to the terminals of a galvanometer by copper wires and one joint is heated, a current starts to flow through the galvanometer from the hot joint to the cold. The effect occurs with other pairs of metals, called couples, and even in couples of a single metal with different degrees of impurity or in which one of a pair of wires has been strained more than the other, the strain causing a structural difference.

The flow of current stems from an effect that occurs at the junctions between the two components of a couple. As mentioned, the ease of movement of free electrons in a metal depends on the strength of the attraction those electrons experience for the nuclei in the metal. At a junction between two metals, electrons tend to drift from the metal whose nuclei exert a weaker grip over free electrons to the metal where that attraction is stronger. Since the number of electrons in each metal perfectly matches the positive nuclear charge, this drift causes an imbalance in charge seen as a voltage difference across the junction.

If a pair of wires is joined at both ends and the temperature is uniform, the voltage differences at the two junctions are of equal magnitude but opposite signs following a path around the circuit. Hence, no current flows due to these voltages.

The situation changes when the temperature at one junction differs from that at the other. At the high-temperature junction, electrons have greater thermal energy than they do at the low-temperature junction. Their random thermal motion is therefore more vigorous and thus counteracts to some extent the trend for electrons to drift to the metal whose nuclei exert more pull. Hence, the voltage difference caused by this pull is smaller than at the cool junction.

The imbalance in the potential differences between the hot and cold junctions causes a current to flow. The direction of current flow is such that the more electropositive metal—the one whose nuclei exert less pull on electrons—gives up electrons to the other metal at the cold junction and accepts electrons at the hot junction.

Peltier effect. In 1834, the French physicist Jean Peltier discovered an effect that is the converse of the Seebeck effect: when a current is forced to flow around a couple of dissimilar conductors, one junction becomes hotter and the other junction becomes cooler. For a given couple, the junction cooled by the Peltier effect is the one that would be the hot junction if a Seebeck current were to flow in the same direction. The Peltier effect also accompanies the Seebeck effect in such couples; its influence is seen as heating of the cold junction and cooling of the hot junction, unless external heating and cooling maintain the junction temperatures at constant values.

An examination of the balance between electrical potential energy and thermal kinetic energy explains how these heating and cooling effects occur. At the junction that gets cooler, the electrons that constitute the current pass from a conductor whose nuclei exert a stronger pull to one where the pull is weaker. This is the electrical equivalent of climbing a mountain, since the electrons must move from a region of low (electrical) potential energy to one of high potential energy.

Since energy is conserved, the energy needed to climb that mountain must be found from some other source. In fact, the energy that makes up the shortfall comes from the thermal energy of the electrons, hence the Peltier cooling effect.

If current is driven in the opposite direction—equivalent to pushing electrons over a "cliff" of electrical potential in the previous analogy—excess potential energy is transformed into kinetic energy. This phenomenon is the origin of the heating effect.

Thomson effect. In the 1850s, the British scientist William Thomson (Lord Kelvin) produced a mathematical analysis that connected the Seebeck and Peltier effects. His work also predicted a related third effect that was later demonstrated and now bears his name. In the Kelvin effect, the flow of current along a conductor in which a temperature gradient exists results in the absorption or release of heat, depending on the sense of current flow.

This effect is easily understood when it is realized that the temperature gradient produces an electrical field (voltage gradient) within the metal. Thus, the Thomson effect is similar to the Peltier effect, except that the field is not produced by a junction but by a temperature gradient.

The mechanism by which the electrical field arises is thermal: electrons at the hot end of a conducting bar move faster and are more likely to migrate to the cool end than vice versa. Hence,

▲ A gas water heater relies on a thermocouple as a safety measure. If the pilot light fails, the hot junction cools, and the drop in the output voltage closes the main gas valve.

▶ An assembly of gas pilot jet, thermocouple, and spark igniter (top right) under inspection as part of routine maintenance.

positive charge accumulates at the hot end, where there are insufficient electrons to match the nuclear charge, and negative charge accumulates at the cool end. If a current pushes electrons from the positive to the negative end—up the hill of electrical potential energy—they lose some thermal energy, and the bar becomes cooler. If the current flows in the opposite direction, the bar becomes warm as electrons gain thermal energy.

Neutral and inversion temperatures

The explanations of thermoelectric effect given so far hold up well for most systems at low temperature. However, for reasons beyond the scope of this work, higher temperatures see a fall in the rate of increase of thermoelectric voltages (Seebeck) and heating and cooling effects (Peltier and Thomson) with increasing temperature.

Above a certain temperature that is different for each system—the neutral temperature—the trends so far described start to diminish. Beyond a second temperature, the inversion temperature, the effects act in reverse.

In the case of iron at room temperature, experiments show the metal to be above its inversion temperature for the Thomson effect, as can be seen by the release of heat when a current flows so that electrons move from the hot end to the cold end of an iron bar.

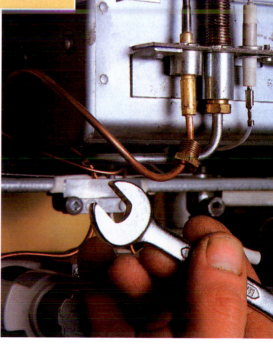

Thermocouple

Thermocouples are devices that use the Seebeck effect to measure temperatures in applications as diverse as household gas heaters, laboratory experiments, and industrial processes. The voltages produced by thermocouples are quite small, as can be seen in the case of the copper–bismuth couple: if one junction is kept at 32°F (0°C) and the other at 33.8°F (1°C), the emf (electromotive force, or voltage) is only slightly greater than 70 µV (millionths of a volt). The emf between junctions is measured using a high-precision voltage-measuring device, such as a millivoltmeter or a potentiometer. The reading obtained can be converted into a temperature difference by reference to standard tables or by use of a processor that converts the voltage signal from a thermocouple into a digital temperature display.

More accurate temperature measurement require one junction being kept at a known fixed temperature, called the reference temperature. In the laboratory, this temperature is often 32°F (0°C), obtaintained by immersing the reference junction in an ice–water mixture. In industrial uses, the reference junction is more likely to be maintained just above air temperature and would then have its own heater to maintain the reference temperature. The other junction, mounted in a suitable protective shielding, can be used as a probe for spot temperature measurements.

The temperature distribution along the connecting leads does not affect the measured emf; thus thermocouples are ideal remote temperature sensors. However, because of the possibility of spurious Seebeck emfs at the connections between the leads and the meter, these connections must be held at uniform temperature.

Although thermocouples are convenient and sturdy instruments, they are normally accurate to within only a few degrees in industrial uses. In the laboratory, however, they can be calibrated to give more precise measurements. In fact, the part of the International Practical Temperature Scale from the melting point of antimony (1167°F, 630.5°C) to that of gold (1945°F, 1063°C) is defined by readings of a standard thermocouple, made of platinum and a platinum–rhodium alloy.

Power generation

A thermopile consists of a number of thermocouples connected in series to give an output voltage many times greater than the output voltage of a single couple. Given a good temperature difference and a sufficient number of thermocouples, the output from a thermopile can be used to power equipment. The process is an inefficient way of generating power, wasting a great deal of heat. Nevertheless, a thermopile is robust, has no moving parts to wear out, and can use any practical heat source, advantages that have made them attractive for military and aerospace uses.

Wood fires, paraffin burners, solar energy, and radioactive decay have all been used as heat sources. The Soviet army made portable thermoelectric generators to power radio transmitters during World War II. Also, various satellites and space probes use thermopiles based on radioactive heat sources and silicon–germanium thermocouples. Overall efficiency is low, but heat given out by a source such as enriched uranium does not diminish significantly during the lifetime of a typical space vehicle, so a thermopile of this type is effectively an unending power supply.

Refrigeration

The Peltier effect can be used to refrigerate objects by passing current through an appropriate junction in contact with the object to be cooled. Experimental prototypes as large as conventional home refrigerators have been built, but the main applications today are in technical uses where a compact cooling unit is needed.

The efficiency of thermoelectric refrigeration increases with the ratio of electric conductivity to thermal conductivity for the materials that constitute the couple. Semiconductors exhibit thermoelectric effects and are superior to metals in terms of the ratio of conductivities. This combination of properties is finding semiconducting couples increasing use in small-scale refrigeration.

▶ This thermocouple component provides a robust and compact means of measuring temperature.

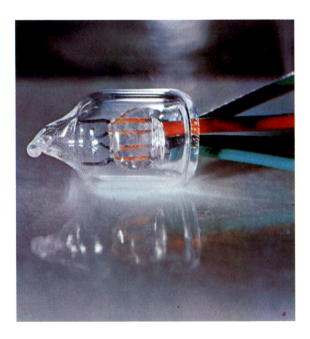

SEE ALSO: CONDUCTION, ELECTRICAL • ELECTRICITY • METAL • METER, ELECTRICAL • REFRIGERATION • SEMICONDUCTOR • TELEMETRY • TEMPERATURE • THERMOGRAM • THERMOMETRY

Thermogram

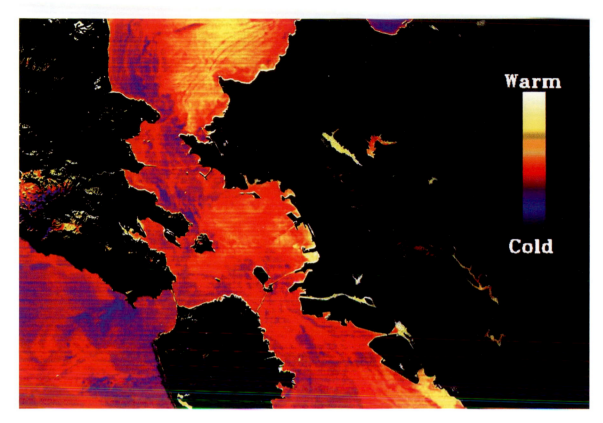

A thermogram is an image in which variations in color represent areas at different temperatures. Thermograms are produced by equipment that measures temperature from a distance by examining the infrared radiation given off by objects. Applications for thermograms are in medicine, in the diagnosis of equipment faults, and in aerial surveys of land and of ocean currents.

Thermal radiation

All objects give off energy in the form of photons of electromagnetic radiation. The intensity and range of frequencies of those photons depends on temperature. Cool objects radiate only far-infrared (low-frequency) photons at low intensity. As temperature increases, the overall intensity of radiation increases, as does the frequency of the most intense radiation. From around 1290°F (around 700°C), objects start to emit visible light—at first glowing only a dull red and then incandescing yellow and eventually white, as the emitted spectrum peaks at ever higher frequencies. Near room temperature, objects emit mainly infrared radiation—the invisible radiation that causes the radiant warmth felt near a fire.

Thermograph

A thermograph, or thermal-imaging camera, works by sensing infrared radiation. By scanning a series of points on an object, it is possible to form a map of the temperature variation across its surface. A typical processor takes that information and creates a false-color image in which each color represents a specific range of temperatures.

The components that detect infrared radiation are based on photoconductors—materials whose electrical conductivity increases in response to being exposed to infrared radiation. Typical examples of such materials include indium–antimony and mercury–cadmium–tellurium alloys.

The sensitivity of a thermograph depends on its working temperature. Thermographs that work at room temperature can produce images of warmer objects, but better resolution and images of cool objects can be achieved only by cooling the thermograph. Cooling can be done using boiling liquid nitrogen, which has a temperature of –320°F (–196°C). Another cooling technique uses the Peltier effect, whereby the passage of an electrical current across a junction between two dissimilar metals causes heat to be absorbed.

Scanning thermograph. One type of thermograph uses a rotating mirror to split views into horizontal lines. A system of lenses focuses an image from the incoming infrared radiation, and the mirror reflects different parts of that image onto infrared detectors as it rotates.

Phased-array thermograph. More sophisticated thermographs are based on arrays of infrared detectors. The outputs from the components of

▲ These thermograms show two people who have been exposed to extreme cold. The person at left, who had been wearing a survival suit during the exposure, returns to normal body temperature (indicated by yellows and reds) more quickly than the person at right.

such an array are combined according to a varying phase relationship; as a consequence, they detect incoming light from a single direction at any given time, and that direction varies with the changing phase relationship.

Image analysis

The basic video image produced from the infrared scanning system is in black and white, with temperature graduations represented by continuously varying gray tones. Isotherms—lines that connect points at the same temperature—can be superimposed on the image to allow temperature measurement. Scanning systems can be switched to cover a number of different temperature ranges, with a typical overall range being from –4°F (–20°C) to 1632°F (900°C). Higher temperatures can be accommodated by the use of gray filters in the imaging system. Sensitivity is high—a temperature difference of 0.2°F (0.1°C) is detectable at 86°F (30°C), for example.

The continuous gray image can be broken up into zones representing a temperature band or converted to a false-color image, typically with 5 to 10 colors, each representing a different temperature range. A permanent record of the thermogram can be obtained by taking photographs of the screen image or by recording the video signals for subsequent replay and analysis.

Early thermographs took around 10 minutes to form images, so they were useful only for scanning fixed objects. Modern systems produce images in fractions of a second, allowing real-time scanning of both moving and stationary objects, thereby broadening the field of applications.

Applications

One of the earliest applications of thermography was in surveillance systems, initially for military use. Such systems enable the identification of concealed personnel or vehicles by their body or engine heat. Handheld thermographs are also used by rescue workers to locate living beings trapped in the rubble of collapsed buildings and to identify the positions of hot spots that could indicate the location of the seat of a fire.

Thermograms are also useful in medical diagnosis. A thermal scan of a healthy body gives a relatively consistent pattern, with the skin temperature varying according to the local blood flow. Areas of poor circulation are cooler than the average body temperature, and areas with unusually high blood flow—typical for inflammation and some types of tumors—show up as hot spots that merit more detailed investigation.

Thermograms of homes or industrial premises help identify areas of high heat loss, such as poorly insulated roofs, faulty wall insulation, and air leakage past inefficient window and door seals. Where energy-saving programs are in operation, aerial scanning can be used to identify buildings whose rates of heat loss are particularly high. Appropriate remedial measures can be taken to reduce the heat losses, and follow-up thermograms can be used to assess their efficiency.

A major industrial application of thermograms is in the examination of electrical and electronic components, which can be monitored in use. In many cases, malfunctioning or overloaded components start to overheat before they fail. Hence, thermal imaging can be part of a preventative maintenance program that minimizes disruptions. Large plants, such as power-distribution stations, can often be inspected from ground level.

Thermal cameras on satellites are useful in producing rapid surveys of large areas. One important use of such devices is in monitoring forest fires, notably in remote rain forests; another is in observing changes in ocean currents, such as El Niño, by their thermal traces.

SEE ALSO: ELECTROMAGNETIC RADIATION • IMAGE INTENSIFIER • SECURITY SYSTEM • SPECTROSCOPY • SURVEYING

Thermometry

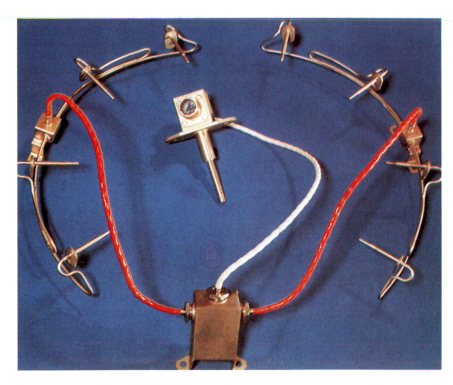

The temperature of a body is one of its most interesting scientific properties, and the measurement of temperature is important in all branches of science from medicine to meteorology and chemistry, as well as in everyday life. The sense organs in the human skin act as a crude thermometer (an instrument for measuring temperature) but suffer from the disadvantage that only a limited range of temperatures, between those that numb and those that burn the skin, can be measured at all. The skin, moreover, is better at measuring temperature differences than the actual temperature.

History

The earliest temperature indicators (thermoscopes) were made just before 1600 by the Italian scientist Galileo Galilei and others, and the important step of attaching a scale to make a thermometer was taken by the Italian physician Santorio Santorio ten years later. These early instruments were essentially barometers, using water in the tube, and so they responded to changes in atmospheric pressure as well as temperature.

By 1654, the Grand Duke of Tuscany, Ferdinand II, had invented the familiar sealed glass tube thermometer with the fluid contained in a bulb. The fluid was a mixture of water and alcohol, which could be used at temperatures below the freezing point of water, an important consideration at a time when thermometers were mainly used for meteorological purposes.

▲ An integral thermocouple array designed to measure the high temperatures within Pratt and Whitney Canada PT6 aero engines. One important advantages of the thermocouple is its small size, which enables it to measure the temperature at a particular point on or within an object.

▶ Bimetallic strip thermometers (center, with samples of hot and cold strips above and below) are fairly accurate, but the clinical thermometer, within its narrower range, is far more precise.

Experiments were also made with the liquid metal mercury, but its expansion is too small to show in the relatively wide tubes current at that time, and mercury thermometers were not widely used until the following century.

Today's thermometers

In the basic pattern of all liquid-in-glass thermometers, the fluid being used is contained in a glass bulb with a narrow tube, or capillary, of as even a bore as possible leading off it. The principle on which they work is that the volume of the liquid increases with its temperature. The expansion is small—about one-thousandth of the original volume per degree Fahrenheit for alcohol—but if the bulb is large and the tube narrow, the expansion will be clearly visible in the capillary. The air is evacuated from the tube above the liquid, to prevent its expansion from interfering with the readings. The glass also expands but to a lesser extent than the liquid.

One of the most familiar types of liquid-in-glass thermometer, is the clinical thermometer, for measuring body temperature. The inner bore of the tube narrows to form a constriction near the bulb so that, when the thermometer is

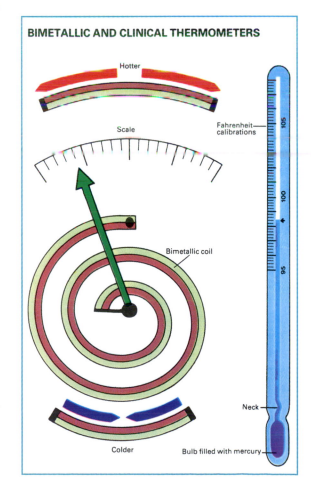

BIMETALLIC AND CLINICAL THERMOMETERS

Hotter

Scale

Fahrenheit calibrations

Bimetallic coil

Neck

Colder

Bulb filled with mercury

◀ The comparison of two mercury-in-glass thermometers shows the differences between the Fahrenheit scale (left) and the Celsius scale (right).

removed from the mouth and the mercury thread begins to contract into the bulb, the thread breaks at this constriction. The temperature can then be read at leisure. The glass bulb of a clinical thermometer is especially thin to allow the mercury to reach body temperature rapidly. The tube is roughly triangular in cross section and acts as a lens to magnify the narrow mercury thread, and it also incorporates a white enamel backing to make the thread more easily visible.

Meteorological thermometers

Although the majority of today's liquid-in-glass thermometers incorporate mercury, pure alcohol is often preferred for meteorological instruments, because temperatures down to –148°F (–100°C) —well below the freezing point of mercury which is –34.6°F (–37°C)—can be measured. Liquids with an even lower freezing point, such as pentane, can be used at temperatures as low as –328°F (–200°C), where air is liquid.

Meteorologists also require thermometers that record the maximum and minimum temperatures reached during the day. One of the most popular, Six's thermometer, includes a short length of mercury in the tube of an alcohol thermometer. Small steel markers at either end of the mercury thread are pushed up or down as the mercury is moved by the expansion and contraction of the alcohol, and the markers are held at their extreme positions by small springs. The maximum and minimum temperatures reached can be read off scales opposite the two markers, which can be reset by a magnet.

To obtain a continuous record of the meteorological temperature, a bimetallic strip can be used. It consists of two long strips of different metals tightly joined and usually formed into a helix. A change in temperature alters the length of each of the strips to a different extent, and so the composite strip bends. A pen attached to the end of the strip records these changes on a slowly rotating drum. Simple versions of this device, with a spiral strip and a dial, are often used.

Other thermometers

The most fundamental thermometer used in physics is the constant volume gas thermometer, because its readings follow the theoretical absolute (Kelvin) temperature scale. A quantity of a gas, usually helium, in a small platinum bulb is brought to the desired temperature, and its pressure is measured. According to the gas laws, the pressure of an ideal gas is directly proportional to the absolute temperature, but as no real gas behaves ideally, a series of readings must be taken with different amounts of gas in the bulb. The result that would be obtained with a negligibly small mass of gas can then be calculated; this result is what an ideal gas would have given. There are many other small corrections that must be made to achieve the most accurate value for the temperature, so that although it can be used for temperatures from 0.5 degrees above absolute zero up to 1832°F (1000°C), the gas thermometer is in practice only employed to measure certain fixed points by which other thermometers can be calibrated. (These fixed points are usually the melting and boiling points of various pure substances.)

Temperatures from –436°F (–260°C) to over 1112°F (600°C) can be measured accurately with a platinum resistance thermometer. The electric resistance of all metals increases with temperature, that of platinum more uniformly than most. Platinum also has the advantage of a high melting point and is very resistant to corrosion. In the thermometer, a thin platinum wire is wound around a mica frame, and its resistance is found by passing a current through it and measuring the resulting voltage. A standard formula converts the value of the resistance to a temperature. At lower temperatures, the resistance of an ordinary carbon resistor can be used instead of a platinum wire, while for higher temperatures, a thermocouple, consisting of a platinum wire in contact at both ends with a wire of platinum–rhodium alloy, is employed.

SEE ALSO: GAS LAWS • MERCURY • TEMPERATURE • THERMOELECTRIC DEVICE • THERMOSTAT

Thermos Bottle

The thermos bottle, also known as the Dewar flask, or vacuum flask, was invented by the Scottish chemist and physicist Sir James Dewar in 1892 for the purpose of storing liquid gases at very low temperatures. Thermos bottles were first made commercially in 1904, when two German glassblowers formed Thermos GmbH.

Thermos (from the Greek *thermos*, meaning hot) was originally a trademark, and is now the common name applied to a form of vacuum bottle protected by a casing. Its basic function is to thermally insulate the contents and prevent heat from flowing either in or out.

The bottle is a glass vessel with double walls, the space between which is evacuated. It is primarily this feature that hinders the transfer of heat to or from the container. The vacuum is created by pumping the air in the wall cavity out through a glass tube, which is an integral part of the outer wall, during manufacture. This tube is then automatically sealed by a machine when the desired degree of vacuum has been achieved.

There are three ways heat can be transferred: convection, conduction, and radiation. A vacuum effectively stops the first two of these as it is a nonconductor. Radiation is reduced to a minimum by silvering the glass, generally on the two internal faces, so that radiant heat waves are reflected. The chief path by which heat can be communicated either to or from the interior of the inner vessel is at the vessel's neck, which is the only junction of the walls, and it is made as small as possible. The stopper is made of a good insulating material such as cork or hollow plastic.

For durability, metal is often substituted for glass, but the latter, being a much better insulator in itself, is the more efficient material. One of the problems of the glass vessel is that it is fragile, so it is generally mounted on pads of cork or rubber within a metal container.

Uses

There are a variety of uses to which the vacuum flask is utilized. Its chief scientific uses are in the field of low-temperature studies, where it is used to store liquid gases at very low temperatures, or to reduce apparatus to very low temperatures by immersing it in liquid nitrogen contained in a vacuum flask. The thermos bottle has been used in various instruments measuring electric power, rate of climb in airplanes, detection of oil deposits, and weather recording. It has also been used to transport blood plasma and serums, bones, tissues, and insulin.

▶ Liquid nitrogen is poured from a vacuum container, where it has been stored, into a cryostat—a machine used in studying materials at very low temperatures.

▼ A complete vacuum container is shown on the right. Beside it is a partly dismantled bottle, revealing its double-wall method of construction. The cavity between the walls is evacuated to minimize radiant heat.

Probably the best-known use is the bottle in which hot or cold drinks are stored. If it is used properly, a thermos flask will keep a fluid near its original temperature for several hours. For best results, the thermos bottle should always be kept upright. Today, the main insulated products used for food and beverages include steel vacuum ware, glass vacuum ware, foam-insulated travel tumblers, and foam-insulated hard and soft coolers and jugs. Heat transfer through foam and the air bubbles it contains is slight, and foam-insulated containers work on a similar principle to thermos bottles, though they are slightly less efficient.

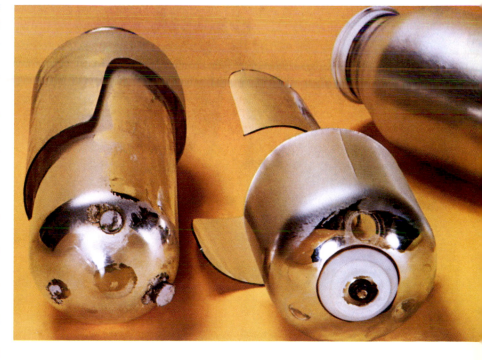

SEE ALSO: CRYOGENICS • REFRIGERATION • VACUUM

Thermostat

A thermostat is a device that controls the temperature of a circulating fluid or of an enclosed space. It has a sensing element, which responds to the temperature, and a control element, which regulates a heating or cooling process on the principle of negative feedback—by suppressing any departure from the desired temperature. Automatic temperature regulation is essential in refrigerators, in central heating and air conditioning systems, in automobile cooling systems, and in a wide variety of industrial processes.

The essential features of any thermostat are well illustrated by one of the earliest known examples, designed about 1660 by Cornelius Drebbel, a Dutchman living in London. The device regulated a furnace that heated an incubator. Hot furnace gases rose around a water jacket surrounding the incubating space. The sensing element, placed in the incubating space, was a vessel filled with alcohol, which expands on heating. One end of the vessel was attached to a tube containing mercury. If the temperature of the water jacket rose, the expanding alcohol pushed down on the mercury column in one branch of the tube. The mercury rose in the other branch and pushed up a rod, which in turn raised one end of a lever. The other end of the lever descended and lowered a damper over the flue through which the furnace's gases vented. This damper restricted the draft to the furnace and slowed its rate of burning. When the temperature fell as a result, the alcohol contracted, and the damper was raised, increasing the strength of the draft and the rate of burning.

The device worked but would have hunted—that is, the thermostat would tend to overcompensate, causing the system to overshoot its precise target temperature. The role of the water jacket in the design was to smooth out these fluctuations by heating up or cooling down slowly. Such devices were used only in isolated instances until the late 19th century, when they were applied to the furnaces and radiators of heating systems in large apartment buildings.

Bimetallic strips

One class of thermostat sensing elements depends on the expansion of materials with a rise in temperature, as did Drebbel's alcohol-filled vessel. One such device, called the bimetallic strip, is made of two strips of laminated metal. The two metals have different coefficients of thermal expansion—that is, they expand by different amounts when heated. Brass, for example,

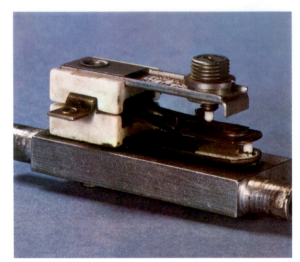

◀ One type of central heating thermostat uses a bimetallic, or two-metal, strip that bends with changes in temperature.

◀ A car's thermostat restricts water flow until the engine is hot, when a wax seal is opened under pressure from the water.

expands by one fifty-thousandth of its length for each degree Celsius that it is heated through. Copper expands by about 90 percent of this amount. Hence, the two components of a bimetallic strip expand by different amounts when heated, and the strip is forced to bend toward the side that expands less. This bending can be used to operate a valve or a damper, or it can be used in a make-and-break electric circuit. When the strip is touching an electric contact, the circuit is closed and current flows; when there is no contact, the circuit is broken.

A bimetallic strip is used in the type of thermostat that regulates home central heating systems. The strip is in the form of a U, one end of which is fixed. The other end makes an electric circuit when the temperature has fallen to a preset level. The position of the contact that the strip touches is varied by twisting a dial; the closer the contact is to the strip, the sooner the circuit is made as the temperature falls. Establishing the circuit causes the water-circulating pump to start.

◀ A remote capillary sensor being attached to a home hot water heater. It controls the water temperature and prevents the system from overheating.

Alternatively, the bimetallic strip may be formed into a coil with the center connected to a temperature-adjustment lever and the outer end attached to a mercury switch. The mercury switch consists of a small amount of mercury (which is a conductor of electricity) contained in a glass tube closed at both ends. Three wires are fixed at different positions in the tube. One wire runs across the bottom of the tube and so is always in contact with the mercury; the other two wires are fixed at either end of the tube so that, as the mercury is tilted by the movement of the bimetallic strip, electrical contacts are formed or broken, and in this way, the heating system is automatically turned on and off.

Another kind of sensing element consists of a light metal vessel with corrugated walls filled with a liquid or a gas. An increase in temperature causes the contents to expand and the vessel to lengthen. Such a vessel can be connected through a fine tube to a bulb, which senses the relevant temperature. When the temperature of the bulb changes, the pressure of its contents changes, too. These pressure changes are communicated to the main vessel, which lengthens or shortens accordingly.

Automobile thermostats

Automobile cooling systems are designed to disperse the excess heat generated by the combustion of gasoline. When the engine is started from cold, however, it needs time to reach the operating temperature. Heat is lost through water flowing around the engine block and through a radiator. The thermostat's role is to stop the water coolant from flowing through the radiator when the engine is below its operating temperature.

The thermostat consists of a block of wax and a spring-loaded plunger, forming a valve. As the engine reaches the operating temperature, the wax melts and the water pressure pushes against the valve and opens it, allowing the coolant to

▶ Radiators can be fitted with thermostatic radiator valves in place of the usual manual type. They are more efficient because they regulate the temperature of each room.

flow through the radiator. When the engine is switched off, the spring closes the valve. As the engine and coolant drop in temperature, the wax solidifies until the engine needs cooling again.

Other devices

The other main class of temperature-sensing elements is electric. The resistance of a metal to the passage of an electric current increases when its temperature goes up. When a fixed voltage is applied across a piece of wire, the current that passes will decrease as the temperature rises. When this effect is used in a thermostat, convenient direct control of a process is provided.

Resistance-based thermostats are extremely accurate—when connected to electronic equipment, they can make minute adjustments to the temperature-regulating system. Resistance-based thermostats are used widely in a range of equipment, from residential heating systems to industrial plants.

▶ The thermostat prevents the coolant from flowing through the radiator when the engine is cold.

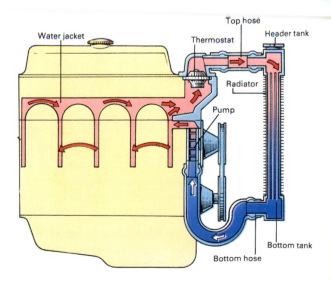

Top hose · Header tank · Thermostat · Radiator · Pump · Bottom tank · Bottom hose · Water jacket

SEE ALSO: Feedback • Heating and ventilation systems • Thermometry

Thunderstorm

Amid the constant shift of air currents in Earth's atmosphere, the conditions for a thunderstorm occur frequently. Computations show that observable lightning flashes happen at a rate of 360,000 times an hour somewhere on Earth's surface. The basic condition for a typical thunderstorm is the meeting of cold, dry air from the polar regions undercutting warm, moist air flowing poleward from the tropical regions. Along the cold fronts, there is a formation of massive convection clouds known as cumulonimbus.

Within these clouds, the hot air rises and expands, producing deep convection currents with warm, moist air bubbling upward and expanding at speeds that can approach 40 mph (60 km/h). As the air rises to colder regions, it cools until water droplets form, but they are too light to fall and are pushed even higher by the strength of the convection currents that have been generated by the movement of air. The topmost layers of cloud will typically be about 6 miles (9 km) above Earth's surface, and when the liquid droplets reach this height, they turn to ice. If the updraft is strong enough, these ice droplets will be too light to drop to the ground through the turbulence, and they will begin to grow rapidly. The convection current that keeps these supercooled droplets aloft is uneven, so they will be swept up and down by the gust. The ice will be brought into frequent collision with water droplets in the lower regions of the thundercloud. Through these collisions, the ice will gain in size until it is heavy enough to fall through the upward air current. Paradoxically, the stronger the convection current produced by warm air, the larger the ice droplets will grow and the more likely they will be to fall on Earth's surface as hailstones.

Not all thunderstorms produce hail, but even when they produce rain, the great strength in the upward air current produced by convection can keep large amounts of condensed water aloft. Consequently, the rainfall that does occur will be heavy, although it will not last long. Normally a large thunderstorm might produce rainwater at a rate of 2 in. (5 cm) an hour, and record rates run as high as 15 in. (40 cm) an hour. So the actual precipitation out of a thundercloud is characteristically violent, and it may be gusted by strong winds generated by the air currents dragged down through the cloud by the falling rain or hail.

The origin of lightning

Actual rates of precipitation are not the most significant feature of thunderstorms. They are also frequently described as electric storms, because of the flashes of lightning, which are accompanied at intervals by peals of thunder. The electrical nature of lightning was long suspected, but it was first proved in 1752 by Benjamin Franklin, an American statesman and scientist, in his cele-

▲ A thunderstorm moves over a city and heavy rainfall starts. A large thunderstorm might tip rain down at a rate of 2 in. (5 cm) an hour, but the rain produced by thunderstorms usually lasts only for a short period.

brated experiment using a kite in a thunderstorm to attract the electric charge.

Lightning develops when there is a special combination of low temperatures, below −4°F (−20°C), and clouds with large concentrations of water and ice. These conditions commonly occur in cumulonimbus clouds that extend to an altitude of at least 4 miles (6 km) but may also arise in other types of thick, unstable cloud.

For lightning to occur, the electric charge must overcome the resistance of air, which is not generally a good conductor of electricity. An immense charge is required to pass a spark through even a few yards of air, yet lightning flashes have been photographed that measure 5 miles (8 km) in length. The presence of water droplets lowers the resistance so that a potential difference of about 10^8 volts will cause a flash. Each flash involves the discharge of several thousand amperes of current and produces temperatures of around 36,000°F (20,000°C), which is three times as hot as the surface of the Sun.

This massive electric charge is generated by the activity within the thundercloud. The way in which this phenomenon happens is still not entirely understood, but the most likely explanation is that convection currents cause cloud droplets to be swept up and down in such a way that they collide against each other. These collisions cause each drop to acquire a small electric charge. By electromagnetic induction, a cloud droplet (an electric conductor) has a voltage produced in it, because it moves in relation to the steady magnetic field. This charge will not be uniform in each droplet, so as they bounce off each other, the large drops will become negatively charged and accumulate at the bottom of the cloud, whereas the smaller, lighter drops become positively charged and are swept by the convection currents to the top of the cloud. In this way, a separation of charges occurs, providing the potential for the discharge of a spark. There are millions of drops within each cloud, which may be carrying as much as 250,000 tons (225,000 tonnes) of rainwater, so there are frequent collisions between them. Each collision adds a fraction to the total charge, which builds up rapidly to a vast voltage.

Positive charges are attracted to the ground area directly below the lower part of the cloud, which is strongly negatively charged. The only thing preventing a discharge of electricity from the cloud in the form of a flash is the resistance of the air to electric conduction. As soon as the negative charge becomes strong enough or the distance between the cloud and a positive charge lessens (as happens where a tall tree or building stands in the cloud's path) the flash between the two points will follow. Even a few yards distance can make a great difference in the exchange, and it is surprising, at first sight, that the lightning chooses a forked, jagged, and indirect path rather than a straight line. In fact, the indirect path is the result of uneven resistance to conduction in the air. Air itself is a good insulator, but water is not, so where there are more water droplets, there will be a patch of less resistance. In some lightning flashes, positive charge may be carried from the cloud to Earth. These flashes tend to occur toward the end of a thunderstorm and are proportionately more common in winter than in the much drier summer.

Cloud ionization

Meteorologists have studied lightning flashes, or discharges, by photography and by measuring changes in the electric field during the lightning flash. Lightning flashes are not single occurrences. They consist of several successive strokes that follow the discharge channel set up by the first stroke and give lightning its characteristic flicker.

A discharge consists of a leader stroke, which may be either continuous, building steadily downward from the cloud base at 9 miles per sec. (15 km/s), or a rapid, flickering stroke, progressing toward the ground in steps of about 330 ft. (100 m), over periods of about 2 microseconds, resting for about 50 microseconds between each step.

The second part of the discharge is the return stroke. This stroke is continuous and runs from ground to cloud. This return stroke follows the path of the first exactly, because the passage of the first has ionized the surrounding air so that its resistance to the conduction of electricity is low-

▼ By leaving the shutter of a camera open for several minutes, photographers capture the many flashes of lightning trying to neutralize the difference in charge between the ground and a cloud. Measurements made from balloons and by high-speed photography have furthered scientific understanding of lightning formation.

cloud lightning), which are in fact the most common form of lightning; and those that flash from cloud to cloud (intercloud lightning). When an electric charge first builds up within a cloud, the positive charge is confined to the top, and the negative charge is separated at the bottom. The wind that blows the storm cloud along may change the shape of the cloud and alter the distribution of charges within it. In this way, a large charge can be built up on one side of the cloud so that the spark of lightning flashes from that side to the other within the cloud.

Intra- and intercloud lightning are both seen as nonlocalized flashes that illuminate the whole sky, whereas forked lightning appears as a jagged spark. In fact, these forms of lightning are the same. Where an observer sees the lightning flash directly, it appears as forked lightning, but when it occurs within a cloud or is obscured by cloud, the light from the flash is dispersed widely.

ered. Ionization occurs when the heat and energy of the lightning changes the atomic structure of the air, giving the atoms of air an electric charge. The return stroke normally lasts about 40 microseconds and is intensely luminous. It moves at between 12,000 and 93,000 miles per sec. (20,000–150,000 km/s) with a maximum current of approximately 20,000 amps.

The final phase follows about 0.1 second later. The dart leader usually but not always descends along the same path, followed by a second return stroke. This process may repeat several times, discharging different areas of charge in the cloud.

Types of lightning

There are three main types of lightning: flashes that occur between the cumulonimbus cloud and the ground; those that travel within clouds (intra-

▲ This is the first color image of a sprite and was taken in 1994 by a team of researchers from the University of Alaska. Red sprites extend upward from the top of storm clouds to the ionosphere and are associated with the most powerful of cloud-to-Earth lightning strikes.

Sprites, jets, and ELVES

In the early 1990s, videotapes taken by the space shuttle and photographs taken from aircraft were used to verify certain atmospheric phenomena in Earth's upper atmosphere that had been reported by pilots and ground-based observers but had not been studied. These electric phenomena, known as sprites, are produced from the top of thunderstorm clouds at the same time that the cloud produces a bolt of lightning that strikes Earth. Sprites are usually red in color and occur as a luminous region that may stretch upward as far as 58 miles (95 km) above the top of the cloud. It is thought that sprites may be caused by the glowing of electrons and ions in response to a strong electrostatic field above the cloud that is in turn produced by a particularly powerful bolt of lightning. Additional phenomena discovered during the

ATMOSPHERIC CHARGE

In a thunderstorm, the negative charge at the base of a cloud induces a positive charge on the ground below. A large voltage builds up until a weak leader stroke flashes down, seeking the path of least electric resistance. A more powerful return stroke then follows, and the cloud once more sends down a leader that usually but not always follows the original path. This process of leaders and return strokes continues until the difference in charge has been neutralized.

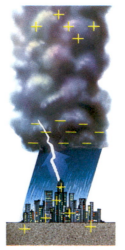
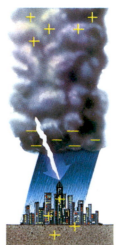

early 1990s include blue jets, which rise above the top of the cloud as cones, flaring out as they reach their maximum height, and ELVES (emissions of light and very-low-frequency perturbations from electromagnetic-pulse sources), which occur above thunderstorms in the lower ionosphere as a bright region perhaps several hundred miles across and which are produced at the same time as a downward lightning stroke. Neither of these phenomena is well understood.

Other electrical phenomena

There are three other distinct kinds of lightning: ball lightning, St Elmo's fire (or corposants), and flachenblitz (rocket lightning). Although the existence of ball lightning has been disputed, it is generally accepted that it consists of a small, roughly spherical mass of glowing air, between 4 and 8 in. (10–20 cm) in diameter. The ball, which may be yellow, orange, or red in color, appears

◀ Thunderstorms occur frequently over the windward slopes of mountain ranges, because they cause warm air to rise rapidly and condense, initiating convection currents.

near ground level and lasts for only a few seconds. Its source and relationship to conventional lightning are uncertain.

St Elmo's fire is a continuous glowing electric discharge under the influence of intense electric fields. It emanates from objects near Earth's surface, such as ships' rigging, weather vanes, lightning conductors, and even hair and is found in snow blowing at ground level or in thunderstorms. Flachenblitz is a rare form of conventional lightning. The flash shoots upward from a cloud top and ends in clear air.

Thunder

Thunder is the sound shock wave produced when the air expands violently as it is heated by the electric discharge. This rapid heating causes the surrounding air to increase in pressure from between 10 to 100 atmospheres. The change causes the air to expand rapidly as shock waves that decay over short distances to sound waves, and it is these sound waves that produce the familiar sounds, such as rumbles and claps, associated with electric storms. Only around 1 percent of the energy in the shock wave becomes an acoustic wave; the rest heats the air of the lightning channel. The pitch of the thunder clap is determined by the energy of the lightning stroke and the ambient air pressure in the region of the lightning stroke. Powerful lightning stokes or low air pressure result in lower-pitched thunder. An interval between the lightning flash and the sound occurs because light and sound travel at different speeds. We see the flash almost instantly, but the sound takes 5 seconds to cover each mile between the storm and the observer. This knowledge can be used to estimate the distance of a lightning strike from an observer.

FACT FILE

- Bogor, in Indonesia, is thought to be the most thundery place in the world. Between 1916 and 1919, an average of 322 thunderstorms per annum were recorded. At least 25 times a year Bogor experiences storms in which lightning strikes within a small area at least once every 30 seconds for half an hour at a stretch.

- Detection devices, such as the Stormscope WX-900, are carried on board aircraft to build up instant maps of electric storms. As thunderstorms intensify, convective wind shear between warm and cold air masses is increased. The Stormscope records and analyzes the electric "fingerprints" of all storms within a range of up to 100 nautical miles.

- Certain Australian eucalyptus trees, known as Darwin Woolly Butts, sometimes explode violently when struck by lightning. The explosions are caused by termite tunnels within the trunk, which expand at enormous speed in the heat of the lightning.

- Car manufacturers use artificial lightning displays to demonstrate the safety of cars when struck. The car acts as a Faraday box, channeling the electricity past the occupants through the wheels to the ground.

Thyristor

A thyristor is a type of diode, a device that will conduct an electric current in one direction but not in the other. The thyristor is named after an electron-tube device called a gas thyratron, whose electrical characteristics are like a thyristor's. A thyristor is usually referred to as a silicon controlled rectifier (SCR) and is made from four layers of semiconductors. A semiconductor is a crystalline solid that, as its name implies, has a lower resistivity than an insulator but a higher resistivity than a conductor. A thyristor is made of four layers of two types of semiconductors, *n*-type (electron rich) and *p*-type (electron deficient), arranged as a *p-n-p-n* sandwich. The device has three terminals: the outer *p*-type layer of the sandwich is the anode terminal, the outer *n*-type layer is the cathode, and the inner *p*-type layer forms the gate terminal.

Operation

If a positive voltage is applied to the cathode and a negative voltage to the anode, then the thyristor is said to be reverse biased. In this state, it will not conduct an electric current. It behaves very much as a reverse-biased diode. If the applied voltages are reversed so that the anode is made positive

▲ The main component of this model railroad's speed-control unit is a thyristor, which is incorporated in a single unit with the step-down transformer and the rectifier.

with respect to the cathode, then the thyristor is forward biased. In this state, however, it will initially oppose an electric current—unlike the diode. In order to make a thyristor conduct, a small voltage, positive with respect to the cathode, has to be applied to the gate so that a small current will flow into the gate. This current turns the thyristor to the on condition, and it will then conduct current in the same way as a forward-biased diode.

▶ Part of a power-controlling unit equipped with thyristors and diodes; the radiating fins, called heat sinks, dissipate the heat.

Once the thyristor is on, the gate voltage may be removed without stopping current from anode to cathode. Thyristors can turn on very quickly, often in less than one microsecond (one-millionth of a second), and consequently, only a very brief voltage pulse (or trigger pulse) needs to be applied to the gate to convert the device from the off condition to the on condition.

A thyristor can be turned off in one of two ways: either by reverse biasing or by reducing the current through it to a very low value, typically ten milliamps. The limiting value of this current is called the holding current. If at any time the current through the thyristor is reduced below the holding current, then the device will turn off. Whatever method is used to turn the thyristor off, it will be necessary to apply the gate voltage again to bring it into operation once more.

It is also possible to make thyristors that are bidirectional so that the direction of current can be changed in either direction by applying a small current between the gate and one of the main terminals. Bidirectional thyristors, or triacs, are used in AC circuits for applications such as temperature controllers and dimmer switches.

Uses

A thyristor can be designed to carry very large currents between its anode and cathode. By comparison, the current required to turn the device on is very small, so a thyristor may be used as a solid-state switch in which a very large current is controlled by a very small one. This characteristic, coupled with the fact that the thyristor automatically switches off when it is reverse biased, makes it an ideal power controller for use with alternating current (AC), and today light-dimmer controls and speed regulators on electric appliances usually employ thyristors. With an AC electricity supply (the home power supply is an example), the current flows first in one direction and then in the other. This sequence occurs many times per second (in the United States the frequency is 60 Hz, or 60 cycles a second). If a thyristor is interposed between the AC supply and the load (for example, an electric motor or light), then it is possible to regulate the amount of power delivered to the load by controlling the point during each cycle at which the thyristor is turned on.

For each cycle of alternating current, the thyristor is first reverse biased and then forward biased. While it is reverse biased, no current, and hence no power, will flow to the load. While it is forward biased, the point at which the trigger pulse is applied to the gate may be varied, thus varying the length of time that the thyristor conducts. The earlier the trigger pulse is applied during the forward-biased period of the cycle, the larger will be the amount of power delivered to the load. The result is that a light can be made brighter or dimmer or a motor can be made to run faster or slower.

Thyristors have several advantages over conventional mechanical switches; they are very fast, require no maintenance, are relatively cheap, and if used correctly, have a virtually unlimited life. They are widely used in industry as power controllers (for example, in electric locomotives), and they can also be found in TVs, washing machines, and electronic automobile ignition systems. They are used a great deal in applications where it is necessary to switch or redirect high currents because they completely eliminate the arcing, which occurs between the contacts of a mechanical switch.

▲ Small thyristors for mounting on an electronic circuit board.

◄ A controlling valve in the electricity supply system in the Democratic Republic of Congo, Africa.

SEE ALSO:	Conduction, electrical • Diode • Electricity • Electric motor • Semiconductor • Voltage regulator

Ticket Machine

A ticket machine is a device that issues or checks the validity of tickets for the use of facilities such as public transportation, entertainments events, and parking lots, for example. They help speed access to such facilities while keeping running costs low and helping to prevent fraudulent use.

Issuing mechanism

Ticket-issuing machines came into use in the early 20th century, when they became standard features of the ticket offices of establishments such as railroad stations. Early machines were operated by cashiers who would take cash, give change, and select the appropriate value of ticket to return to the customer. Some machines of this type are still in use, particularly in movie theaters, but an increasing number of ticket machines are automated to take ticket requests and cash or credit card payments directly from customers. This type of machine is frequently used in conjunction with automatic barriers operated by machines that check ticket validity.

Tickets fall into three categories: preprinted, partially preprinted, and custom printed at the time of issue. In addition to the value and period of validity of the ticket, printed details often include information about the date, place, and time of issue. The same information may also be carried on the ticket in machine-readable form, such as a bar code or magnetic strip.

Preprinted. Fully preprinted tickets are produced as reels with feed holes punched in their margins and sometimes with perforations separating adjacent tickets. The ticket-issuing machine in this case is purely a dispenser—it has no printing function. Tickets issue through a slot under the action of feed wheels whose peripheries have pins that engage with the punched holes in the tickets. A ratchet mechanism advances the feed wheel through an arc that corresponds to the length of one ticket with each action and also prevents the feed wheel from slipping back. In some machines, a guillotine knife snaps forward to sever issued tickets; in others, the ticket is torn off at the perforation.

Partially preprinted. Partially preprinted tickets are widely used by transportation companies. The preprinted blanks carry general information, such as the company details and legal conditions. Finely detailed graphics and holograms are sometimes included as measures against counterfeiting.

A customer or cashier initiates the issuing process by selecting the ticket details on a keypad or using a touch screen. Details specific to each

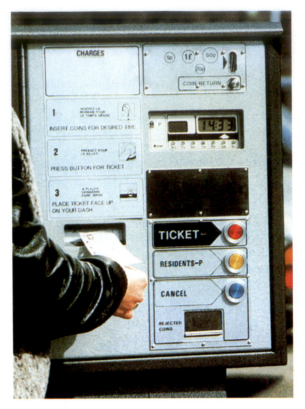

ticket purchase—time, location, destination, and so on—are printed onto the blanks. The obvious advantage in this approach is that one set of blanks serves for various types of transactions.

Early printing mechanisms used engraved type and sequential-number punches that typed through inked ribbons. Modern ticket printers use techniques developed for fax and computer printing, such as dot-matrix, ink-jet, and laser printing. These techniques allow much more flexibility in the details that can be printed, as well as smoother, faster operation. In a typical printer of this type, a preprinted blank card the approximate size of a credit card is fed from a stack into a frame for printing. Before or after printing, the ticket might pass across a magnetic head that records the ticketing information in a magnetic strip on the back of the card for machine reading.

Cash-operated machines require extra equipment to examine the coins and notes for value and validity. If the machine gives change, the coins are stored in hoppers or storage tubes separated by value and released as necessary. The coins taken in payment are stored within the machine in a security vault, which automatically locks to prevent theft when it is removed from the machine. Machines that take credit or debit cards also have telephone links to the clearing agencies that authorize transactions on such cards. In all cases, ticket-issuing machines keep computerized records of the cash and credit card transactions they perform. Most also store information on the types of tickets issued, information that is useful in planning changes to the fares and schedules of transportation systems, for example.

Custom-printed. More basic tickets, such as those for single, short bus trips, for example, are produced by on-the-spot printers fitted at access points or carried on shoulder straps by conductors. These devices print basic trip details onto a roll of plain paper that is cut after each issue.

Checking machines

Increasing use is being made of automatic equipment to check the validity of tickets, normally at the start or end of a journey. For this purpose, the information printed on the tickets also has to be present in a machine-readable form, generally as a bar code or in a magnetic stripe.

The simplest validation machines check that a prepaid ticket is current and of the correct value for the journey concerned and then release a turnstile to allow the passenger to proceed. More elaborate designs, such as those in automatic parking lots, calculate the charges payable from the elapsed time, signaling the sum due to a cash machine, which accepts the appropriate payment before raising a barrier for the vehicle to proceed.

In some parking lots, customers take their tickets with them as a security measure (a vehicle cannot pass through the barrier without a ticket). Parking charges are paid off at the pedestrian entrance to the lot, sometimes with rebates gained through in-store promotions and recorded magnetically on the ticket. The ticket holder then has a time limit for leaving the lot before incurring a penalty. Provided the limit is not exceeded, inserting the ticket at the barrier releases the vehicle without delay.

Multitrip tickets

Many transportation systems offer multitrip and period tickets for better value than single trips as a means of stimulating usage. These types of tickets require slightly different administration than simple one-journey tickets.

Period tickets usually allow unlimited travel within a specific geographical limit and for a fixed period of time; other conditions often apply, such as use in off-peak hours. In this case, ticket-issuing machines print the appropriate ticket type and start date on legible and machine-readable forms. Ticket-checking machines at access or exit points then read the ticket to ensure that the ticket is valid for use at the given time and location and on the given date. These checks are often backed up by manual inspections during journeys.

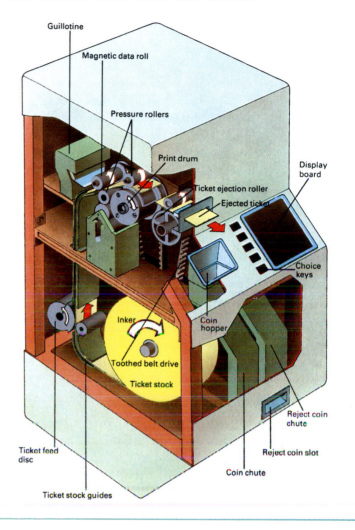

AUTOMATIC TICKET MACHINE

Automatic ticket-issuing machines are a feature of all major transportation interchanges. In the type illustrated below, customers press the key for the required ticket from a number of options. On payment, a card of preprinted ticket stock is cut from a roll and fed first through a magnetic roller, where it receives its machine-readable information. An offset roller then prints the details in ink before the ticket is issued to the customer.

Guillotine

Magnetic data roll

Pressure rollers

Print drum

Display board

Ticket ejection roller

Ejected ticket

Choice keys

Inker

Coin hopper

Toothed belt drive

Ticket stock

Reject coin chute

Reject coin slot

Ticket feed disc

Coin chute

Ticket stock guides

Multijourney tickets allow a fixed number of trips on a single ticket. The value of one trip must be canceled at the start of each journey, either by automatic barrier equipment or by hand-fed cancellation units on buses, for example.

In some systems, the ticket-printing machines have access slots to take such tickets and overprint them with the appropriate trip details. At the end of a trip, another machine calculates the fare due from the starting-point data recorded by the entry machine and deducts it from the ticket value to leave a new total for subsequent use.

SEE ALSO: AUTOMATIC TELLER MACHINE (ATM) • CASH REGISTER • COMPUTER • COMPUTER PRINTER • DIGITAL DISPLAY • GEAR • MASS TRANSIT AND SUBWAY • VENDING MACHINE

Tidal Power

The idea of extracting energy from the ceaseless motion of Earth's tides is not new—the basic principle was used to mill grains in Britain and France from the 12th century, when farmers would trap sea water in mill ponds to power their water mills as the tide dropped. In modern times, tides have been considered seriously as a renewable energy source for the last 50 years.

The global electricity market stands at $800 billion annually and is steadily increasing. To meet future demand without increasing the production of so-called greenhouse gases, which warm Earth's atmosphere, renewable energy sources such as tidal power will play an important part.

Tidal power works by taking advantage of the variation in sea level caused twice a day by the gravitational effect of the Moon and to a lesser extent the Sun on the world's oceans. Earth's rotation is also an important element in the creation of tides. The interactions involved are quite complex but can be explained by looking at the gravitational effects of the Moon and the Sun and the effect of centrifugal forces on the ocean.

As the Moon travels around Earth on its 28-day orbit, the oceans bulge out toward it owing to its gravitational pull. On the opposite side of Earth, the Moon's gravitational effect is partly shielded by the mass of Earth itself, so the oceans on that side of the planet are not constrained by the Moon's gravity but instead bulge outward owing to centrifugal force. This effect is known as the lunar tide. Centrifugal force is caused by Earth's spinning on its axis, which makes the oceans move outward just as the spinning motion of a washing machine causes water to be thrown to the edge of the drum.

The Sun also influences tides by exerting a smaller but significant gravitational pull on the oceans in exactly the same way—the oceans on the side facing the sun bulge slightly toward it, and those on the opposite side bulge away from it. This phenomenon is known as the solar tide.

The Sun and Moon change their relative positions in the skies throughout the year as a result of the motions of Earth and the Moon in their orbits. As their position relative to each other changes, their influence on the difference between low and high tide (the tidal range) is also affected. For example, when the Moon and the Sun are in the same plane as Earth—in other words, all the bodies are aligned in a straight line (during a full moon)—the tidal range is the combination of the lunar and solar tides. This phenomenon causes the high spring tides. On the

▼ The Rance barrage has produced energy from the tides since the early 1960s. When each of its turbines is in operation, the barrage delivers 24,000 kW of energy into France's power supply.

► Barrages are effectively dams that allow water to pass beneath them and generate electricity by turning the blades of a turbine. They are fitted with sluice gates that can be raised or lowered in combination with pumping in order to generate power at low tide. Turbines can operate in two directions to take advantage of the flood and ebb tides.

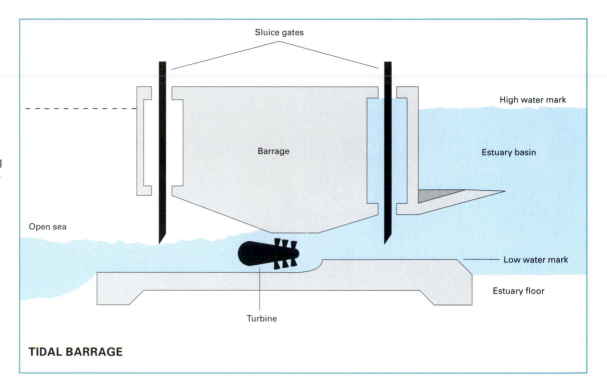

TIDAL BARRAGE

other hand, when the Moon and Sun are at right angles to each other (a half moon), their forces tend to cancel each other so the tidal differences are smaller, the result being the low, or neap, tides. Coasts experience two high tides and two low tides in a period of slightly over 24 hours.

Capturing the tide

Since the mid-20th century, engineers have been trying to find ways of developing tidal and wave power on an industrial scale. However, until recently, particularly in Europe, wave power and tidal power were both seen as uneconomic. Pilot projects showed that energy could be generated but that, even without considering the costs of generation, it was difficult to make equipment that could stand up to the harsh conditions of the marine environment.

Generating electricity from tides is similar in principle to hydroelectric generation, except that as the tide ebbs and flows, the water must generally be able to flow in both directions through the turbines that generate the electricity. Tidal turbines use the force of the flowing tidal waters to turn the blades of the turbine, and it is this motion that is turned into energy. Turbines are mainly used for currents that move at velocities of between 4 and 6 knots (4.5–7 mph, or 2–3 m/s), generating between 4 and 13 kW per square yard of water surface passing through. Although tides contain very large amounts of energy, it is practical to generate power only from sites with extremely high tidal ranges. The higher the tidal range, the greater the amount of energy that can be generated from it.

Tidal barrage

The simplest generating system for tidal plants is known as an ebb generating system. This involves a dam, or barrage, being constructed across an estuary. The barrage is fitted with sluice gates to enable the tidal basin to fill when the incoming high tides arrive and to exit through the turbine system on the outgoing ebb tide. Some systems also generate power from the incoming tide; these are less common than ebb generating systems because the incoming tide is less controllable.

The first commercially and technically feasible tidal power plant built on this principle was developed by French engineers. The Rance power plant was built in the Gulf of Saint Malo, Brittany, France, between 1961 and 1967. It consists of a dam that has reversible bulb turbines that can generate energy in both directions as the tide flows from the sea to the tidal basin during the flood tide and from the basin to the sea during the ebb tide.

The Rance plant has 24 power units, each capable of producing 10,000 kW of energy. Much of the power, around seven-eighths, is produced during the ebb tide, as the trapped waters behind the dam can be more easily controlled than the incoming tide from the ocean. A set of sluices fills the basin during flood tide and closes during high tide. The emptying of the basin does not begin until there is enough depth of fall between the basin and the ebb tide to operate the turbines.

The Soviet Union finished building a tidal power plant soon after Rance was completed, in 1969, on the White Sea. This plant generates around 1,000 kW. There is also a 40,000 kW pilot

plant in Russia on the Barents Sea, and in the intervening years a number of tidal power devices have been constructed.

In systems that use bulb turbines, water that flows around the turbines at all times makes them difficult to access for maintenance purposes. Rim turbines, such as those used at the Annapolis Royal barrage in Nova Scotia, lessen maintenance difficulties: the generator is mounted in the barrage at right angles to the turbine blades. Tubular turbines have been suggested for use in Britain's proposed Severn tidal project. In this configuration, the turbine blades are connected to a long shaft at an angle that allows the generator to be sited on top of the barrage. It has been estimated that if the Severn project went ahead, it could provide up to 10 percent of the UK's power needs (12 GW).

The main disadvantages of tidal barrages are that they affect the tides within and outside the enclosed basin—a potentially life-threatening change for the creatures that live in the intertidal zone—and that they increase siltation within the basin. They also create an impassable barrier for both fish and shipping.

Tidal fence

A different type of tidal power-generating device, the tidal fence, does not have the disadvantages of a barrage. The tidal fence is a structure that acts not unlike a giant turnstile. Unlike barrage power generators, tidal fences do not need to be constructed in confined basins—they can sit in unconfined channels, such as the gap between two islands. The important feature in terms of generating power is that they are constructed across the width of the channel. With the entire force of the tide forced through the device, the amount of power that can be generated is maxi-

▲ The Rance barrage in operation. The barrage has 24 turbines, all or some of which can be used depending on how much power is needed and the state of the tide.

▼ Tidal fences resemble turnstiles that can reverse direction with the movement of the tide. Unlike barrages, they can be placed anywhere that is affected by the tide, such as a channel between an island and the coast.

mized. There are advanced plans for a tidal fence across the Dalupiri Passage between the islands of Dalupiri and Samar in the Philippines.

Circular dam

Another tidal power device is under development in the United States—it takes the form of a circular dam, built on the seabed near to the shore. The turbines are sited in a generating house within the impounding structure, with power transmitted to the shore via connecting cables. Water can be pumped out of the dam at low tide if extra energy is needed or pumped in through the turbines, a process effectively increasing the tidal range and thus the energy generated. Preliminary projects for the circular dam have been identified in Africa, Mexico, England, and Chile, and there are feasibility studies for projects in India and Alaska. Alaska is attractive because of the significant tidal ranges along its southern coast.

One of the other sites that is being actively considered is the tidal record holder—the Bay of Fundy in Canada. The bay is an inlet of the Atlantic Ocean between the Canadian provinces of New Brunswick (north and west) and Nova Scotia (south and east). It extends 94 miles (151 km) inland, is 32 miles (52 km) wide at the entrance, and is noted for its fast-running tides, which may produce rises as great as 70 ft. (21 m), the highest in the world.

Tidal power has the potential to generate significant amounts of energy, but the environmental consequences of building barrage-type structures are complex and the costs of construction are high. However, as the cost of fossil fuels continues to rise, such systems may become increasingly popular.

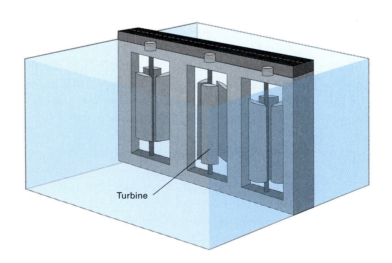

Turbine

SEE ALSO: ELECTRICITY • ENERGY RESOURCES • HYDROELECTRIC POWER • POWER SUPPLY • TIDE • TURBINE • WATER • WAVE POWER

Tide

◀ The ancient monks of Mont St. Michel off the coast of Brittany in France took advantage of the island's strategic position when building their monastery. It can be reached only twice a day, when the tide is at its lowest point. When it is on the turn, the tide races back in extremely quickly to cover the causeway and can outrun a galloping horse.

The twice-daily rise and fall of the seas has always been very important to people dwelling by the coast, especially to seafarers. The traditional connection between tides and the position of the Moon was interpreted astrologically, in learned circles as well as in country folklore, until Sir Isaac Newton showed that by attributing the property of gravitation to all bodies, the Moon would naturally have the power to attract the water of the seas. Although tides are an inconvenience to shipping, they have also been used as an energy source, first for mills and more recently for the generation of electricity.

Equilibrium tide

The tide rises because of the falling off of the gravitational attraction of the Moon from one side of Earth to the other. Both Earth and the Moon orbit around their mutual center of gravity, which actually lies inside Earth, so if Earth is regarded as stationary, there appears to be a fictitious centrifugal force, which balances the gravitational attraction at the center of Earth. On the side nearer the Moon, however, the gravitational force of the Moon is stronger, and anything on Earth's surface feels a slight upward force.

On the farthest side, the Moon's gravitational force is less than the centrifugal force about the common center, and the resulting force is away from the Moon, that is, upward with regard to the surface of Earth. The water on an ocean-covered Earth would therefore be at a higher level at the point immediately below the Moon and at the diametrically opposite point, and as Earth rotates, the water level would rise and fall twice a day. Because of the orbital motion of the Moon, the position of the tidal bulges rotates with a period of 29½ days so that the interval between successive high tides is not exactly 12 hours, but 12 hours and 25 minutes. However, the tidal force due to the Moon at the surface of the sea is only one ten-millionth of Earth's gravity, and these equilibrium tides would have a range between low and high water of only about 20 in. (50 cm).

Actual tides

Large tidal ranges are due to the phenomenon of resonance. Any body of water has a natural period of oscillation—the time it takes a disturbance to travel from one end to the other. This phenomenon can be seen by tilting a pan containing water—it takes a certain time for the water to pile up at one end. If the pan is rocked at intervals equal to this time, the water level will oscillate violently at both ends, but if the frequency of rocking is significantly different, the variation in water level will be small. Exactly the same effect occurs in an enclosed sea, where the tilting force is the tidal effect of the Moon, with a period of 12 hours and 25 minutes.

A sea that is connected to the ocean is usually dominated by the tides from the latter. The North Atlantic tides, for example, flow around the north of Scotland into the North Sea and up the English Channel, producing a tidal flow in the opposite direction from the equilibrium tidal flow. The Coriolis force, resulting from Earth's rotation, also affects the flow of water, causing the tide to veer to the right (in the Northern Hemisphere).

Resonance also occurs in inlets and estuaries, where the periodic force of the ocean tides can build up to give tides as much as 70 ft. (20 m) in the Bay of Fundy, Nova Scotia. Even an ordinary tide in an estuary can push water up the river that flows into it, forming a wall of water several feet high. These bores occur on the rivers Severn and Trent in Britain, the Seine in France, and the Amazon in South America, among others. There are usually local names for this impressive phenomenon, such as the aegir, mascaret, and pororoca. The largest tidal bore is that on the Tsien-Tang-Kiang River, in China, which can be 26 ft. (8 m) high and occurs in an estuary that is several miles wide.

The Sun also produces a tidal force on the seas, but because it is less than half the force due

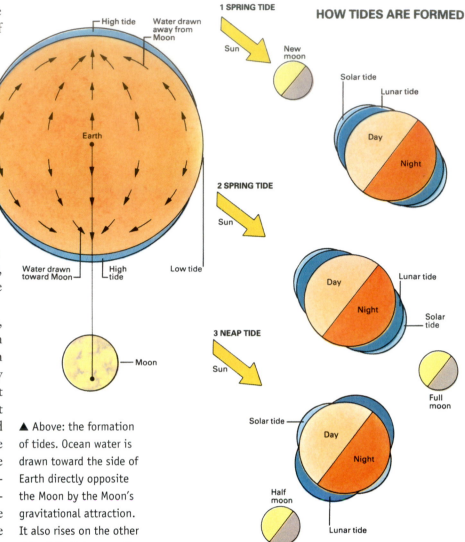

▲ Above: the formation of tides. Ocean water is drawn toward the side of Earth directly opposite the Moon by the Moon's gravitational attraction. It also rises on the other side of Earth because the gravitational attraction there is less than that acting on the solid sphere of Earth.

Above right: A similar but weaker effect is produced by the Sun. When the Sun and the Moon act in the same direction (at a new moon), they give the higher and lower than usual spring tides. At neap tides, the tidal range is minimized because the solar and lunar tides oppose each other.

to the Moon, its principal effect is to reinforce the lunar tides when Sun and Moon are in line (spring tides) and to reduce the tidal range when they are 90 degrees apart (neap tides). There are two spring tides and two neap tides each lunar month.

Planetary tides

The gravitational pull of the Sun and Moon not only induce tides in the oceans but also in Earth's solid interior. So-called Earth tides produce a bulge in the surface as the result of friction and the slightly greater rotation velocity of Earth relative to the Moon. This effect causes the bulge to be carried slightly forward of Earth's rotation and delays the time of the oceanic high tides. Gravitational tides are observed in other planets and moons, particularly Io, whose active volcanism arises from the strong pull of nearby Jupiter.

FACT FILE

■ *The tidal bore on the Bay of Fundy, between New Brunswick and Nova Scotia, Canada, is 3 ft. (1 m) high and more than 2,500 ft. (760 m) wide. Subsidiary bays within the Bay of Fundy have a tidal range during spring tides of up to 50 ft. (15 m).*

■ *Sea tides have their equivalent in the air, which are known as lunar winds. These movements are extremely delicate, at 0.05 mph (0.08 km/h), and can be detected only by careful study of weather statistics. High and low air tides occur twice a day, as do sea and ocean tides, with high air tides equivalent to oceanic spring tides.*

SEE ALSO: ASTROPHYSICS • EARTH • GEOPHYSICS • GRAVITY • OCEANOGRAPHY • TIDAL POWER • TSUNAMI • WAVE POWER

Time

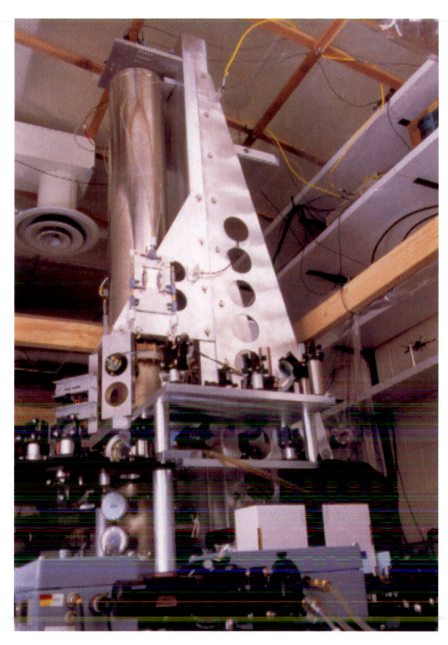

▲ The cesium fountain clock at the National Institute of Standards and Technology (NIST) is accurate to 1 second in nearly 20 million years.

The idea of time is difficult to describe in scientific and philosophical terms. In science, since the acceptance of the theory of relativity, the rate at which time passes has been seen as analogous to the speed a distance is traveled, so time has been thought of as a fourth dimension—in addition to the three spatial dimensions of length, breadth, and height.

The feeling of time passing is an intuitive one, but the measurement of an interval of time requires a regularly repeating process against which it can be compared. On Earth, the most important recurrent phenomenon is the day, the alternation of light and dark. Many species have a built-in biological clock that controls the animal's biochemistry roughly in time with day and night.

Calendar

The year is another important time interval, and because, historically, people have required an interval of intermediate length, the time between successive new moons has also been used for the division of time. Here problems arise in establishing a calendar, because none of the three intervals is an exact multiple of any other. For example, the time taken for Earth to rotate on its axis with respect to the Sun is called a day, but the number of days in a year, which is the time Earth takes to orbit the Sun, is not an exact number.

There are approximately 365¼ days in a year, 29½ days in a lunar month (the interval between new moons), and 12⅓ lunar months in a year. The calendar at present in use in the Western world ignores the lunar month and is divided into 12 months of 30 or 31 days. The month of February normally has only 28 days, with an extra one added every four years (the leap year), to make the average length of the year 365¼ days. This calendar is based on that established by Julius Caesar in 46 B.C.E., which left a difference of 11 minutes between the calendar year and the real year. By 1582 C.E., this discrepancy had accumulated to ten days, and Pope Gregory XIII made a small correction to the Julian calendar by requiring that, thereafter, in the case of centennial years, only those divisible by 400 should be leap years. Hence, the year 1900, which would have been a leap year in the Julian calendar, was not a leap year. The Gregorian calendar is only inaccurate by 26 seconds per year and will remain accurate for thousands of years. Although it was adopted by Britain and its American colonies in 1752, Russia did not adopt it until 1918 and has since developed a variant arrangement for the computation of leap years.

Other calendars have been, and still are, in use. The Jewish calendar, for example, is based on the lunar month and requires some years of 12 months and some of 13. This extra month is 30 days long and occurs on the 3rd, 8th, 11th, 14th, 17th, and 19th years of a 19-year cycle.

Clocks

The earliest clocks for measuring time during the day were sundials, on which a stick or gnomon threw a shadow on a scale to mark the hour. Until the 13th century, daylight was divided into a fixed number of hours, the length of which varied with the time of year. The introduction of mechanical clocks, beginning with the clepsydra, or water clock, about 1500 B.C.E., led to the division of the

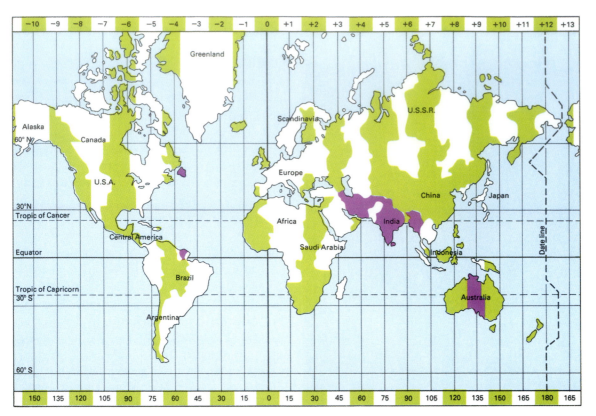

day into 24 equal hours. The first weight-driven clocks were made toward the end of the 13th century, but they were not accurate, because their time-keeping ability depended on the friction acting on a horizontal swinging beam and it was impossible to keep this swing constant. The pendulum clock, invented by Christiaan Huygens in 1656, was based on Galileo's observation that the period of swing of a pendulum is constant.

The most accurate clocks available, however, are not mechanical but utilize the vibrations of atoms or of the electrons in atoms. Quartz clocks, introduced in 1929, were immediately ten times more accurate than the best pendulum clocks and have subsequently been improved, and cesium atomic clocks, accurate to better than a millionth of a second per day, are now being produced even in a portable form. The standard unit of time, the second, is now based on the average time as shown by several cesium clocks around the world, rather than on the length of the day. From a study of the places at which eclipses were observed in early historic times, the day is known to be increasing at a rate of a thousandth of a second per century.

Although time is now actually measured by atomic clocks, it is important for practical reasons that it does not differ greatly from the time defined by the rotation of Earth, which is measured by observations of stars at several observatories around the world and is known as Universal time (UT). This measurement superseded the earlier Greenwich mean time, GMT. It subsequently corrected for the fact that Earth's axis of rotation moves slightly and for a variation during the year due to the movement of air masses with the seasons. This time is known as UT_2, and whenever it becomes more than half a second different from atomic time, an exact second is added to atomic time to bring them into line. Atomic time incorporating these leap seconds is called Universal coordinated time (UCT) and is the basis for all accurate timekeeping. Clocks in different parts of the world can be synchronized with it to an accuracy of a millionth of a second by satellite. The second is currently defined in the International System of Units as the duration of 9,192,631,770 periods of the radiation corresponding to the transition between the two hyperfine levels of the ground state of the cesium 133 atom.

Time in physics

From the physicist's viewpoint, most processes can occur identically whether time is flowing in the direction we experience or in reverse. One of the few properties that does determine an arrow of time in physics is entropy (a measure of the disorder of a system), because the second law of thermodynamics states that the entropy of an isolated system never decreases.

The Special Theory of Relativity, developed mainly by the German-born U.S. physicist Albert Einstein between 1905 and 1915, shows that there is no absolute time that is the same for all

CESIUM FOUNTAIN CLOCK

Laser

Cesium
atoms

Microwave
cavity

Laser

Detector

Laser

Laser

Laser

Laser

Laser

Laser

**In this atomic clock, a gas of cesium atoms
enters a vacuum chamber, where it is slowed by
the action of six lasers, causing the temperature
of the atoms to drop near to zero. The atoms
form into a spherical cloud at the intersection
of the six lasers. Two of the lasers then move the
cloud upward until they pass though a microwave-
filled cavity. The lasers are then switched off,
allowing the cloud to pass back down through the
cavity under the force of gravity. The microwaves
have the effect of partially altering the cesium
atoms' atomic states. The atoms then pass
through another laser, causing those that were
altered by the microwaves to emit light, which
is then measured by a detector. This process is
repeated until a maximum fluorescence is
reached, which corresponds to the resonance
frequency of cesium. The second is then defined
using this resonance frequency.**

observers, as assumed by the English physicist
Isaac Newton and his successors. A clock in motion
seems to go more slowly than one at rest relative
to any observer (time dilation). In 1971, cesium
clocks were carried around the world in opposite
directions by supersonic aircraft and then com-

pared with clocks that had remained on the Earth.
The difference between the clocks was about the
same as that predicted by Einstein's theory. In the
extended version of Einstein's theory, the general
theory of relativity, Einstein linked his theory of
space-time and motion with gravity. One conclusion of this theory is that, just as motion slows
time, so does gravity. As the strength of the gravitational field builds up, the time warp climbs with it.
In 1963, the idea was tested directly by comparing
atomic clocks at the top and bottom of a tower.
The effect was confirmed: time is slowed at ground
level compared with an elevated location.

Black holes and time

The dilation of time by gravity is minute in the
case of Earth and even the Sun, but astronomical
objects exist where gravity is so intense that time
actually stops. They are the black holes, which
form when a star implodes under its own gravity,
forming an extremely dense point known as a sin-
gularity, from which nothing, not even radiation,
can escape. One of the stranger predictions that
cosmologists make about black holes is that, for
an observer watching a body falling into a black
hole, the body seems to take an infinite time to
reach a certain distance from the center, known as
the Schwarzschild radius—around 6 miles (10
km) for a black hole formed from a typical massive star. For the object, however, the fall to zero
radius seems to take a very short time indeed, perhaps 10 to 100 microseconds. To fall into a black
hole is to travel beyond the end of time, because
in the brief duration that it would take to travel
down, all of eternity will have elapsed in the
Universe outside.

▶ A jet of electrons
produced by a black hole
at the center of galaxy
M87. In black holes,
gravity is so intense that
time stops. To an external
observer, it seems to take
an infinite amount of time
for an object to fall into
the center of the black
hole. Paradoxically, for the
object, it seems to take a
very short time, perhaps
10 to 100 microseconds,
to reach the center.

**SEE
ALSO:** Astronomy • Black hole • Clock • Navigation •
Relativity • Sundial

Timing Device

Timing devices of varying complexity and accuracy are widely used both in the home and in industry. They provide control of an event or a series of events on a time basis and have a wide range of applications, such as in controlling central heating systems, in industrial processes, in ovens, and in refrigerator defrosting cycles. In general, timing devices fall into three broad categories according to their use: period timers, time switches, and event timers.

Period timers

The most common type of timing device is undoubtedly the period timer, which gives fixed or adjustable timing periods for applications such as appliance control, process timing, and cooking control. The timing sequence is started either manually or automatically on receiving a signal, usually electric, from some other equipment. Some models incorporate automatic resetting for continuous recycling applications—others have to be reset by hand. Many of these simple timers are merely refinements of mechanical clockwork movements with spring-driven escapement mechanisms.

Electric timers are usually driven by a battery and an escapement mechanism or by a small synchronous electric motor powered from the alternating current (AC) local electricity supply. These devices are able to control virtually any process or appliance, and they are incorporated in a wide range of home and industrial equipment ranging from photocopiers and washing machines to ovens and automatic exposure devices in cameras.

Electronic digital period timers fulfill exactly the same functions as the electromechanical ones. However, because they have a digital readout and because they use AC frequency (which is accurately controlled at the power plant) as a timing standard, they are capable of much greater accuracy. The period to be timed is normally set up digitally to the nearest second, and the timer will often be accurate to within a fiftieth of a second.

Where a fixed timing period is required, it is often accomplished by means of a time-delay relay. This is a simple electromechanical relay with an electronic circuit that delays its operation by a predetermined amount after application of the actuating current. Delays of up to about three minutes are obtainable with these devices, which are often built into electric equipment to ensure that the various sections are switched on or off in the correct sequence. Where the delay does not need to be very accurately timed, a pneumatic device may be used. Typically, a spring-loaded switch is operated manually by a push button coupled to a piston moving in a cylinder. Once the switch has been turned on, the spring urges it back to the off position, but the operation is delayed by the piston traveling back along the cylinder. The speed of travel of the piston, and hence the delay interval, is determined by the size of a small aperture that allows air to flow slowly back into the cylinder. A one-way valve allows air to escape rapidly from the cylinder as the switch is turned on.

Time switches

The essence of time-switch operation is that it can be programmed—usually on a 24-hour basis, but time switches are also available with a seven-day cycle for commercial users. This feature enables events or sequences of events to be preselected to occur automatically at certain times throughout the day or week without any human supervision.

The heart of a modern time switch is nearly always a synchronous motor driven directly from the local electricity supply. Because the time switch has no internal time standard of its own, it must rely on an external timing reference, in this case the AC supply frequency, for its accuracy. The speed of the synchronous motor is dependent on the AC frequency, and the clock dial of the time switch is advanced by a gear train that gives

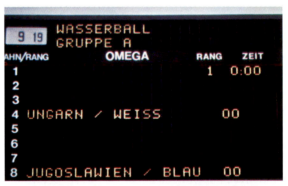

◀ Electronic scoreboards incorporating event timers (shown on the right) as well as ordinary clocks (shown at top left) are standard equipment in many sports stadiums.

◀ Solar-dial time switches are often used in street lights; this type operates at preset timings during the day and has a cam mechanism for altering the timing according to the season.

◀ A time switch for automatically switching electric equipment on and off at predetermined times throughout the day (large dial) and week (small dial to right).

the required speed reduction. Once set, the time switch should not need any further adjustment.

It will, however, require adjustment if the power supply is interrupted for any reason. Usually an interruption represents no real problem, but in particular applications, such as public street lighting systems (where resetting would be a time-consuming operation), it is often necessary to incorporate a spring reverse mechanism, kept fully wound by the synchronous motor, to give a carry-over period of several hours so that short electricity supply interruptions have no effect on the time-switch operations.

Time switches used in the home normally carry a calibrated clock dial that shows the correct time of day against a reference mark. Around the edge of this dial is a set of adjustable tappets that are arranged to actuate a simple mechanical switch capable of controlling an appliance, such as a central heating boiler or pump, at the times set by the tappets. Several sets of tappets can be provided on the dial to allow as many on and off operations each day as required. A manual override button provides instant control whatever the settings.

There are many variations of the basic time switch. Time switches for home central heating can incorporate separate switches for the independent control of the hot water and heating circuits, using electrically operated valves in the

▼ A central feature of this design for variable valve timing is a Metronic microprocessor unit, which senses engine speeds and regulates a solenoid-operated plunger that turns the camshaft to advance and retard the ignition timing.

water circuit. Other time switches are designed for portability and can be used directly at the electric wall socket as a simple means of controlling a wide variety of appliances in the home. To deter burglars, for example, timing devices may be plugged into wall sockets to automatically turn on lighting. During evenings when a person is absent from the home, the automatic turning on of lights gives the impression that the house or apartment is occupied.

Town and city lighting schemes commonly use a solar-dial time switch equipped with a specially contoured cam that automatically advances or retards the switching times, depending on the season. In this way, variations in the times for turning on the street lights can be accounted for without any manual intervention.

Event timers

Event timing involves measuring the period between two events, such as the start and finish of a race or industrial process. For many sporting events, accuracies down to a few hundredths of a second can be achieved with either a mechanical escapement or an electrically driven synchronous motor. At the heart of modern electronic timers and of all devices based on microchip technology is a crystal clock, which was originally developed by NASA as an accurate lightweight timing device for the spacecraft in the Apollo program. Quartz crystals oscillate at a fixed frequency of about 100,000 Hz (100 kHz) when a voltage is placed across them. Quartz clocks, watches, and timers have a precisely grown and cleaved sliver of

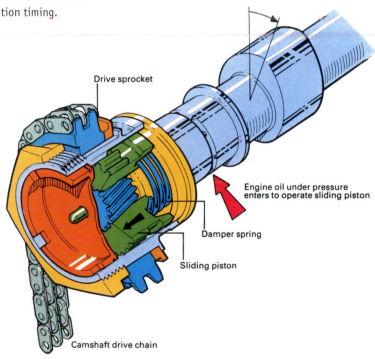

Drive sprocket

Engine oil under pressure enters to operate sliding piston

Damper spring

Sliding piston

Camshaft drive chain

quartz crystal and a small battery or a power supply converter, to yield the low voltages needed by the crystal. The crystal's oscillations are counted, the timing device using its behavior much as a mechanical clock uses the oscillations of a pendulum to move the hands.

Many purely electronic timers now on the market manage to combine high accuracy with high resolution by employing digital displays with light-emitting diodes or liquid crystal displays to indicate the elapsed time in hours, minutes, seconds, and fractions of a second. Systems have been developed for major sporting events where several competitions must be simultaneously timed and displayed. These public systems usually employ neon displays. It is common practice to trigger each timing period directly from contacts built into the starter's pistol and to terminate it by breaking a light beam or the tape itself at the finishing line. In this way, any possible sources of human error are completely eliminated; the measuring accuracy is that of the timing circuits themselves. In marathon races, competitors now have transducers in their shoe laces that enable transmitters at various points in the race to record the runners position and time, and in swimming events, touch pads rather than photocells are used to record the competitors' times. In sailing and yachting events, conventional systems for timing are now used in conjunction with satellite information that enables the position of the vessel to be assessed to within 3 ft. (1 m).

Current developments

With the increasing need for miniaturization, engineers have developed microelectromechanical systems (MEMS) for timing devices that operate electrostatically. Two very fine strings are mounted on actuator frames through which a voltage is set up, causing the strings to oscillate at a regular rate and therefore keep time. These timing devices, which are about the size of a pollen grain, may be incorporated on integrated circuits, leading to complete electromechanical systems on a single chip. The MEMS clock may come to replace quartz crystal clocks in many applications.

Computer chips made from superconductors operate at extremely high speeds and require timing devices that can function at these high levels. Currently it is possible to make clocks for circuits that run at 50 gigahertz, and engineers hope to increase this frequency to hundreds of gigahertz, thus increasing the rate at which computers can process data.

▲ An electronic meter giving digital readouts is used to check the accuracy of camera shutter speeds in a camera assembly plant.

SEE ALSO: CLOCK • INTEGRATED CIRCUIT • SOLENOID • THERMOSTAT

Tin

Tin is a soft, silvery-white metal whose melting point at 450°F (232°C) is lower than that of most other metals. It is a component of bronze and has been known since the third millennium B.C.E. Tin has a wide variety of applications because it is resistant to corrosion, is nontoxic, has a good appearance, and forms alloys with most other metals. It also forms many chemical compounds and is extensively used in the chemical industry. The chemical symbol for tin is Sn, derived from the Latin word for the element, *stannum*.

Although tin has a wide variety of applications, the total world consumption is small compared with that of other metals, being about 240,000 tons (218,000 tonnes) annually. For every ton of tin, about 3 tons of nickel, 17 of lead, 22 of zinc, and 32 of copper are consumed. The United States is the biggest consumer, followed by China.

Occurrence and production

Significant economic deposits of tin minerals are found in very few places in the world. The principal producing countries, in order of importance, are China, Indonesia, Malaysia, Brazil, Bolivia, Russia, and Thailand. These countries together account for about 90 percent of world tin production. Tin is also mined in Australia, Nigeria, and South Africa. In 1996, the world production of tin metal was 229,000 tons (208,000 tonnes).

The principal tin mineral, the oxide cassiterite, SnO_2, is very dense and widely disseminated—often there is as little as 7 oz. (200 g) of cassiterite per ton of earth mined. The tin mineral must therefore be concentrated before it can be smelted to recover the metal. The prepared concentrate is heated in a reverberatory furnace together with anthracite, limestone, sand, reclaimed slag, and other refinery by-products. The purpose of the anthracite is to reduce the cassiterite to tin metal by reacting with the combined oxygen—the other components are added to the furnace in order to form a slag in which impurities in the concentrate are collected. The basic reaction can be written as follows:

$$SnO_2 \ + \ C \ \rightarrow \ Sn \ + \ CO_2$$

tin oxide (cassiterite)	carbon (anthracite)	tin	carbon dioxide

Molten metal and slag are tapped from the furnace, the impure tin being cast into ingots and sent for further refining. The slag is collected and returned for reprocessing. When the tin has been refined to a purity of about 99.8 percent, it is cast into ingots weighing 100 lbs. (45 kg).

▲ Strengthened by a coating of tin compounds, a glass bottle can withstand an impact equivalent to a weight of 1lb. (0.45 kg) falling from 25 in. (0.625 m).

◀ Concentrating tin ore by gravity. Water flows down the grooved table; as the ore travels across it, the lighter and heavier impurities are filtered out.

Metallic tin

As a metal, tin is almost always used in combination with other metals, either as a protective coating or as an alloy. Solders, which are low-melting-point alloys of tin and lead (and occasionally a third and even a fourth metal), use about 31 percent of total tin production. Pewter is another alloy of tin; it contains 92 percent tin, 6 percent antimony, and 2 percent copper. Most plain bearings, as opposed to ball bearings, con-

▲ A scoop trolley carrying tin ore in a tin mine in Cornwall, England. Although Cornwall was one of the oldest sources of tin, the main producers in the world are now China, Indonesia, and Malaysia.

tain tin. The proportion varies from high-tin white metals (used in heavy engineering) to aluminum–tin and bronze (copper–tin) alloys that are used in high-performance engines.

Tin is also used as an alloying element in cast iron, where as little as 0.1 percent improves the wear resistance and machinability of iron castings. Tin powders are used in some powder metallurgy products, ferrous (iron containing) and nonferrous.

Tinplate, chiefly for food-can manufacture, accounts for about 30 percent of the tin produced. Tinplate is generally made by a continuous, high-speed electrolytic process that does not require much tin, the average coating being less than 0.00004 in. (0.001 mm) thick. This small amount of tin provides the essential corrosion resistance, formability, and malleability. Other tin and tin-alloy coatings are applied to a wide variety of manufactured goods for decorative purposes and to provide protection and solderability.

Chemical compounds

Inorganic tin compounds are used in electroplating solutions for tin and alloy deposition. Stannous sulfate, $SnSO_4$, is most commonly used in acid electroplating baths, and sodium stannate, $Na_2Sn(OH)_6$, is used where the bath is alkaline.

The distinction between stannous and stannic compounds is one of valency. In stannous salts, the tin has a valency of two, whereas in stannic salts, it has a valency of four. Tin forms two chlorides: stannous chloride, $SnCl_2$, and stannic chloride, $SnCl_4$ (chlorine has a valency of one).

Tin oxides are employed as pigments and opaque glazes in ceramic ware and for the manufacture of electric resistors. The glass surfaces of lightweight bottles and jars are often coated with tin compounds to strengthen and protect them. Other chemical compounds of tin find use as catalysts and curing agents in the production of polymers, especially urethane foam rubber and silicone rubbers.

Polyvinyl chloride (PVC) may be stabilized against discoloration and becoming brittle by means of an organotin compound, often a dioctyl tin compound. Compounds in which a tin atom is bonded to three carbon atoms are found to have a powerful biocidal activity, and this property has led to their use in fungicides, timber preservatives, and antifouling paints for ships. Environmentally, organotin compounds are not a hazard because natural weathering degrades them to nontoxic, inorganic forms of tin.

FACT FILE

- White tin, which has a crystalline structure, emits an unusual sound when subjected to certain sorts of stresses. The crackling noise is known as the cry of tin.

- In the course of the Bronze Age, tin, one of the constituents of the bronze alloy used for implements and weapons, became worked out in Caucasian and Persian mines. Phoenician and Greek traders sought supplies from as far away as Cornwall in England and Brittany in France for use in the Middle East. Early English tin, mined from 500 B.C.E., was 99.9 percent pure.

- Tin was once used as a pure, unalloyed metal. Siberian grave goods and Egyptian artifacts dating back to the second millennium B.C.E. are of pure tin, as is jewelry found in the Low Countries dating from as early as 3000 B.C.E.

SEE ALSO: ALLOY • BRONZE • CANNING AND BOTTLING • ELECTROLYSIS • METAL • SURFACE TREATMENTS

Index